Saving Energy
in the Home

Saving Energy in the Home

Princeton's Experiments at Twin Rivers

Edited by
Robert H. Socolow
Center for Environmental Studies
Princeton University

Ballinger Publishing Company • Cambridge, Massachusetts
A Subsidiary of J.B. Lippincott Company

This book is printed on recycled paper.

The eleven chapters of this book are also being published by Elsevier Sequoia S.A. as a special issue of *Energy and Buildings* (vol. 1, no. 3, April 1978).

This research has been supported by the Department of Energy and by the Energy Research and Development Administration under Contract Nos. EC−77−S−02−4288, E(11−1)−2789 and EY−76−2−02−2789; the Department of Commerce under Contract No. 6−35758; and the National Science Foundation under Grant Nos. S1A 72−03516 and AER 72−03516.

International Standard Book Number: 0−88410−080−4

Library of Congress Catalog Card Number: 78−2598

Printed in the United States of America

Library of Congress Cataloging in Publication Data

Main entry under title:

Saving energy in the home.

 Reports of research conducted by the Center for Environmental Studies, Princeton University.
 "Also being published by Elsevier Sequoia S.A. as a special issue of Energy and Buildings, vol. 1, no. 3."
 1. Dwellings—New Jersey—Twin Rivers—Energy conservation. I. Socolow, Robert H. II. Princeton University. Center for Environmental Studies.
TJ163.5.D86S28   696   78−2598
ISBN 0−88410−080−4

※

Contents

List of Tables

List of Figures

✳

Preface

We have learned how to eliminate three-quarters of the energy used by the furnace in quite ordinary, reasonably well-built townhouses in Twin Rivers, New Jersey. The combination of retrofits that accumulates these savings includes many that are unconventional at the present time, but none that is unreasonably costly. The story of how, over five years, a multidisciplinary group at Princeton University learned how these particular townhouses functioned is told in this book.

The presentations are technical. The primary audience addressed consists of the professionals and policymakers who are working in the previously neglected territory where housing concerns and energy concerns overlap. The book's eleven chapters appear in nearly the same form in a new journal, *Energy and Buildings*, created for that audience.* Nonetheless, I believe that readers with more casual interest in these problems—someone who wants to do something about his or her own house or an amateur futurist who is looking for some clues about the coming Age of Conservation—will find much that will interest them.

The first chapter is a distillation of insights and results. The busy policymaker should read at least its first section. Many of the conclusions stated starkly there are controversial, but they have become our group's orthodoxy. The second and third sections of that chapter give a general impression, through photographs and graphs, of what kinds of measurements we have taken and how we have reduced our data.

Energy and Buildings (Elsevier Sequoia S.A.) vol. 1, no. 3 (April 1978).

The second, third, and fourth chapters in this book describe the retrofitting of Twin Rivers townhouses. Collectively, they contain our group's experience of learning by doing. Our first retrofits, described in the fourth chapter, were largely conventional. They were consistent with the recommendations found in most guides and manuals. They saved both energy and money. But as we understood the townhouses better, we realized that other strategies were available that were even more cost-effective.

The three-fourths reduction in annual energy consumption by the furnace results from a combination of the insights presented in the second and third chapter. The house is modified; nothing is done to the furnace itself, and no changes are made in interior temperature.

The 75 percent reduction comes about by (1) a reduction in the heat loss rate ("lossiness") of the townhouse by roughly 60 percent, from its original value of about 320 W/$°$C (600 Btu/hr$°$F) to about 130 W/$°$C (250 Btu/hr$°$F); and (2) the amplification of this savings that results when the nonfurnace energy sources (electricity and sunlight), which heat the house during the winter at an average rate of between 1.5 and 2.0 kilowatts, are better retained in the less lossy house and thus take over a larger fraction of the space heating. The second chapter reports a reduction of lossiness by about 50 percent of its original value that was demonstrated in one townhouse, which gets amplified into a two-thirds reduction in annual space heating.

The third chapter identifies still other sources of heat loss (bypasses of the attic insulation) that were not fully addressed in the work described in the second chapter. We are currently checking our hypothesis that these residual bypasses can be virtually eliminated at reasonably low cost and that they are responsible alone for between 10 and 20 percent of the initial lossiness.

These dramatic reductions far exceed what is ordinarily projected by those who prognosticate about energy policy. But these reductions do not seem to us at all exceptional. Energy use for space heating at Twin Rivers was already half the national average (based on annual energy use divided by floor area) before our efforts started, reflecting relatively careful construction and the incorporation of some insulation and double glazing. Space heating could surely become a minor energy use for most climates, over the next few decades, if conservation receives sustained attention.

We have been brooding about the significance of having found several strategies for retrofit that depart from conventional wisdom but that emerge naturally once one has become familiar with particular buildings. We find ourselves pleading with those national and state governments that are embarking on major and costly programs to promote the retrofitting of millions of homes, urging (1) that retrofits be selected following field examination of buildings, (2) that both homeowners and new cadres of professionals be trained to conduct such diagnoses, (3) that both instrumentation and analytical tools be developed to facilitate this process, and (4) that mechanisms for after-the-fact evaluation of results be built into all major programs to make learning easier.

If one had perfect information in hand, the first billion dollars spent on house retrofit would save more energy and money than the second billion dollars, because one would come immediately upon diminishing returns. But the opposite is likely to be true, if a society is sensible; the energy and money saved as a result of the second billion dollars spent on house retrofit will be greater if one has arranged to learn from the experience of spending the first billion dollars.

The important Twin Rivers retrofits are likely to apply widely. We have already verified that attic bypass mechanisms canceling much of the function of attic insulation are found in many different kinds of housing in New Jersey. There appears to be justification for recommending a fairly simple exercise to nearly all the residents of houses with insulated attics. Early on a cold winter morning with low wind, take a thermometer into your attic and take the attic's temperature. Also read the temperatures outdoors and upstairs. If the attic temperature is not a lot closer to the outside temperature than to the house temperature, and there is insulation in your attic floor, you have some variant of the Twin Rivers attic diseases: one or more short circuits perforating the thermal cap on your house. Most of these attic bypasses can be found by looking carefully for gaps and shafts and can be stuffed closed or sealed with caulking material. Some may be more elusive, such as the bypass through the interiors of the hollow cinderblocks in the dividing walls between Twin Rivers townhouses. Add to your attic insulation without attending to these bypasses and you will save substantially less energy and money than the handbooks say; attend to the bypasses while adding to attic insulation and you will save substantially more.

The fifth and sixth chapters in this book describe some of our attempts to understand air infiltration, the most important and least documented form of heat loss from houses. Together with the seventh chapter, a quick tour of all our instrumentation, they give a glimpse of the interactive approach to house diagnosis that, in forms we hope will soon be simplified, may characterize house analysis in the future.

Our field experimentation has been conducted in one townhouse that we rented for several years and were free to modify and treat as a laboratory, and in numerous other houses occupied by families who continued to go about their business with our instruments in place. We have found that research in occupied houses is different from research in laboratory houses in ways not unlike the ways that astronomy is different from physics. In laboratory townhouses, intervention is essentially unlimited; in one instance we toasted our rented townhouse to 35°C (95°F) and then watched the temperature drop over time. Intervention, moreover, can occur at almost any time, so we could plan experiments appropriate to particular kinds of weather and set them in motion when that weather arrived. By contrast, at the front of our minds when we worked in homes occupied by the owners was a desire to minimize the intrusion, not only to reduce the perturbation on the house-occupant system being studied, but also to avoid being thrown out. (Our own group's record has been remarkable; never have the people in one of our project homes asked us to leave.)

The distortions of research brought about by the constraint of minimum intrusion need to be recognized, for they will apply as well to any approach to house diagnosis that involves leaving instruments behind to be picked up at a later date. Components need to be rugged, reliable, quiet, safe, and inconspicuous; we were led to replace squeaky metal bearings by plastic ones, to paint thermistors and wires to match walls, to place thermistors just below the ceiling, where no one could walk into them. This last constraint led us to fail to document the significant vertical temperature gradients within rooms until experiments were done in the rented townhouse.

Constraints on the quantity of data obtained in instrumented, occupied townhouses are almost completely absent. In particular, one can sample data at whatever frequency is desired. This freedom is useful, but it can be abused, such that far more data are collected than anyone wants to process. As discussed briefly in the seventh chapter, one wants quite different sampling intervals depending on the question being addressed. The optimum frequency of data acquisition is usually determined by the characteristic time constants of the problem.

The eighth and ninth chapters probe another dimension of house diagnosis—those insights that can be extracted at a distance, directly from the records of monthly energy consumption obtained by utilities for billing purposes. These huge data sets have hardly been tapped as sources of detailed information about energy use in buildings. As both chapters illustrate, these records promise to be especially useful in separating, on a statistical basis, the roles of building structure and of occupant behavior. Further development of the ideas in these chapters will be required before their full potential and their limitations are well understood.

The final two chapters in this book concern our research directly with the Twin Rivers residents. Residents inclined to conserve energy currently get little help from the machines and meters around them. Our feedback experiments, which confirmed well-established doctrine, show how this could be otherwise. The speculations in the concluding informal chapter give a glimpse of how the principles established in another area of social psychology, that governing the generation of consumer action, may find application in the attempts to lower the thresholds for homeowner initiative in modifying the house to conserve energy. Judiciousness in this area will be required so that as more technically elegant houses and appliances are developed, they are also deployed on the landscape.

This book concludes with four appendixes. Appendix A gives considerable technical detail about Twin Rivers—the cost of energy, the weather, the chronology of construction, the pattern of land use, the thermal characteristics of the townhouses, and some of the operating characteristics of the appliances inside them.

Appendix B lists our research reports; the key results in many of these reports have been captured in chapters of this book. But this book is not a complete summary of our program, and considerable detail is to be found elsewhere.

Appendix C lists those at Princeton and many of those outside the university who have participated in this research. We ourselves were surprised by the length of the list of students who have contributed, through independent work for course credit and through paid work during school year and summer. A delightful characteristic of this program has been its ability to "calve," like an iceberg, and thereby to give birth to projects that float on their own but can be mastered by individual students in a reasonable period of time.

Appendix D presents many of the equivalences between the international (SI) units now used by the scientific community and the "American" units in which America's building professionals and researchers are still mired. As often as was practicable, I have used a double set of units in this book in order to communicate with a wider audience; those who join us in this new research field will find that their Appendix D will become well thumbed.

More than any of us expected, our program at Twin Rivers has been productive of insights into what lies ahead as the world gears up to increase the energy efficiency of its housing stock. We credit our own cleverness hardly at all in considering why this is so. We are struck most particularly with the extraordinary payoff from gaining control of the great variability that plagues this subject by focusing on a single site for an extended period of time and by bringing to bear the standard operating procedures of several disciplines at once.

The initial idea of a strongly controlled experiment conducted over an extended period of time was imitative on my part—it was borrowed from the extraordinarily successful experiments in ecosystem performance and stress that have been conducted for more than twenty years by H. Bormann, G. Likens, and other ecologists at a single site, the Hubbard Brook Experimental Forest in New Hampshire. I like to think that the Twin Rivers study will come to hold a comparable place in conservation research; this partly depends on not totally abandoning the site now that we know many of its most important physical features.

Twin Rivers is a normal place, in terms of construction practices, and its buildings are of few types, with certain basic units repeated hundreds of times. Its residents are in the population targeted by many of the programs to conserve energy—young, reactive, and buying now the machines that will go on consuming energy for ten to twenty years. These characteristics of Twin Rivers have enhanced our research. But many other sites exist where all this is true. "Twin Rivers" should be done again, in other kinds of houses, in other climates, in other cultures.

Robert H. Socolow
Princeton, New Jersey
January 1978

✳

Acknowledgments

When Chapter 1 stood alone, there was a risk that my summary remarks would be perceived as private thoughts. With the other ten chapters for company, I am more confident that the reader will grasp the nature of the interaction that characterizes our daily rounds. Responsibility has been widely shared.

David Harrje has directed all of the experimentation in the field, assisted, for a crucial period, by George Mattingly. Harrje has also directed the program of retrofits, and he has been the principal link with the buildings professionals and with the researchers in the energy companies.

It was Richard Grot's conviction in 1971 that he could measure what was going on in houses in new and better ways that led to our first funding from the National Science Foundation in 1972, when conservation of energy was not yet on any political agenda. Grot has proven his contention year after year, continuing to spend long days at Twin Rivers even after moving to the National Bureau of Standards in 1974.

Frank Sinden has given lustre to the program's physical modeling since his arrival in 1976. With the help of Gautam Dutt and Jan Beyea, Sinden has pointed the program in several new directions.

Lawrence Mayer, from 1974, and Thomas Woteki, from 1975, both statisticians, have rescued the program from the well-known disaster where data displace ideas, supplying professional data management and greatly expanding the range of hypotheses that can be evaluated and reported in ways that are respectable. Mayer, too, has been the one in our group most insistent on having us address the needs of policymakers, not just of our own professional colleagues. The orientation of Chapter 1 reflects his persuasiveness.

The social science experimentation initially addressed issues of design and decisionmaking and was led by Harrison Fraker, Jr., an architect, assisted by Elizabeth Schorske. It has changed emphasis and escalated in intensity under the direction of Clive Seligman, Lawrence Becker, and John Darley, all psychologists, who, while they educate the rest of us, are carving out new territory in their discipline.

From the length of the list of students involved (see Appendix C), one correctly gathers that there has been a continuous effort to make a program of research simultaneously a valid activity in educational terms. Robert Sonderegger has now gained the program's first doctorate, after a stretch of research that included two years at Twin Rivers conducting clever experiments in his home. Sonderegger helped me prepare a detailed but informal review of the program containing all of the figures and photos now appearing in Chapter 1 and much of the material in Appendix A. This book could not have emerged without that first exercise.

The program has had the help of three master's students and more than forty undergraduates. John Fox, who followed his MSE with study at the Wharton School, did the first analyses of the variations in consumption across nominally identical houses. Thomas Schrader, now with the Wisconsin Gas Company in Milwaukee, extended that analysis to reveal the hidden difficulties that complicate the analysis of gas consumption in terms of degree days. Nicholas Malik, now with the consulting firm of Gamze, Korobkin and Caloger in Chicago, played a principal role in the development of equipment and the analysis of data bearing on air infiltration. Of the undergraduates involved, I accept the charge of favoritism in identifying the particularly critical roles played by Malcolm Cheung, Jon Elliott, Shawn Hall, Peter Maruhnic, Mark Nowotarski, and Alison Pollack. The dedication of our students has reflected a commitment to the subject matter as well as amazing personal standards of excellence. Student work underlies nearly all of our most cherished conclusions.

Anyone who knows experimental research in a university knows how indispensable is the role of the supporting staff. The program has enjoyed unusual dedication from its technicians: Kenneth Gadsby, Roy Crosby, Jack Cooper, Victor Warshaw, and Richard Whitley; from Stephen Kidd in the office of grants and contracts; and from Jean Wiggs, Selma Lapedes, Deborah Doolittle, and Terry Brown at home base. Our advisory committee, whose membership is found in

Appendix C, gives the group invaluable insights into its strengths and weaknesses in regular, spirited day long sessions. The guidance from above, from Professors George Reynolds and Irvin Glassman, successive directors of the Center for Environmental Studies, has been a model of intelligence and tact.

The management of the program has been subject to an unusual amount of interaction with our sponsors, the result of its topicality, its accessibility, and the large number of disciplines into which it has intruded. The relationships with our monitors at the Conservation Division of the Energy Research and Development Administration (now Department of Energy) and at the National Science Foundation, Division of Research Applied to National Needs, have always included assistance in the substantive aspects of the program.

Throughout this program, and to an increasing degree every year, we have profited from the numerous probing questions of visitors from industry and government "passing through" and by visits of members of our group to their offices and laboratories. Three of these relationships deserve to be singled out: The public utilities who service Twin Rivers, Public Service Electric and Gas, and Jersey Central Power and Light, have cooperated with our program since its inception, and the collaboration has steadily widened. Norman Kurtz and his consulting firm, Flack and Kurtz, were especially helpful in bringing real world experience to the early stages of this program. The National Bureau of Standards (the guardians of a lean program of conservation research through the years of energy affluence), with parallel grants from our sponsors, has assisted in numerous ways, providing the prototype devices for the measurement of air infiltration, carrying out infrared thermography, collaborating in the reduction of data, and sharing in our decisions about overall strategy.

I wish to thank Dr. Richard Eden for providing the hospitality of the Energy Research Group at the Cavendish Laboratory, Cambridge, England, where Chapter 1 was prepared. That chapter benefited from critical readings by Aart Beijdorff, John Eyre, Joseph Stanislaw, and Philip Steadman and from the wondrous typing of Jan Jenkins. The sojourn at the Cavendish was made possible by fellowships from the German Marshall Fund of the United States and from the John Simon Guggenheim Memorial Foundation.

**Saving Energy
in the Home**

Chapter 1

The Twin Rivers Program on Energy Conservation in Housing: Highlights and Conclusions

Robert H. Socolow
*Center for Environmental Studies
and Department of Aerospace and
Mechanical Sciences
Princeton University*

Abstract

Key results and conclusions of a five year field study of residential energy use are reviewed. Our multidisciplinary research is being undertaken in a set of nominally identical townhouses in Twin Rivers, New Jersey, a recently built community of standard construction with gas space heating, electric central air conditioning, and a full set of appliances.

Average levels of energy consumption and their dependence on weather and building type have been established, thereby permitting detailed quantitative studies of the sources of remaining variability. Starting from this baseline, we have established the level of change in energy consumption that followed the "energy crisis" in the autumn of 1973, and we have performed two kinds of controlled experiments: (1) experiments where a set of modifications (retrofits) are made to the building structure, and (2) experiments where "feedback" is provided to residents on a regular basis, reporting their level of consumption of energy. Conclusions drawn from our modeling and experimentation are presented here, with emphasis given to those results bearing directly on the character of programs to retrofit the national housing stock.

Photographs of the site, of building defects, and of our retrofits are included, as well as a selection of graphs, each indicating a kind of analysis we have found useful and are prepared to recommend to others who wish to help develop an understanding of how houses work.

INTRODUCTION

Since July 1, 1972, our research group at the Center for Environmental Studies at Princeton University has been engaged in an enterprise to document, model, and learn how to modify the amount of energy used in homes. The principal target has been the energy used for space heating; subordinate targets have been water heating and air conditioning. Our research approach has strongly emphasized field studies at a single site, the recently built planned unit development of Twin Rivers, New Jersey, twelve miles (nineteen kilometers) from our campus, where about 12,000 people are living in approximately 3,000 homes. Our group has monitored the house construction, interviewed many of those responsible for energy-related decisions in the planning and construction phase, formally surveyed and informally interacted with the residents, obtained a complete record of monthly gas and electric utility meter readings, built a weather station at the site, and placed electronic instrumentation in thirty-one townhouses (all identical in floor plan). We have rented and occupied one of these townhouses ourselves, turning it into a field laboratory. Our sponsors have been the National Science Foundation (since 1972) and the Department of Energy (since 1975).

The opening section of this chapter, "Principal Goals and Conclusions," presents our major messages for the policymaker. They address four subjects:

1. The effective retrofit;
2. The effective pilot program;
3. The role of the resident;
4. The larger context of space heating.

In addressing the effective retrofit, we emphasize that real houses depart in important ways from the textbook idealization of the house as a warm box sitting in cold air. There are usually numerous ways of reducing energy consumption in real houses that are at least as cost-effective as those that textbook models prescribe and that can best be detected on site. We envision the evolution of cadres of workers with various levels of on the job training—workers having various employers, including themselves.

Diagnostic tools for these workers must include both simple methods of measurement and simple methods of data reduction. For the most part these do not exist. Our research program has addressed the question: Given an hour or a day in a house, and the objective of advising on the most effective strategies to reduce energy consumption, how should those giving advice spend their time?

Answers to this question will come, in part, from carefully structured pilot programs, on the scale of our program or larger. Ours might be considered a pilot study of pilot programs, and it provides insights into the opportunities and limitations inherent in disciplined, subsidized projects where a set of houses are modified and the resulting changes are monitored and interpreted.

Our data confirm the significance of resident behavior in determining energy consumption. We have been testing ways of helping the resident to conserve by providing feedback, and we have obtained some clues about attitudes and beliefs that differentiate residents according to level of energy use.

Although most of our conclusions bear particularly on energy conservation in space heating, several conclusions emphasize that space heating must be considered in the context of all uses of energy in the house—especially in the United States, where energy use by appliances has been increasing much faster than energy use by heating systems. This chapter does not explore the still larger context of energy in buildings—the economic and social forces that have led to a housing stock so far from optimal. Nonetheless, the reader will appreciate that successful implementation of programs responsive to our conclusions requires a sophisticated understanding of a housing market that has long been skewed to respond to first costs rather than operating costs. The historic reluctance of government to invest research and development funds in end use technologies, relative to production technologies, will also thwart implementation unless confronted and overcome.

The remaining two sections of the chapter are cinematic. The first contains ten pages of photographs that give an orientation to our program and a brief history. The second presents ten pages of figures with annotations. Each figure is illustrative of a kind of analysis that we have found useful and are prepared to recommend to others who wish to help develop an understanding of how houses work.

PRINCIPAL GOALS AND CONCLUSIONS

Goal No. 1   The effective retrofit: To clarify the technical requirements for an effective national program to retrofit the existing housing stock to reduce the energy consumption for space heating.

Conclusions

Real Houses.   An effective retrofit program must emphasize measurements in actual houses. The textbook idealization of houses as simple shells with well-defined levels of insulation, which underlies nearly all legislation and regulatory activity, has serious shortcomings. This idealization directs attention nearly exclusively to levels of insulation in the walls and roof and to window glazing, but once there is some insulation in place in all surfaces, attention must be directed more widely. Real houses reflect a haphazard accommodation to efficient energy utilization: both good and bad design, as far as energy is concerned, are largely accidental. As a result, attention to a range of issues more difficult to model but no less difficult to appraise in the field frequently should become the first order of business.

For example, one target for the field assessment of the thermal performance of a building will be the semiexterior volumes—those volumes that, because of patterns of use, can be kept considerably colder in winter and warmer in summer than the living space. The Twin Rivers basement, whose volume is 50 percent of the volume of the living area, is frequently warmer than the living area in winter and colder in summer because it contains the furnace and uninsulated ducts. The Twin Rivers attic, in spite of substantial floor insulation, provides unintended heat loss mechanisms through air exchange with the basement and through conductive links across the upstairs walls that short circuit the attic floor. Both basement and attic have proven worthy targets for design-specific retrofits. In other dwellings, semiexterior spaces might include hallways, crawl spaces, and attached garages.

Other targets for a field assessment of thermal performance include:

1. The levels and paths of air infiltration;
2. The heat distribution system and its controls;
3. The performance of the windows as solar collectors;
4. The fraction of appliance-generated heat recovered within the living area.

Our experience at Twin Rivers suggests that some of the shortest payback periods for specific retrofits are associated with a house "tune up" that addresses these issues.

Diagnostic Methods. Cheap and simple diagnostic field tests can be devised to determine those parameters of a house that help discriminate among retrofit strategies. We have shown, for example, that the efficiency of delivery of heat from a furnace can be clearly separated from the quality of heat retention by the shell of the house when an electric heater is run intermittently in the house for a test period, modulating the heating ordinarily provided by the furnace. Such a test can help decide whether to emphasize the furnace or the shell in a retrofit program. Other tests being pioneered in our research include (1) on the spot measurements of air infiltration rates, either by bag sampling or by continuous injection to maintain a constant concentration of tracer gas; (2) rapid assessments of the effectiveness of attic insulation by simultaneous reading of interior, attic, and outside temperatures; (3) measurements of heat capacities by regular readings of interior temperature as it "floats" with the furnace shut off; and (4) assessments of the furnace and distribution system by frequent (once a minute) temperature readings during a furnace cycle. Although all of these tests need further development, they appear at this point to lend themselves to routine implementation in the field, with hard-wired minicomputer programs more than adequate to reduce output to useful form.

Performance Indexes. Energy consumption in housing can be usefully discussed in terms of a simple performance index analogous to the miles per gallon (or, more precisely, gallons per mile) performance index for vehicles. The index has units of energy per degree day. (The degree day is a measure of the coldness of a time interval.) The Twin Rivers townhouse, for example, functions at about 30 MJ/°C day (megajoules per Celsius degree day) in international (SI) units, or at about 15 cf/°F day (cubic feet per Fahrenheit degree day) in the energy units registered by conventional U.S. gas meters.

This performance index has shortcomings, but to the extent that we have been able to examine this index at Twin Rivers, in several extensive investigations, these appear less serious than we had expected and no more serious than those that make miles per gallon an imperfect measure of vehicle performance. Analogous to the specification of a standard driving cycle for automobiles, one might want to specify the average outside temperature (say, $32°F = 0°C$) and the duration of the measurement (say, one month). The index is less precise when the outside temperature is warmer or the duration of the measurement is shorter, but straightforward modeling procedures can be used with considerable confidence to extract the performance index from data obtained in milder weather or over shorter periods of time. For example, we have found average monthly gas consumption at Twin Rivers to be more nearly proportional to a modified measure of degree days, where a "best" value of 62°F (16.7°C), estimated from our data, is used as the reference temperature for the calculation of degree days, rather than the conventional reference temperature of 65°F (18.3°C) used by the U.S. National Weather Service.

Energy consumption for space heating is likely to be proportional to degree days (with a suitable reference temperature that must be independently determined) for most houses and furnaces in most climates. Straightforward data analysis can be used to include effects such as sun and wind if they have large seasonal fluctuations or directional biases.

Lower Inside Temperature. Relative to most other quantitative statements about energy conservation in residential heating, estimates of the savings obtainable from lowering the inside temperature are less uncertain. This is because all of the dominant heat loss mechanisms for a house are nearly proportional to the temperature difference between indoors and outdoors. Consider Figure 1–1, which is a schematic rendition of several important issues. Vertical distances represent temperature differences, and the area bounded by the thick dashed line (constant interior temperature) and the curve (a year's average daily outside temperature) is proportional to the annual heat loss. This heat loss is seen to be replaced in part by heat from the fur-

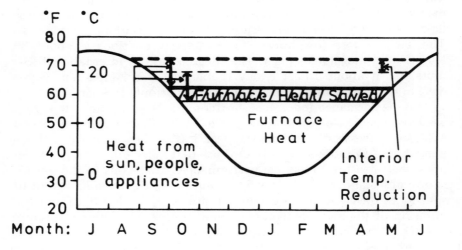

Figure 1–1. Reduction in Furnace Heating When Interior Temperature is Lowered

nace (area below the heavy solid line) and in part by heat from the sun, appliances, and people (area above the heavy solid line). Fixing the interior temperature at a lower value (while making no other changes) results in a smaller annual heat loss, proportional to the area bounded by the thin dashed line and the curve. The resulting reduction in the heat required from the furnace is proportional to the area of the horizontal strip between the thick and the thin solid lines.

The fraction of annual energy consumption at the furnace that is saved by lowering the interior temperature one degree is given (in this simple model) by the length of the heating season, in days, divided by its severity, in degree days—both referred to the outside temperature below which the furnace is required. Figure 1–1 shows an initial interior temperature of 72°F (22.2°C) and a contribution from heating by sun, appliances, and people that lowers the temperature at which the furnace is first required by 10°F (5.6°C) to 62°F (16.7°C). The curve of outside temperature in Figure 1–1 is the National Weather Service's average daily temperature profile for Trenton, New Jersey (fifteen miles from Twin Rivers). The savings at the furnace are found to be about 220 days/4200°F days, or about 5 percent per °F reduction (9 percent per °C reduction) in interior temperature, for locations near Trenton.

Lowering the interior temperature for part of the day gives proportionately smaller savings that nonetheless are significant. For example, lowering the interior temperature at night by 10°F (5.6°C) for eight hours (in a house of light enough construction to fall rapidly to the lower temperature setting) results in a savings of roughly $1/3 \times 10 \times 5 = 17$ percent in annual energy consumption at the furnace. This makes "night setback" (and day setback, as well, when houses are unoccupied for a period of the day) one of the most attractive strategies for retrofit programs—one, moreoever, largely complementary to those that address the furnace and shell.

Solar Energy. Houses are already heated by solar energy, which substitutes for energy at the furnace when it enters through windows (and to a lesser extent, through walls). At Twin Rivers, gas consumption at the furnace provides 60 percent of the annual space heating (compare Figure 1–1), appliances 20 percent, body heat from occupants 5 percent, and solar energy 15 percent. All attempts to increase the efficiency with which incident sunlight displaces energy consumed at the furnace are directly comparable from a public policy standpoint—those that improve the retention of incident sunlight (like better insulation) are equivalent to those that increase the amount captured. At Twin Rivers, enlarging the south window and giving it shutters, a strategy we are currently studying, is a cheaper approach to partial solar space heating than installing a collector on the roof; as long as one is not trying to cut loose entirely from the existing energy supply systems, the same conclusions will apply widely. A serious problem with very large windows—overheating of the living space in mild weather—needs solutions based on architectural design, thermal storage, and internal air movement that remain to be developed.

Side Effects. The national retrofit program is imperiled by universal ignorance about the side effects of prominent retrofit strategies in areas of health, safety, and comfort. As a case in point, our measurements of the range of air infiltration rates in a single house obtained under varying conditions of outside weather draw attention to the possibility of creating an overtight house in low wind and mild weather in the process of reducing average air infiltration rates; but "overtight" is imprecisely understood at present. Other effects in need of research would appear to include health effects of insulation fibers, effects of humidity on the durability of materials, and possible conflicts with both noise control and fire prevention.

Learning by Doing. Because quantitative indexes (like energy per degree day) are easily employed to obtain rough indications of the savings obtained in retrofit programs, the monitoring of programs as they occur should be relatively inexpensive and instructive. Such monitoring can have high payoff. In the United States alone, there are more than sixty million homes, and in nearly all of them, retrofitting is warranted. Only a few percent of these homes will be retrofitted each year, and many initially unfamiliar situations will be encountered again and again. The first retrofits will not be as cleverly designed or as cost-effective as those a decade from now. But improvement will come much more quickly if provision is made in the early retrofit programs for detailed evaluation of the level of success achieved.

Goal No. 2 The effective pilot program: To clarify the role of controlled field experiments and demonstration programs in the evaluation of specific retrofits and retrofit packages.

Conclusions

Uncertain Outer Limits of Savings. The outer limit of financially sensible conservation cannot be probed without an aggressive field program based on a succession of retrofits. First round retrofits may be expected both (1) to include some that, upon subsequent evaluation, turn out to have a low return on investment, and (2) to omit retrofits that have high returns. In our program, unanticipated and significant channels for heat loss revealed themselves only as known channels were closed off. Even our second round of retrofits, which appears to have reduced annual gas consumption to one-third of the preretrofit value, has not exhausted the list of cost-effective retrofits at Twin Rivers.

Uncertain Estimates of Savings. Without the underpinning of field experiments under controlled conditions, quantitative claims for percentage reductions in energy consumption associated with specific retrofits will be and should be viewed skeptically. Our first round retrofit experiments with eight- and sixteen-house samples showed a wide spread in the size of the effects obtained that was not easily attributable to prior differences among houses. Our standard retrofit package reduced energy consumption for space heating by 15 to 30 percent, with interior temperatures unchanged. Apportioning the savings among the components of the package (addressing attic, windows, and basement ducts) has proved difficult, and effects are probably not additive. Pilot programs to estimate savings should not use samples any smaller than ours.

Uncertain Estimates of Costs. The dollar costs of retrofits are difficult to assess because most retrofits are labor-intensive yet not very difficult to perform. Costs, therefore, are sensitive to the treatment of the residents' own labor in the accounting. Several retrofits that have been slow to spread at Twin Rivers have very low costs if performed on a do it yourself basis. This suggests that one objective of demonstration programs should be the investigation of how confidence and skill can be generated in a community such that specific labor-intensive retrofits, once introduced, will be adopted widely.

Early Warnings.   The side effects of retrofits (as discussed above) are likely to be visible even in small experiments. Positive side effects in terms of increased comfort were found in the Twin Rivers retrofit program when increased attic insulation and decreased basement duct losses reduced an inequality (perceived to be annoying) between temperature upstairs (cold) and downstairs (warm). Gaining familiarity with positive and negative side effects appears a significant reason to conduct controlled experiments.

Goal No. 3 The role of the resident: To clarify the role of behavior in energy consumption for space heating.

Conclusions

The Resident Matters. The observed variation in energy consumption for space heating (in townhouses with identical floor plans, furnaces, and appliances) is substantially assignable to the resident rather than to structural features that persist independent of the resident. Strongest evidence comes from studies of houses where there has been a change of owner: new occupants of the same structure have consumption levels nearly unrelated to their predecessors. Additional evidence comes from studies of houses receiving common retrofits: the rank ordering of consumption (highest, second highest, and so forth) remains largely intact in spite of major physical modifications.

Variations Among Residents. Profiles of the high and low users of energy have proved to be very difficult to establish. Relative use of energy in summer correlates with only a few answers to questions designed to probe attitudes, preferences, and general knowledge posed in questionnaires administered to Twin Rivers residents. Attitudes toward expending effort to conserve energy are particularly salient, as captured, for example, in the degree of agreement with the statement: "It is just not worth the trouble to turn off the air conditioner and open the windows every time it gets a little cooler outside." Also significant are beliefs about comfort and health.

Our questionnaires have been even less definitive in illuminating the reasons for variation in winter, other than beliefs about comfort. Moreover, it is still unclear what specific behavior brings about high or low energy consumption for space heating, other than choice of interior temperature. There is very little window opening at Twin Rivers in winter. Opening of outside doors, positioning of interior doors, and management of drapes are probably all associated with variations in gas consumption, but this remains to be proved.

Feedback. Residents of Twin Rivers reduce their summer electricity consumption by 10 to 15 percent and their winter gas consumption by up to 10 percent when information about their level of consumption is supplied on a daily basis in controlled "feedback" experiments. Such savings were anticipated by our psychologists who look on energy conservation as a problem in learning new skills. Our results lead away from the meter in the basement and the bill in the mail that record consumption in inscrutable units. The analog of the future meter is the sportscar's dashboard, giving consumption (in money units?) separately for the major appliances, with buttons to reset some meters to zero. The future bill makes comparisons with one's own past performance and with the current performance of one's peers.

The Response to the "Crisis."   At Twin Rivers, the alteration in the pattern of energy consumption that followed the "energy crisis" during the autumn of 1973 can be approximated by a one shot, 10 percent response, occurring during the 1973–1974 winter, with no subsequent relaxation but (through the 1975–1976 winter) only minimal further conservation. The response occurred across all levels of consumption (high users and low users) and was greater (in amount of energy saved) in colder weather. The response must have taken the form, primarily, of lower interior temperatures because it occurred too quickly to reflect retrofitting. The response may be described as price anticipation since the price of gas rose steadily, not abruptly. (During the period 1971–1976, the price approximately doubled, in current dollars, and rose 50 percent in constant dollars.) Alternatively, it may be described as a prompt response to a pulse of exhortation and information.

Goal No. 4   The larger context of space heating: To clarify the relationship of energy conservation in space heating to energy conservation elsewhere in the residential sector of the economy.

Conclusions

Appliances. Energy conservation in domestic appliances is receiving inadequate attention, given its relative magnitude and the potential for retrofit and replacement. Over a year, the Twin Rivers resident spends more money on water heating than on space heating. (The 8,000 kWh of electricity used annually for water heating corresponds to 100GJ of coal or oil consumption at the central station power plant, compared to 80GJ of gas consumption at the home furnace; hence water heating is also more costly in energy terms.*) Nearly as much dollar expense and energy consumption is associated with the combined tasks of air conditioning and refrigeration as with space heating. A simple retrofit to the water heater at Twin Rivers, in the form of a jacket of insulation to reduce losses from the tank, reduces the electricity used by the water heater more than 10 percent and has a payback period of less than a year.

Systems Within a House. Energy conservation in domestic appliances should not be considered in isolation from space heating. At Twin Rivers, about 20 percent of annual space heating is already provided by appliance heat, and the potential is present to reach 40 percent through improved retention of appliance heat (especially waste hot water) in winter. Appliances, moreover, may be usefully coupled together (for example, using waste heat from the refrigerator to preheat hot water) so as to reduce energy consumption simultaneously for two or more services. We have been struck by the particular potential for encouraging such innovation at the time of construction of communities, like Twin Rivers, where the builder supplies the basic appliance package and purchases hundreds of identical models at one time. With appropriate subsidies, such communities become laboratories for field research on appliance systems.

Scale. Consideration of Twin Rivers as a community reveals that the residents spent about $2.5 million for gas and electricity in 1975,

---

*1 GJ = 1 gigajoule = 10^9 joules is an amount of energy roughly equivalent to the energy content of seven gallons of gasoline, or seventy pounds of coal, or the food consumed daily by one hundred people, or a thirty Watt bulb burning for a year. Its monetary value in New Jersey currently ranges from about $3 as residential natural gas to $12 as electricity. Tables to convert among energy units are found in Appendix D at the end of this book.

$800 per dwelling unit in 3,000 dwelling units. The community consumed gas at a rate of 200 million cubic feet (6 million cubic meters) per year and electricity at an average rate of 6 megawatts. There is an obvious need to investigate economies of scale in energy systems at the ten-house level (the townhouse building), at the fifty-house level (the street of buildings), at the three-hundred-house level (the "Quad"), and at the level of the community as a whole (which also contains shops, offices, and light industry). Energy end use systems at all of these scales are totally absent at Twin Rivers, with the exception of some water heating on a ten-unit scale where there are rented apartments. Several promising technologies, among them thermal energy storage (including annual storage) and on-site cogeneration of electricity and heat, might play a central role in advanced retrofits in communities like Twin Rivers and might be usefully assessed in communities where good data at the single house level already exist.

Summers. Energy consumption for air conditioning shows even more variability at Twin Rivers than energy consumption for space heating. Moreover, the levels of consumption for air conditioning and for space heating are uncorrelated across houses. In response to the energy crisis, there appears to have been no conservation in summer electricity consumption, one-half of which is for air conditioning, even though opportunities for conservation (at the thermostat, front door, and drape) are as readily available as in winter space heating.

The modeling of the summer energy balance of a house is complicated by the absence of any single term as dominant as the losses due to conductive heat flow in the winter energy balance. Yet careful models that include solar effects, variable air conditioner efficiency, humidity, appliance heating, and thermal storage are a necessary precondition to the refinement of cost-effective retrofits to reduce summer electricity consumption.

A PHOTOGRAPHIC TOUR
OF THE PROGRAM

The sets of photographs in this section were taken by various members of the research group over the past five years. They should offer a quick grasp of the program. Each facing page contains a commentary on issues raised by the photographs.

Figure 1–2A. Aerial View of Twin Rivers Quads I and II, Looking Southeast. Dark Roofs are Apartments; Light Roofs are Townhouses; Circular Building in Foreground is the Bank, where our Weatherstation is Located; Geodesic Dome at Top is School.

Figure 1–2B. Front View of Quad II Townhouse Rented by Princeton. Masonry Firewalls Project Beyond the Structure in Brick; Central Projection (with Windows of Living Room and Master Bedroom) Terminates One Foot Above Ground Level (Behind Bushes).

The Site

Roughly one-fourth of the houses in Twin Rivers, New Jersey, may be seen in the aerial view (Figure 1–2A). Twin Rivers was New Jersey's first planned unit development, and its beginnings are associated with new state and local zoning legislation to permit a mix of industrial, commercial, and residential structures, the latter including detached houses, townhouses, and apartments [1–3]. Twin Rivers is governed as a portion of East Windsor township. In an average year, the heating degree days total 4900°F days (2700°C days), based on a reference temperature of 65°F (18.3°C).

Also shown (Figure 1–2B) is the townhouse rented by our program. It is located in the townhouse complex (Quad II) at the top left of the aerial photo, where most of the other nominally identical townhouses studied in our program are also found. These townhouses are of conventional construction, with masonry bearing walls and wood framing for floors and roof. They provide approximately 720 square feet (67 square meters) of space on each of two floors, above a full, unfinished basement. They sold for approximately $30,000 when they were built in 1972, and for about $40,000 in 1977.

Figure 1–3. Type YSI #44204 Linearly Compensated Thermistors Read Temperature Above Door to Basement in Hallway of Two "Identical" Townhouses.

Identical Houses

Figure 1–3 shows two thermistors measuring "hall temperature" above the door to the basement in two of the more than thirty, three bedroom townhouses where we have made that same measurement. The pair of photographs symbolize our attempt to standardize not only houses but also measurements. Thereby, experimental artifacts are highly unlikely to be the source of observed house-to-house variations in interior temperature, or in appliance use, or in furnace gas consumption [4].

Several further sources of variation are largely absent in our sample. Nearly all of the families have small children, typically one when they moved in and another since. Their townhouse is the first home most have owned. Many of the adults grew up in apartment houses in New York City. About half are Jewish; 96 percent are white. Nearly all of the wage earners are mobile professionals, and many of them commute to New York City on buses that leave Twin Rivers every five minutes in the morning. (The town is one-half mile (one kilometer) from Exit 8 of the New Jersey Turnpike, and the fifty-mile (80 kilometer) trip takes fifty-five minutes.) The annual family income of townhouse owners at the time of purchase averaged $20,000, and it did not vary greatly.

However, the residents of Twin Rivers townhouses are far from a homogeneous population in many other respects. They differ in their "temperature preference," with interior temperatures showing a standard deviation of about $2°F$ ($1°C$) in winter. They differ in their commitment to modifying their homes, such that six years after purchase some of the originally unfinished basements have dropped ceilings and paneled walls, while others are unchanged. They differ in level of knowledge about the equipment in their home, in their attitudes toward sun and toward dryness, and in their (at least expressed) concern for saving money. Psychologists have played a central role in our research program since 1974, and they have helped greatly in sharpening the exploration of this wide class of behavioral and attitudinal variables [5–9] (see also Chapters 10 and 11).

Figure 1—4A. Bank of Electric Meters in Townhouse Basement Separate the Usage of Air Conditioner, Water Heater, Range, Dryer, and Everything Else.

Figure 1—4B. Electric Water Heater Following Retrofit, Wrapped in Foil-Backed R—7 Insulation.

Appliances

The bank of electric meters that separates the electric load into its major components is seen in Figure 1−4A. Our estimates of the major contributors to an average annual consumption of 16,200 kilowatt hours are:

Water heater	8,000	kWh/year
Air conditioner	2,500	
Refrigerator	2,000	
Range (cooker)	700	
Dryer	500	
Other	2,500	
Total	16,200	kWh/year

Also shown (Figure 1−4B) is a water heater, following a retrofit in which two inches (five centimeters) of foil-backed fiberglass insulation are wrapped around the tank. The payback period for this retrofit is less than one year [10]. With a gas water heater, care must be taken to leave adequate air flow for combustion and exhaust gases.

Figure 1–5A. Infrared Equipment in Master Bedroom Being Tuned by Richard Grot (N.B.S.), Watched by Lynn Schuman (N.B.S.) and Owner of Home.

Figure 1–5B. Infrared Thermograph Reveals Anomalous Cold Patch in Upstairs Ceiling.

Looking for Trouble

In Figure 1–5A, Richard Grot, now of the National Bureau of Standards and a principal investigator in the research program, 1972–1974, when at Princeton, adjusts the controls of the bureau's infrared thermographic unit [11]. The equipment is in the master bedroom. In another such bedroom, when Grot scanned the ceiling, he detected a thermal anomaly (Figure 1–5B), confirmed to be a missing panel of insulation (Figure 1–5C).

Infrared devices have been made smaller and less costly than the research device shown in Figure 1–5A. Surface temperature probes, moreover, often can be substituted for thermography. It is a central and continuing goal of our research group to assist in the invention of a kit of instruments and algorithms that can diagnose problems in the thermal characteristics of a house with minimal time, minimal cost, and minimal bother to the resident [12, 13] (see also Chapter 7).

Figure 1–5C. Cause of Patch in Figure 1–5B is Traced to Missing Batt of Attic Insulation.

Figure 1−6A. Living Room Overhang at Time of Construction.

Figure 1−6B. Ducts Passing into Living Room Overhang, Casually Insulated.

Figure 1—6C. Insulation of Duct and Overhang, Part of Princeton Retrofit Package C.

Heat Distribution

The heat distribution system is a neglected subject in discussions of energy conservation in housing, but it offers significant opportunities for productive retrofits. Energy as hot air at the furnace plenum is distributed by forced convection through a network of ducts branching off the plenum and leading to nine individual registers located next to the outside wall in each room. The five ducts feeding the downstairs run along the basement ceiling, while the four ducts feeding the upstairs are embedded in the interior walls and in the first floor ceiling for about two-thirds of their length. In all, 160 feet (49 meters) out of the 246 feet (75 meters) of ducting run along the basement ceiling. A basement duct is seen before retrofit in Figure 1—6B and after retrofit in Figure 1—6C.

The entire hot air distribution system delivers only half of its heat to the rooms via the registers, one-third of the heat flowing initially into the basement and one-sixth flowing initially into the interior structure above the basement. Much of the heat not entering the living area through the registers nonetheless heats the living area, and it is not clear whether the flow of heat into the interior of the structure above the basement (in the spaces between interior studs, for example) should be avoided. But the loss of heat to a cold overhang, like the one shown in Figure 1—6A, is surely undesirable. In Figure 1—6C, the overhang is packed with insulation [14—16].

Figure 1—7A. View of Open Shaft Around Furnace Flue from Basement to Attic. In Foreground, Duct to Upstairs Bedroom Passing Through First Part of Shaft; Attic End of Shaft (Not Visible) will be Sealed as Part of Princeton Retrofit Package D.

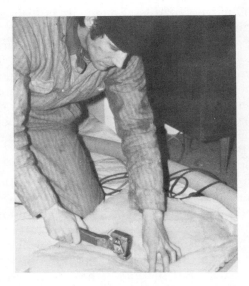

Figure 1—7B. Insulation Batt Being Stapled onto Attic Floor Trap Door, Part of Princeton Retrofit Package A.

An Open Shaft

An adverse impact of building codes on energy conservation is revealed in Figures 1–7A and 1–7B: an open wooden shaft, with a 1.8 square foot (0.16 square meters) cross section, is built around the flue. Many building codes require such a shaft to insure that the hot flue is not a fire hazard. The shaft at Twin Rivers is open top and bottom and thus provides a path of communication for air moving between basement and attic. The view (Figure 1–7A) of the shaft from below shows that this flow will be doubly enhanced when the furnace is firing because a duct to upstairs runs through the lower part of the shaft. This shaft is one of several paths by which heat can reach the attic, which is unexpectedly warm in spite of insulation. One of the less important paths is through and around the hatch to the attic, shown (Figure 1–7B) being given a backing of insulation.

Our retrofit to the shaft is a tight-fitting fiberglass plug at the attic floor. The temperature at the surface of the flue at this elevation is about 130°F (55°C), compared to a char temperature for fiberglass of about 800°F (430°C). The plug, formed simply by wrapping the flue with a four foot (1.3 meter) section of six inch (fifteen centimeter) unbacked fiberglass and pressing it tightly into the opening, not only improves the retention of heat but also reduces the likelihood that a fire could spread through the house (see Chapter 4).

Figure 1—8. Four Views of Gaps Between Wall Framing and Masonry Firewall.

A: Seen at Time of Construction, Downstairs.

B: Gaps at Attic Floor.

C: View from Outdoors. Caulking Comes Away at Wood-Masonry Joint.

D: Plug of Gap from Basement by Fiberglass,
Part of Princeton Retrofit Package B.

Other Open Passages

Additional unintended paths for air flow are created behind the interior side walls of the living area, as seen in Figure 1−8. As a result of differential settling over time, a gap opens up between the floor joists and the masonry firewall that separates townhouses from one another (photo B). The cross sectional area for flow between basement and attic through these gaps ranges up to one square foot (0.1 square meters) in the Twin Rivers townhouse. Access to these passages behind the side walls (photo A) is also provided through cracks in the caulking material that initially sealed the joints between the firewall and both front and back walls (photo C). The net effect is to open up paths for the movement of cold air into the firewall cavity from outside, and then into the basement and attic through the gaps (see Chapter 3). In our retrofit program, we have both recaulked from outside and stuffed the gaps at attic and basement with fiberglass (bottom) (see Chapter 4).

Defects such as the shaft shown in Figure 1−7 and the gaps and cracks shown here apparently degrade energy performance rather uniformly across townhouses. They have a measurable effect, for their repair leads to reduced consumption. On the other hand, these defects cannot be responsible for much of the observed house-to-house variation in gas used for space heating, because (1) such defects would be likely to persist when a townhouse changed owner, but (2) we have found almost no "memory" in a townhouse, when occupied by a new family, as to whether previously it was high or low on the scale of relative use of gas (see Chapter 9).

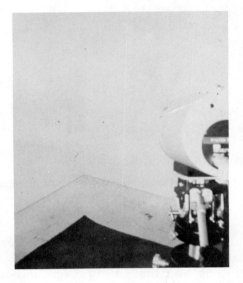

Figure 1—9A. Infrared Unit Scans a Corner, with Outside Wall to Left, Wall Fronting a Firewall to Right.

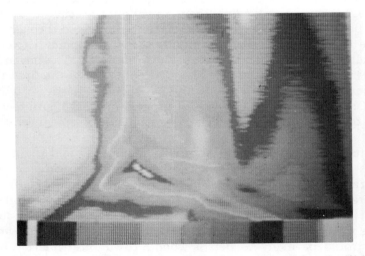

Figure 1—9B. Infrared Thermograph of Same Corner Reveals Interior Wall to be Several Degrees Colder. Dip in the Pattern is First Vertical Stud, Separating Two Pockets of Cold Air.

Figure 1—9C. Characteristic Corner Pattern: Cold Air Flows from Outside Through Space Between Firewall Masonry and Sheet Rock Panels and Merges with Warm Air from Basement.

Cold Walls

The National Bureau of Standard's infrared unit, shown in Figure 1—9A, dramatizes the heat losses at the corners of the house through the interior walls that parallel the firewalls. The corner patterns seen on Figures 1—9B and 1—9C have proved to be the rule rather than the exception in inspections of more than ten townhouses [11]. These patterns shrink (for a given temperature scale) following retrofit, reflecting warmer surface temperatures. Much of the information about surface temperature is lost in these black and white prints, compared to the colored thermographs that clearly distinguish ten temperature levels. (A temperature scale may be discerned at the bottom of the two infrared photographs.) The surface temperature of the window in Figure 1—9C has exceeded the temperature scale; the window is nearly always the coldest interior surface, even when double glazed.

Cold surfaces are readily perceived by the human body as a result of radiative heat loss to these surfaces. Whereas the window may be covered by a curtain or drape when it is cold, the cold interior wall is not as easily dealt with and is widely perceived to be a source of discomfort at Twin Rivers.

Figure 1—9C was the cover (in color) of the August 1975 issue of *Physics Today* to illustrate an article [17] giving highlights of the American Physical Society's summer study, "Efficient Use of Energy," held at Princeton in July 1974 [18].

Figure 1–10. Four Aspects of Princeton's Air Infiltration Research.

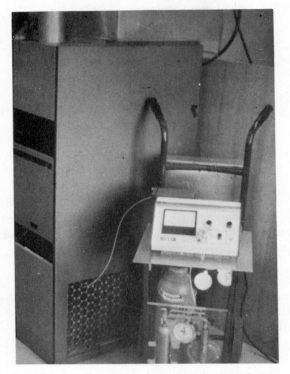

A: Air Infiltration Measurement Device, Alongside Gas Furnace.

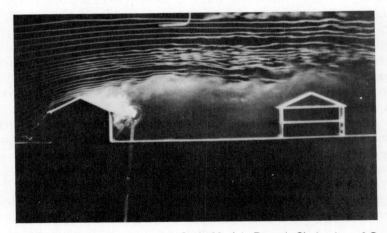

B: Wind Tunnel Smoke Test with Scale Models Reveals Sheltering of One House by Another.

Air Infiltration

Once a house has wall insulation complying even with today's minimal standards, heat losses through air infiltration usually constitute at least one-third of heat losses through the shell. Very little is known about these heat losses, which are caused by outside weather forcing air through a multitude of cracks—in contrast to what happens in a modern commercial building where forced ventilation is almost entirely controlled by electrically driven fans forcing air through clearly defined passages.

Instrumentation to measure air infiltration rates in houses (photo A) has been developed over several years, in collaboration with the National Bureau of Standards [19, 20]. Using the hot air distribution system, about 10 cc of sulfur hexafluoride (SF_6) are injected into the house (whose volume is about 3×10^8 cc, so that the initial concentration is about thirty parts per billion), and concentrations are read at regular intervals until the concentration drops by a factor of two to ten, when reinjection occurs. The rate of decay of concentration is a measure of the air infiltration rate. Measured values range from 0.25 to 2.5 exchanges per hour and average about 0.75 exchanges per hour.

The very large exchange rates occur in high winds. (In fact, the design day for sizing of a home furnace should be a very windy day rather than a very cold day.) To study the pressure distribution at the house under high winds, scale models were placed in a wind tunnel (photo B). These tests [21] facilitated the choice of dimen-

Figure 1—10. Four Aspects of Princeton's Air Infiltration Research *(cont'd.)*

C: Windbreak of Trees Installed Behind Highly Instrumented Townhouses in Collaboration with U.S. Forest Service.

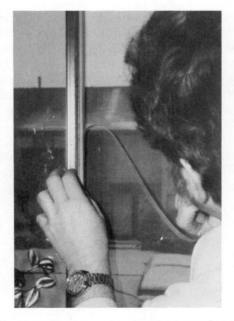

D: Kenneth Gadsby Installs Weatherstripping in Sliding Panel of Patio Door, Part of Princeton Retrofit Package B.

sions for a full-scale test of a windbreak (photo C). The experiment, performed in collaboration with the U.S. Forest Service, appears to have reduced air infiltration rates in westerly winds by about 0.2 exchanges per hour, according to direct measurements in one townhouse before and after the windbreak was erected [22].

Air infiltration is also driven by buoyancy (hot air flowing out of the top of the house and replaced by cold air below). Air infiltration rates can approach one exchange per hour on a very cold day with no wind. The effects of buoyancy and of wind add in nonlinear ways that have proved difficult to model (see Chapters 5 and 6); but both effects are reduced by attention to the larger cracks such as those along the metal window frames (photo D).

Will well-built or well-retrofitted houses become overtight on mild days with little wind? Our group is currently attempting to formulate this issue more precisely, and several designs for passive devices to regulate the air exchange rate have been proposed [23−25].

Figure 1–11A. Blown Fiberglass Insulation Lies on Top of Original Batt Insulation on Attic Floor, Part of Princeton Retrofit Package A.

Figure 1–11B. Early Morning View of Frost Pattern on Back Slopes of Attics of the Three Highly Instrumented Townhouses at a Time when the Middle One has not yet Received Retrofit Package A. Dark Color Indicates Greater Heat Flow Through Roof and Less Frost Formation.

Attics

On a frosty morning, one can tell which attics have been retro-fitted. The middle roof shown in Figure 1–11B belongs to a house whose attic is untouched, at a time when extra insulation has been added (Figure 1–11A) to the attic floor of its two neighbors. The frost is maintained longer on colder roofs, and roofs are colder when less heat flows into the attic from below.

Thus, the rare frosty morning at Twin Rivers offers the opportunity for advertising one's citizenship. It also provides the opportunity for neighbors to monitor one another and for authorities to monitor everyone. The latter do not have to wait for frosty mornings because infrared photography easily picks out the insulated attic, whatever the weather (as long as it is cold).

It is not hard to imagine ways in which campaigns to encourage retrofits by homeowners could develop such that the protection of civil liberties became a pressing concern. The attic has been rendered useless as a storage area by the retrofit shown here, and it is quite possible that for some residents, the choice between more storage and more fuel conservation would be decided in favor of more storage. A sensitive campaign would at least offer a more elaborate attic retrofit that left the attic more usable for those who wanted it. It would, hopefully, also offer the choice of doing nothing [26].

The retrofits shown in Figures 1–4, 1–5, 1–7, 1–8, 1–10, and 1–11 were the principal components of Princeton's first retrofit experiment and were undertaken in varying combinations and sequences in thirty-one townhouses (see Chapter 4).

SOME CHARACTERISTIC
QUANTITATIVE RESULTS
IN GRAPHICAL FORM

The sets of figures in this section distill some of our most important quantitative results. Several also represent innovative methods of data reduction that others may consider adopting. Each facing page contains a commentary on issues raised by the figures.

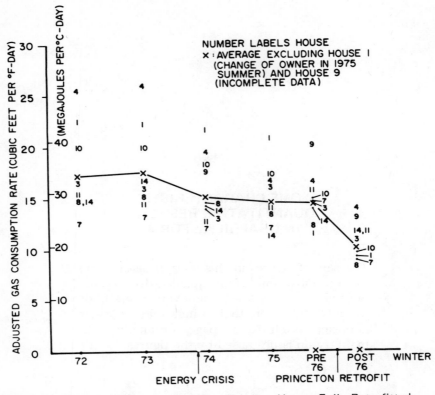

Figure 1–12. Five Year History of Nine Omnibus Houses Fully Retrofitted by Princeton in Winter 1976.

Five Year History of Nine Houses

Four issues central to our research program are evoked by Figure 1–12: variation across houses, a performance index for gas consumption in variable outside weather, conservation in response to the energy crisis, and further conservation as a result of our retrofits. The nine houses shown, coded by an integer label, all participated in the Princeton retrofit experiment during the 1976 winter. Monthly meter readings for these houses provide a full record of winter gas use from the date of first occupancy four years earlier.

Variation Across Houses. All nine houses are three bedroom interior units in Quad II of Twin Rivers. They have identical floor plans, furnaces, and basic appliance packages. Yet the gas consumption in House 4 is seen to be a bit more than twice the gas consumption in House 7 in each of the first two winters of occupancy. The same houses are "high" gas consumers, winter after winter, with only minor changes in rank ordering. A glaring exception is the plunge of House 1 from highest to lowest between the winters of 1975 and 1976, which corresponded to a change of owner in House 1 during the summer of 1975, the only change of owner over the five years for the nine houses.

Performance Index. The vertical scale has units of energy per degree day; a central finding of our research program is that such an index is adequate for most discussions. The calculation of degree days in the United States is usually done relative to a reference temperature of 65°F (18.3°C), and such a reference temperature is also adequate. It is always safer, however, to do comparisons for the same average outside temperature, as is essentially the case when entire winters are compared. Comparisons of gas consumption for two periods with differing outside temperature may be made more accurate by fitting simple curves to previous data for such houses. At Twin Rivers, winter gas consumption is found to be nearly directly proportional to $(R - T)$, where T is the average outside temperature and for the average townhouse $R = 62°F = 16.7°C$. A simple adjustment to the index that reduces its sensitivity to outside temperature can therefore be devised; it is applied here for the data of the two fragments of the 1976 winter before and after retrofit.

Energy Crisis. All of the houses shown here reduced their gas consumption between the 1973 and 1974 winter in response to the "energy crisis" of the autumn of 1973. A new plateau was established in the average consumption, one that persisted until the Princeton retrofit.

Princeton First Round Retrofit. The performance index of the average of seven houses coded 3, 4, 7, 8, 10, 11, and 14, which had dropped from 17 cf/°F day to 15 cf/°F day following the energy crisis, was brought down to 10 cf/°F day by Princeton's first round retrofit package (see Chapter 4). (In System International (SI) units, it fell from 33 to 28 to 20 MJ/°C day.) The retrofit package had only a small effect on the rank ordering of the nine gas consumers, however, suggesting that faults in house design addressed in the retrofit package probably do not play a crucial role in creating variability in gas consumption.

A second round of retrofits has been performed on one townhouse, featuring thermal shutters on the windows. Combined with the first round retrofits, it appears to have reduced annual gas consumption to about one-third of the preretrofit level (see Chapter 2).

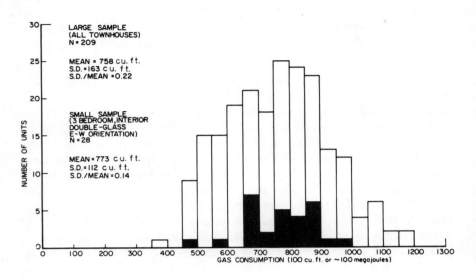

Figure 1–13.   Average Gas Consumption over Two Six Month Winters (1971–1972, 1972–1973).

Variation in Gas Consumption

Figure 1–13 presents two histograms (a sample and one of its subsamples) that are characteristic of our data. The gas consumption plotted here is the average of two six month winters (November 1971 to April 1972 and November 1972 to April 1973).

The large sample differs from the small sample in that:

1. The large sample contains units with two, three, and four bedrooms. All units in the subsample are three bedroom units with common floor plan.
2. All compass orientations are found in the large sample. All units in the subsample face either east or west.
3. Units in the large sample occupy both interior and end positions in the townhouse row. All units in the subsample are interior units.
4. Units in the large sample differ in amount of double glazing, an option at the time of purchase. All units in the subsample have double glazing throughout.

As expected, variability is reduced when these four variables are held constant. Winter gas consumption for space heating varies by more than three to one for the large sample (209 townhouses), by two to one for the subsample (28 houses), and the ratio of the standard deviation to the mean drops from 0.22 to 0.14.

The variability in both samples is one of the startling results of our program. Natural gas is used exclusively for space heating, so that the entire variability must reflect variations in the structures or in the way people use those structures. The reduction in variation in passing from the large sample to the subsample can be apportioned among the four physical variables just described, using the methods of linear regression analysis. Double glazing, averaged over the winter, is found to reduce the rate of gas consumption by 14 ± 4 watts per square meter of double glass installed, or 4 ± 2 percent for a three bedroom unit (194 ft^2 or 18.0 m^2 of glass), about half of the 9 percent savings predicted by heat load calculations. The 13 percent penalty for the end wall, the 9 percent penalty for the interior four bedroom unit, and the 26 percent benefit for the interior two bedroom unit, relative to an interior three bedroom unit, are close to the values expected from heat load calculations. Orientation effects are buried in the statistical noise, an indirect consequence of nearly equal glass area front and back [27−29].

The remaining variation confounds a conventional approach: the usual computer programs, which make no allowance for variable patterns of use, would predict a single value for the gas consumption of the twenty-eight-unit subsample. Evidence that factors specific to the residents are responsible for much of the variation in such subsamples has been obtained by comparing gas consumption in two different winters for houses having the same owner and houses having two different owners [29] (see also Chapter 9).

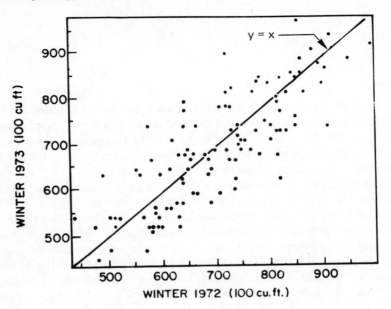

Figure 1–14A. Winter 1972 versus Winter 1973 Gas Consumption.

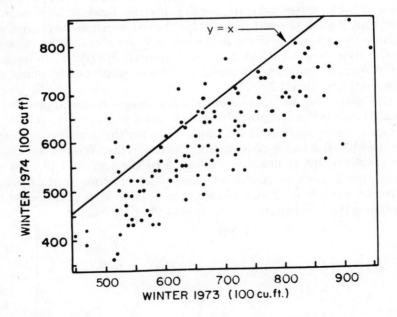

Figure 1–14B. Winter 1973 versus Winter 1974 Gas Consumption.

The Pattern of Response to the Energy Crisis

The short-term response to the energy crisis is rendered in a striking fashion by the two cross-plots in Figure 1—14. Here gas consumption for the four month winters of 1972, 1973, and 1974 are compared using the gas meter readings for the split-level townhouses in Twin Rivers (a set of townhouses adjacent to those from which all other figures in this section are drawn). At the nearby station of the National Weather Service at Trenton there were, respectively, 3,291, 3,151, and 3,251 °F days during each four month period, and so one might have expected a drop in consumption of 4 percent from the first winter to the second and a climb of 3 percent from the second winter to the third, if outdoor temperature were the only determinant of consumption.

The cross-plots tell a different story. The winters of 1972 and 1973, plotted against one another in the upper cross-plot, both preceded the energy crisis; the houses (each a dot on the graph) scatter nearly symmetrically about the straight line, on which gas consumption is the same in both winters. The two winters plotted in the lower cross-plot, 1973 and 1974, straddle the "energy crisis" in the autumn of 1973; the pattern of the upper cross plot is displaced downward, corresponding to conservation of roughly 10 percent of expected gas consumption in 1974 [30, 31].

Conservation in 1974 is seen to take place among high users and low users to roughly the same extent, with individual users varying greatly in the degree of response. The ratio of variance to mean, in fact, remained unchanged by the crisis. The extent of variation in any single winter is comparable to that displayed in the histograms in Figure 1—13.

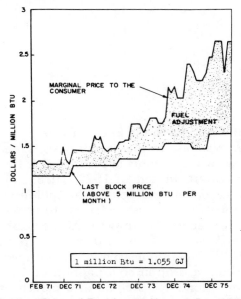

Figure 1—15A. Marginal Price of Residential Natural Gas, 1971—1976

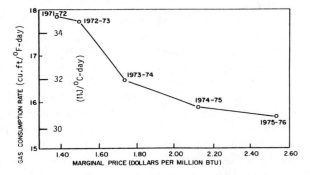

Figure 1—15B. Price versus Rate of Consumption of Gas

Conservation and Price

In Figure 1—15, the upper graph shows the price of natural gas paid by the Twin Rivers resident, which approximately doubled, in current dollars, from 1971 to 1976. The lower graph shows the reduction in average rate of gas consumption (normalized by degree days) that has accompanied this rising price. The price shown is the price for the last block of the rate structure and applies to all gas consumption above five million Btu (50 therm, or 5.1 GJ) per month. This is the marginal rate faced by all Twin Rivers residents in December through March and by all except a few very low consumers in the months of November and April; this is, therefore, the traditional price for economic analysis. It is seen to be the sum of two components: a regulated price, revised once or twice a year by the New

Jersey Public Utility Commission; plus a fuel adjustment, computed monthly, by means of which short-term changes in the price paid by the utility for gas are passed through to the customer. The price shown is not adjusted for inflation. One regional price index (consumer price index—city average, as reported in the *Monthly Labor Review*, a monthly index covering New York City and northern New Jersey) climbed from 128 to 170 from November 1971 to November 1975 (relative to 1967 = 100). The marginal price rise by a factor of 2.0 in current dollars in the four year interval is, thus, a rise by a factor of 1.5 in constant dollars.

Plotted against the marginal price (in current dollars) in the lower graph is the gas consumption rate, averaged over 151 Quad II townhouses (a sample that excludes houses that have had a change of owner). The rate is normalized by dividing by degree days (with $65°F = 18.3°C$ reference temperature); the resulting performance index drops from 17.8 cu.ft./°F day (34.5 MJ/°C day) to 15.7 cu.ft./°F day (30.5 MJ/°C day) in five years, a drop of 12 percent, much like the drop observed for the seven house average in Figure 1–12.

Based on the data for the winters of 1972 and 1975, a four winter elasticity of demand of −0.5 may be computed, the ratio of an increase in marginal price (in constant dollars) of 23 percent and a reduction in the performance index of 11 percent. The pattern of consumption versus price, however, is inconsistent with a constant elasticity of demand operating for the whole interval because most of the reduction in demand occurred in the winter immediately following the crisis, whereas most of the increase in price occurred later. One may describe the pattern shown in Figure 1–15B equally well as price anticipation or as a fast response to the pulse of exhortation that characterized the 1974 winter. It is significant that no deterioration of the performance index is observed since the energy crisis, in contradiction to a frequent prediction that over time the residential consumer would "relax" [31, 32].

Following the energy crisis, Twin Rivers residents appear to have reduced their electricity consumption marginally, if at all. This result confounded our expectations, as the price history for electricity has been similar to that for natural gas, and strategies to reduce electricity consumption appear to be no more difficult to execute. Median winter electricity consumption was down 6 percent in 1974, relative to 1972 and 1973, an effect that vanished when mean values were compared. Summer electricity consumption was at the same level in 1974 and 1975 as in 1972 and 1973, when periods of equivalent cooling degree days were compared. These results strongly suggest that levels of air conditioning were not curtailed following the energy crisis [31, 33].

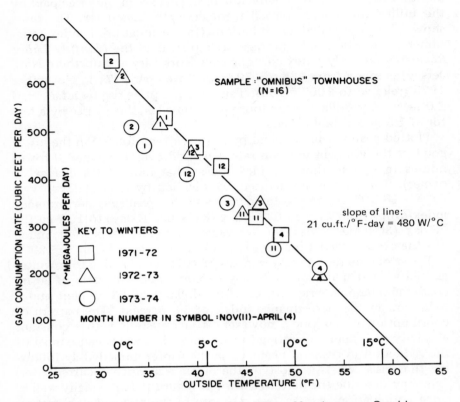

Figure 1-16. Mean Gas Consumption Over Winter Months versus Outside Temperature

Outside Temperature: The Critical Variable

The average rate of gas consumption of sixteen townhouses later to be retrofitted by Princeton is plotted against the average outside temperature in Figure 1-16. The monthly data shown cover three winters of six months each. The first two winters precede the "energy crisis," and the twelve data points fit a single straight line extraordinarily well. The last six data points correspond to months of the 1974 winter, and the conservation of gas at Twin Rivers during these months reappears here. The amount of gas conserved is seen to be largest in the coldest months, a pattern confirmed in studies of a larger sample of houses and one inconsistent with a constant reduction of interior temperature throughout the winter. The reduction of interior temperature, relative to the previous two years, appears to have been 4°F (2°C) in the colder months, but only 1°F (0.5°C) in the milder months [32].

A linear relationship between gas consumption and outside temperature is not unexpected. It follows, for example, if the auxiliary heating from the sun and the electrical appliances, the average air infiltration rate, the furnace efficiency, and the interior temperature are all constant over months, and in fact none of these varies substantially at Twin Rivers. A prolonged investigation of solar, appliance, furnace, and wind effects has led us to the following energy balance in the Twin Rivers townhouse:

1. Appliances, people, and sun lower by 10°F (5.6°C) the temperature at which the furnace is required for space heating, from 72°F (22.2°C; the interior temperature, now constant) to 62°F (16.7°C); of the total, 6°F (3.3°C) represents auxiliary heating from appliances and people, and 4°F (2.2°F) represents solar heating.
2. The efficiency of the furnace as a converter taking chemical energy from gas and delivering heat to a volume defined by basement plus living area is about 70 percent.
3. The heat losses by which the heat from furnace and auxiliary sources is dissipated are distributed: 40 percent by air infiltration, 30 percent by conduction through windows, and 10 percent each by conduction through attic, walls, and basement. The heat loss rate is roughly 640 Btu/hr°F (340W/°C), when long-term (monthly) data are considered [28, 34] (see also Chapters 2 and 3).

For most house-furnace systems in most locations, a linear relationship between the energy consumption for space heating and the outside temperature, similar to Figure 1-16, should represent the data quite well. Then the determination of two parameters (slope and intercept) from an analysis of data for various outside temperatures will suffice to make useful quantitative statements about conservation strategies. In a few special situations, such as houses with heat pumps (whose efficiency drops with colder weather), three parameter fits to the data may be warranted. Field determinations of the parameters in simple models of energy consumption can form the core of an effective retrofit program, helping initially in choosing among retrofits and later in verifying the degree of success of those implemented [35–37] (see also Chapter 8).

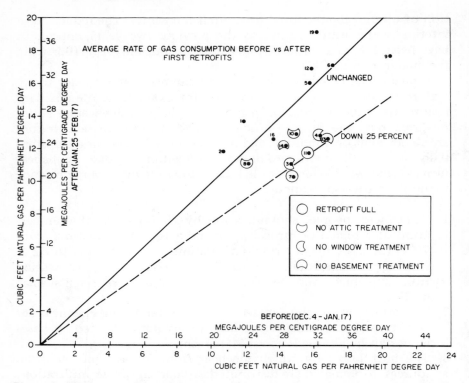

Figure 1–17. Average Rate of Gas Consumption Before versus After First Retrofits

Savings Due to First Round Retrofits

The display of house-by-house gas consumption in Figure 1–17 provides an accurate view of the effectiveness of the retrofits installed in the Twin Rivers townhouses as confirmed by subsequent, more detailed analysis. A performance index, gas consumption per degree day, is calculated for each house for time intervals on both sides of a period of retrofit, and a cross-plot is constructed with the "before" and "after" indexes as coordinates. It is desirable for the weather to be as nearly the same in the two time intervals as possible; here the outside temperature averaged 34.5°F (1.4°C) in the six week period before and 36.7°F (2.6°C) in the three week period after the one week period of retrofit.

Our experimental design simplified the interpretation of the cross-plot. Eight of the sixteen houses were left untouched (the control group), while the other eight received differing combinations of the components of the full retrofit package. The cross-plot strongly suggests that all of the retrofits had some effect and that the relative effectiveness, in terms of amount of gas conserved, is window treatment (smallest), then basement treatment, then attic treatment (largest). The combined winter savings appear to be up to 30 percent, relative to a control group manifesting a slightly larger rate of consumption "after" than "before" [10, 15] (see also chapter 4). Summer conservation appears to be very small, for reasons not fully understood [38].

More detailed analysis has revealed two pitfalls in this method of winter data reduction. First, spurious effects of house orientation are easily enhanced in such cross-plots, making it necessary to take care when the sample of houses contains a mix of orientations. In the figure here, Houses 7, 9, 10, 11, 13, and 16 are oriented east and west, and the sun systematically shifts them downward on this plot, relative to the other houses (nine oriented north and south, one—House 5—oriented northeast and southwest). This shift is a special case of the following solar effect: in periods of comparable sunniness, the sun improves (lowers) the performance indexes of houses with east and west windows by an amount that becomes increasingly significant the further the time interval under assessment is from December 21; no comparable enhancement occurs for south windows, the effect of longer days being almost exactly canceled by the effect of a higher sun. In the assessment of the Princeton retrofits, the inclusion of this solar shift turns out to reduce estimates of the savings by about ten percentage points [39].

The second pitfall of calculating the percent fuel saved for a short period in midwinter is not recognizing that the percent fuel saved over the whole winter will generally be larger. There are two consequences of improving either the tightness of a house or the thermal resistance of its shell: not only does less heat flow out of the house at each outside temperature, but also the auxiliary heat generated by sun, appliances, and people is more effectively retained. The second effect leads to a shortening of the heating season, that is, to a 100 percent reduction in amount of gas consumption required on certain mild days. The percentage reduction in gas consumption resulting from most retrofits will be smallest in coldest weather, and the annual average reduction will be that of a stretch of average winter days rather than that of a stretch of cold ones. Given data for a limited period, the accomplishments of a retrofit over a winter can, however, be estimated quite accurately with a simple model of daily winter temperature (and, possibly, sunlight and wind). Of course, one is not likely to have to contend with either of these two pitfalls if one has a full year of data "before" and "after" a retrofit, but this requires a long wait for results.

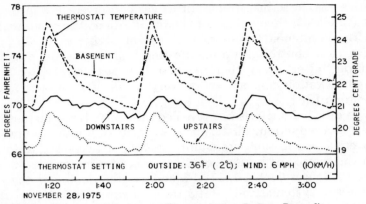

Figure 1–18A. Room and Basement Temperatures Before Retrofit.

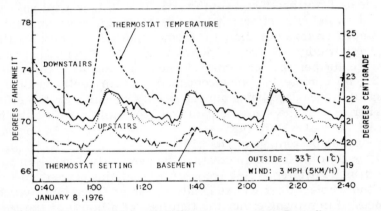

Figure 1–18B. Room and Basement Temperatures After Retrofit.

Details of Interior Temperature

Four interior temperature traces are shown in Figures 1–18A and 1–18B. Three cycles of furnace operation last approximately two hours, during two cold winter nights, one before and one after Princeton's full retrofit package was installed in this townhouse.

The following results of the retrofits may be discerned:

1. The basement has become $5°F$ ($3°C$) colder.
2. The basement temperature rises less sharply and less far and it falls more slowly.
3. Conversely, the downstairs temperature rises more sharply and further, and it falls more rapidly.
4. The upstairs and the downstairs temperature have become much more nearly equal, the downstairs having previously been $2°F$ ($1°C$) warmer.

The basement retrofit is responsible for the first three effects: insulation of basement ducts means less heat lost to the basement and more heat delivered immediately to the living area through the registers rather than delivered slowly through the basement ceiling. The fourth effect, a warmer upstairs, is brought about principally by the attic retrofit, which reduces the heat flow through the attic and upper side walls [40].

A detailed look at a single furnace cycle reveals significant information about the furnace controls. The temperature inside the thermostat (located downstairs) rises far more steeply ($1°F$, or $0.6°C$, per minute) than the temperatures in the rooms. The difference in rates of climb is reflective of a resistive heating element within the thermostat, the "anticipator," that is active when the furnace is on and shuts off when the furnace shuts off. The length of time the furnace will fire during any cycle (for a given "dead band" on the thermostat) is actually more sensitive to changes in the size of the resistance in the anticipator than to changes in the size of the furnace.

It is often argued that furnaces are oversized. Figure 1–18A shows that, when the outside temperature is $36°F$ ($2°C$), this Twin Rivers furnace runs for seven minutes (while the temperature within the thermostat rises $7°F$, or $4°C$), then stays off for thirty-three minutes, thereby firing only 18 percent of the time. Such a furnace is oversized by any usual criteria. The case against "oversizing" is a very loose one, however, grounded in a vaguely formulated case against "transients" in furnace combustion and in duct heat transfer. Moreover, such transients can be reduced, without changing the fraction of time that the furnace is on, either (1) by increasing the dead band at the thermostat, or (2) by reducing the rate of heating by the anticipator. Both are more modest changes than resizing the furnace. The penalty for making such changes at the controls, however, is a larger temperature rise within the rooms during a furnace cycle, with possible adverse consequences for comfort [15, 16].

The anticipator setting in the Twin Rivers thermostat (and many others) is easily adjusted by an accessible lever. It is not at all clear exactly where the lever should be set, however, so it may be just as well that hardly any resident knows the lever is there.

The data here were logged by an acquisition system belonging to the National Bureau of Standards that is capable of scanning twenty data points per second. The system can collect data either periodically (as here, once a minute) or in an event-activated mode (see Chapter 7).

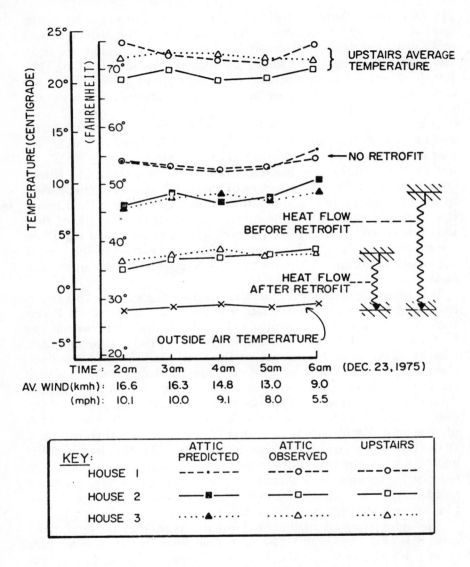

Figure 1–19. Effect of Attic Retrofit on Attic Temperature

The Attic Temperature Index

The attic temperature is particularly easy to measure, and we are convinced that it is also particularly informative if one is seeking to characterize the thermal properties of a house. In many cases, this temperature is an immediate index of the quality of the thermal system that isolates attic from living area. The homeowner can monitor attic temperature before and after an attic retrofit to obtain a nearly immediate assessment of its efficacy.

An attic temperature at night predicted from a simple linear model is compared with the temperature actually observed, for three attics, in Figure 1–19. Two of the three attics had been retrofitted (floor insulation added and air passages from the basement blocked) between the period of time during which the parameters of the model were established and the night shown here. The third attic (House 1) was untouched. The retrofitted attics are seen to be $10°F$ to $14°F$ ($6°C$ to $8°C$) colder than predicted, the expected result of better isolation of the attic from the living area; the attic of House 1 is seen to have the expected temperature, within $1°F$ ($0.6°C$) [36, 41].

The linear model used in these predictions involved only upstairs temperature, outside air temperature, and wind velocity. Parameters are established using standard linear regression techniques. The model has been found to be broadly useful in extensive tests. The parameters in the model, however, have turned out not to be easily interpretable in terms of the thermal properties of the building materials in the townhouse, an unexpected result. The attic is much warmer, both before and after retrofit, than was anticipated. Detailed investigation of air flow and thermal storage in the attic is underway to establish the detailed correspondence between the parameters of the model and the physical properties of the attic. Large, unexpected channels for heat flow into the attic that bypass the attic insulation have been found. It is becoming clear that retrofits that block these channels are even more cost-effective than conventional attic insulation [42–44] (see also Chapter 3).

Linear regression models have been developed for other variables, notably the air infiltration rate and the rate of gas consumption, with the same expectation that the parameters in these models may be useful numerical surrogates for complex physical effects [45, 46]. This approach has enabled us, for example, to model buoyancy-driven and wind-driven air infiltration (see Chapter 6), and to produce simple measures of the effectiveness of solar heating through windows and walls. We expect that, very generally, field assessments of the quality of a building and the priorities for its retrofit will rely heavily, in the near future, on the determination of the parameters in such relatively simple models and on the comparison of such parameters against norms determined by experience to be desirable [34, 47–49].

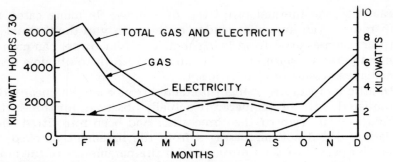

Figure 1–20A. Rate of Thermal Energy Release at the House by Gas and Electricity Use

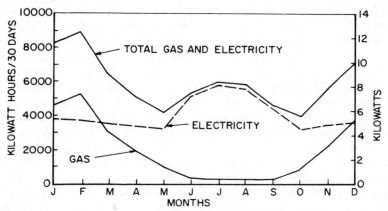

Figure 1–20B. Rate of Fossil Fuel Energy Consumption for Gas and Electricity Use

Gas and Electricity

Gas consumption and electricity consumption are superimposed in two different ways in Figure 1–20. Figure 1–20A presents the thermal energy content, *at the house*, of the chemical energy in the gas and the electrical energy in the wires. Figure 1–20B presents the fossil fuel energy consumed *by the economy* to provide the gas and electricity: to do this, the electrical energy is simply weighted by a factor of three, which approximates the conversion inefficiency of the electric power plant, while the gas energy is left unchanged. (A complete consideration of conversion losses would include various 10 percent effects, like the energy to pump the gas from the wellhead and the energy lost in electric power lines and transformers. Slightly larger multiplicative weights would result.)

The rates of energy consumption across months shown here are averages over the 248 two floor townhouses in Quad II at Twin Rivers. In these townhouses, gas is used exclusively for space heating (and, rarely, for outdoor barbecues). Electricity is used for all other purposes. We use data on gas and electric consumption from 1973, and we normalize the variable (and noncoincident) periods between meter readings to thirty-day periods.

Figure 1–20A is appropriate for judging the significance of the electrical energy consumed by appliances as an auxiliary source of space heating, relative to the gas consumed by the furnace. In the mild months of April and November, the energy content of the electricity is roughly 35 percent of the total energy consumed at the house, and even in the coldest month, February, it is 20 percent. The second role for electric appliances as auxiliary sources of residential heating needs to be addressed in an overall program of residential energy conservation. Considerations of appliance location and heat recovery are relatively unfamiliar, for the relative role of appliances in residential space heating has only recently grown to the levels shown here. Our detailed studies suggest that the potential for increasing the fraction of the heat recovered from appliances is a task comparable in significance to the task of increasing the effectiveness of the heat source represented by the sunlight striking the building.

The bulge in the summer months in an otherwise flat electricity profile represents consumption by the air conditioner; the air conditioner accounts for nearly half of total electricity consumption in July and August. The summer gas consumption (700 cubic feet, or 0.8 GJ, per month) is attributable to a single pilot light on the furnace, shut off in very few houses, a heat source equivalent to a 300 watt bulb burning continuously. As Figure 1–20B shows, this is about 20 percent of the energy consumption rate for electrical appliances other than the air conditioner. Minimizing the "second role" of gas and electric appliances in summer, as sources of unwanted heat, requires strategies complementary to those designed to retain winter appliance heat. Summing over the twelve months yields annual totals: 780 hundred cubic feet (800 therms, or 84GJ) of gas and 16,200 kWh (58GJ) of electricity consumed in the average townhouse.

Figure 1–20B is appropriate for judging the drain imposed on natural resources by space heating relative to that imposed by the electric appliances. Roughly one-third of the fossil fuel combustion required to "power" the Twin Rivers townhouse for a year occurs at the furnace and two-thirds at the electric power plant. Moreover, as the relative dollar costs paid by the resident closely parallel Figure 1–20B, it also is appropriate for judging the drain on the pocketbook. A cost profile over months that has two nearly equal winter and summer peaks is characteristic of most gas-heated, electrically air conditioned houses in a climate like New Jersey's.

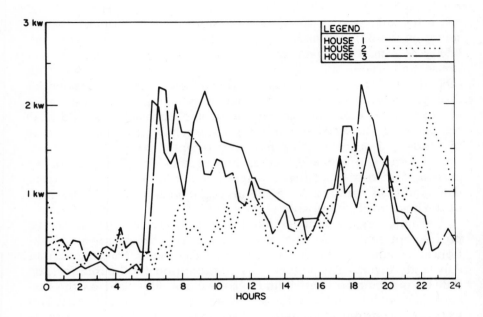

Figure 1-21. Load Profiles of Water Heaters in Three Adjacent Townhouses

The Water Heater

The electric water heater uses 8,000 kWh of electricity over the year in an average Twin Rivers townhouse, roughly half of the total electricity. The annual cost of electricity for hot water (about $300 in 1975) exceeds the annual cost of gas for space heating (about $220 in 1975). The provision of hot water clearly merits attention!

Figure 1–21 shows the distribution of electricity consumption over the hours of the day for three water heaters. The data for each hour, in these "load profiles," are obtained by averaging the consumption during that hour for ninety-seven winter days in 1975. Electricity consumption is seen to be very uneven, with peak to trough ratios exceeding ten to one. Moreover, the peaks occur at nearly the worst possible times, from the point of view of the electric utility system—not during the nighttime hours when the system is operating its least costly baseload plants, but rather during the morning and evening, when the system is operating its more expensive (and less efficient) peaking capacity [50].

The electric consumption of the water heater can be approximated by the sum of two terms: (1) continuous consumption at a rate of about 200 W, compensating for the steady loss of heat into the basement through the poorly insulated sides of the tank (visible as the minimum level of consumption between midnight and six A.M.), and (2) intermittent consumption, averaging 700W, occurring nearly simultaneously with the use of hot water in the house. Assuming that the water is heated from 60°F (15.6°C) to 145°F (62.8°C) before use, 700 W corresponds to eighty gallons (0.24 cubic meters) of hot (145°F, or 62.8°C) water consumption per day.

The Twin Rivers water heater contains two 4.5 kW heating elements, only one of which is on at a time. These enable near instantaneous response to demand for hot water, but evidently with the result that the water heater operates only 0.9 kW/4.5 kW = 20 percent of the time. The capacity of the water heater, eighty gallons, is approximately equivalent to one day's use, so shifting the time of heating to off-peak hours, with such large heating elements and a well-insulated tank, should not be difficult. Time of day pricing, to be sure, would provide an incentive to do so.

Approaches to energy conservation in water heating include (1) improving the insulation on the tank (see Figure 1–4B); (2) lowering the thermostat setting at the tank to reduce tank heat losses; (3) providing heat exchange between incoming cold water and waste hot water; (4) capturing heat rejected by appliances, like the refrigerator; (5) capturing heat vented up the furnace flue; and (6) capturing solar energy. A combination of the six strategies (in conjunction with strategies, like faucet design, that reduce water consumption directly) should permit energy consumption at the water heater to be eliminated entirely [51].

REFERENCES*

1. Fraker, H., Jr., and Schorske, E. 1973. Energy husbandry in housing: an analysis of the development process in a residential community, Twin Rivers, N.J. CES Report No. 5.
2. Hackney, L.D. 1975. A political analysis of the development process in East Windsor Township. Senior thesis, Department of Politics, Princeton University.
3. Socolow, R.H. 1975. Energy conservation in housing: concepts and options. In *Future Land Use: Energy, Environmental and Legal Constraints*, eds. R.W. Burchell, and D. Listokin, pp. 311–23. New Brunswick, N.J.: Rutgers University Press.
4. Fox, J.; Fraker, H. Jr.; Grot, R.; Harrje, D.; Schorske, E.; and Socolow, R.H. 1973. Energy Conservation in Housing: First Annual Progress Report (1973). CES Report No. 6.
5. Seligman, C., and Darley, J. 1977. Feedback as a means of decreasing residential energy consumption. *Journal of Applied Psychology* 67: 363–68.
6. Seligman, C.; Darley, J.; and Becker, L.J. 1976. Psychological strategies to reduce energy consumption. CES Report No. 41.
7. Becker, L.J. 1978. The joint effect of feedback and goal setting on performance: a field study of residential energy conservation. *Journal of Applied Psychology* (in press).
8. Seligman, C.; Kriss, M.; Darley, J.J.; Fazio, R.H.; Becker, L.J.; and Pryor, J.B. 1978. Predicting residential energy consumption from homeowners' attitudes. *Journal of Applied Social Psychology* (in press).
9. Becker, L.J., and Seligman, C. 1978. Reducing air conditioning waste by signaling it is cool outside. *Personality and Social Psychology Bulletin* (in press).
10. Harrje, D.T. 1976. Retrofitting: plan, action, and early results using the townhouses at Twin Rivers. CES Report No. 29.
11. Grot, R.; Harrje, D.; and Johnston, L. 1976. Application of thermography for evaluating effectiveness of retrofit measures. In *Third Biennial Infrared Information Exchange*. St. Louis, Mo.: AGA Corporation.
12. Socolow, R.H. 1973. New tasks for the energy industries. *Public Utilities Fortnightly* 91 (12): 40–43.
13. Hall, S., and Harrje, D. 1975. Instrumentation for the Omnibus experiment. CES Report No. 21.
14. Sinden, F. 1976. Conductive losses from basements. Twin Rivers Note No. 4.
15. Socolow, R.H., and Sonderegger, R.C. 1976. The Twin Rivers program on energy conservation in housing: four-year summary report. CES Report No. 32.

*Unpublished works were produced for Princeton University. They have been disseminated from the Center for Environmental Studies (CES), Princeton University.

16. Harrje, D.T.; Socolow, R.H.; and Sonderegger, R.C. 1977. Residential energy conservation—the Twin Rivers project. *ASHRAE Transactions* 83, pt. 1.

17. The Study Group on Technical Aspects of Efficient Use of Energy, 1975. Efficient use of energy. *Physics Today* 28 (8): 23–33.

18. Ford, K.W.; Rochlin, G.J.; Ross, M.; and Socolow, R.H., eds. 1975. *Efficient Use of Energy: A Physics Perspective.* AIP Conference Proceedings No. 25. New York: American Institute of Physics.

19. Harrje, D.; Hunt, C.; Treado, S.; and Malik, N. 1975. Automated instrumentation for building air infiltration measurements. CES Report No. 13.

20. Harrje, D., and Grot, R. 1977. Automated air infiltration measurements and implications for energy conservation. In *Proceedings of the International Conference on Energy Use Management* (Tucson, Arizona; October 1977), eds. R.A. Fazzolare and C.B. Smith, I, 457–64. New York: Pergamon.

21. Mattingly, G., and Peters, E. 1977. Wind and trees—air infiltration effects on energy in housing. *Journal of Industrial Aerodynamics* 2:1–19.

22. Malik, N. 1977. Air Infiltration in Homes. MSE thesis, Department of Aerospace and Mechanical Sciences, Princeton University.

23. Sinden, F. 1978. Theoretical basis for tracer gas measurements of air infiltration. *Building and Environment* 13:21–28.

24. Sinden, F. 1977. Passive device for controlling ventilation. Patent disclosure dated January 31, 1977. CES.

25. Sinden, F. 1977. Decentralized heat recovery devices. Patent disclosure dated March 8, 1977. CES.

26. Socolow, R.H. 1978. Four anxieties about a vigorous energy conservation program in the United States. *Annals of the New York Academy of Sciences* (in press).

27. Grot, R., and Socolow, R.H. 1974. Energy utilization in a residential community. In *Energy: Demand, Conservation, and Institutional Problems*, ed. M.S. Mackrakis, MIT Press. Cambridge, Mass.: pp. 483–98.

28. Fox, J. 1973. Energy consumption for residential space heating—a case study. MSE thesis, Department of Aerospace and Mechanical Sciences (also CES Report No. 4).

29. Mayer, L., and Robinson, J. 1975. A statistical analysis of the monthly consumption of gas and electricity in the home. CES Report No. 18.

30. Cheung, M. 1974. The effect of the energy crisis on the winter gas consumption of quad II split-level townhouses at Twin Rivers, New Jersey. Junior independent work, Department of Statistics, Princeton University.

31. Mayer, L.S. 1976. Estimating the effects of the onset of the energy crisis on residential energy demand. *Energy and Resources* (in press).

32. Horowitz, C.E., and Mayer, L.S. 1977. The relationship between the price and demand for natural gas. *Energy Research* 1: 193–222.

33. Alpert, R.A. 1976. Electricity: residential consumption and conservation. Senior thesis, Department of Statistics, Princeton University.

34. Sonderegger, R.C. 1977. Dynamic models of house heating based on equivalent thermal parameters. Ph.D. thesis, Department of Aerospace and Mechanical Sciences (also CES Report No. 57).

35. Schrader, T.F. 1978. A two-parameter model for assessing the determinants of residential space heating. MSE thesis, Department of Aerospace and Mechanical Sciences, Princeton University.

36. Socolow, R.H. 1976. Energy utilization in a planned community in the United States. In *Energy Conservation in the Built Environment*, ed. R.G. Courtney, pp. 447−57. Proceedings of the CIB Symposium held at The Building Research Establishment, Garston, Watford, April 1976. Hornby, Lancaster, England: The Construction Press.

37. Socolow, R.H. 1977. The coming age of conservation. *Ann. Rev. Energy* 2: 239−89.

38. Pollack, A. 1977. Residential energy conservation: the effects of retrofits on summer electricity demand. Senior thesis, Department of Statistics, Princeton University.

39. Woteki, T. 1976. The Princeton Omnibus experiment: some effects of retrofits on space heating requirements. CES Report No. 43.

40. Woteki, T. 1977. Some effects of retrofits on interior temperatures in a sample of houses. CES Working Paper No. 31.

41. Pollack, A. 1976. Modeling attic temperature in three highly instrumented townhouses in Twin Rivers, New Jersey. Junior independent work, Department of Statistics (also CES Report No. 28).

42. Dutt, G.S., and Harrje, D.T. 1977. Influence of attics on residential energy conservation. CES Working Paper No. 33.

43. Woteki, T., and Dutt, G. 1977. The two-resistance model for attic heat flow: theory and results from a retrofit experiment. CES Report No. 52.

44. Dutt, G., and Beyea, J. 1977. Attic thermal performance: a study of townhouses at Twin Rivers. CES Report No. 53.

45. Socolow, R.H. 1975. Time-series models for the energy balance in a house. CES Working Paper No. 19.

46. Socolow, R.H. 1975. A model of heat flow in an attic. CES Working Paper No. 20.

47. Socolow, R.H. 1976. Energy conservation in existing residences: Your home deserves a house call. Presented at the conference, Energy Efficiency as a National Priority, Washington, D.C., May 20, 1976.

48. Sonderegger, R.C. 1977. Modeling residential heat load from experimental data: the equivalent thermal parameters of a house. *Proceedings of the International Conference on Energy Use Management* (Tucson, Arizona; October 1977), eds. R.A. Fazzolare, C.B. Smith, II, 183−94. New York: Pergamon.

49. Sonderegger, R.C. 1977. Diagnostic tests determining the thermal response of a house. Presented at the ASHRAE meeting in Atlanta, Georgia, February 1978.

50. Robinson, J., and Yeung, J. 1975. Summer air conditioning and appliance use patterns: a graphical analysis. CES Report No. 22.

51. Meyer, J.; Niemiec, D.; and Harrje, D. 1974. Energy efficient design of household appliances. CES Report No. 11.

Chapter 2

A Two-Thirds Reduction in the Space Heat Requirement of a Twin Rivers Townhouse*

Frank W. Sinden
Center for Environmental Studies
Princeton University

Abstract

A Twin Rivers townhouse received a series of retrofits more extensive than those deployed in previous experiments at Twin Rivers, and a 67 percent reduction in annual energy use for space heating resulted. The retrofits included interior window insulators of various designs, basement and attic insulation, and systematic attention to routes of air infiltration. The 67 percent reduction was approximately the savings anticipated by a simple model in which the "second role" of insulation in improving the retention of the nonfurnace heat from sun, appliances, and people appears explicitly. (In the absence of nonfurnace heat, the savings of gas achieved would have been only 50 percent.) The retrofits appear to be a financially attractive investment at the present price of natural gas and a 10 percent return on investment. Further retrofits are discussed.

INTRODUCTION

Among the ways of conserving household energy, there are no spectacular technical fixes. There is only a catalog of small fixes, many of them drab and unimpressive in isolation. It is therefore easy to dis-

*I am indebted to our former graduate student, Robert Sonderegger, who lived in the house, for his assistance in planning and supplying important information; to Adrienne Lavine for her outstandingly competent assistance with the data analysis; to Kenneth Gadsby and Roy Crosby for their craftsmanlike construction and technical work; to Terry Brown and JoAnn Poli for their patient manuscript preparation; and to many others who helped along the way.

miss conservation of household energy as an incremental business and to seek bigger solutions elsewhere. But the catalog is fat, and many of its entries are cheap. With patience, groups of small and even tiny fixes can be put together into large assemblies that overall can produce impressive results.

Some of the items in the catalog can only be perfected and applied by large or technically sophisticated industries (solid state controls, heat pumps, better refrigerators, and so forth), but many others, and among them some of the most economically attractive measures, use only low technology and are accessible to small businesses, individual designers, and householders.

Of all the fuel that is consumed to run a Twin Rivers townhouse, about a third is for space heat. The other two-thirds is consumed at the power plant to provide the house's electricity. Space heat is the largest single item in the energy budget and possibly the one that offers the simplest, most accessible, and most numerous opportunities for conservation. For this reason, we chose to concentrate on space heat in this experiment. That is not to say, however, that important reductions cannot also be achieved in the other two-thirds of consumption by equally economical, though possibly more sophisticated, means.

In past Twin Rivers experiments, simple conservation measures or "retrofits" were systematically tested in groups of similar townhouses. These retrofits resulted in fuel savings of between 20 and 25 percent. The purpose of the experiment reported here was to follow through on these efforts, though on a smaller, more exploratory scale, to see what could be achieved with more extensive and less conventional retrofits. Using a single, rented Twin Rivers townhouse, we aimed to assemble a package of small measures that in aggregate would reduce losses by 50 percent or more. This, we felt, would give us a useful benchmark for judging the feasibility of large reductions in the use of fuel for heating houses.

We did not intend that the particular set of retrofits we chose should be regarded as unique or optimal in any way. Rather, we merely aimed to find, out of the many possibilities, one simple and economical set that would do the job. Altogether, our retrofits reduced thermal loss in the house by about 50 percent. This resulted in an estimated 67 percent reduction in the yearly fuel requirement. The reason for this magnification of effect is explained in the next section, which defines the simple model on which our analysis is based. In its elements, this model is little different from the ones usually used in studies of this kind. However, we have reformulated it somewhat in a way that we think improves its clarity and convenience. In particular, we have avoided the customary degree day measure because of its inappropriateness for very well-insulated houses whose breakeven temperatures are well below the 65°F (18°C) conventionally assumed. As more and more low loss houses appear on the scene through retrofit and new construction, the degree day measure will become increasingly awkward to apply. We believe the formulation offered here may be a useful alternative.

The third section of the chapter gives handbook estimates of the components of heat loss in our test house, while the fourth discusses some problems in retrofit design and in particular describes the designs we used. The fifth section gives the experimental results, and the sixth discusses briefly some further conservation measures not included in our tests. The final section is a summary and conclusion.

ANALYTICAL FRAMEWORK

The rate at which a house uses fuel-supplied heat is given approximately by the equation:

$$F = [L(T_i - T) - H]_+ \tag{2.1}$$

where:

F = rate at which heat passes through the house's shell (Btu/hr or kW);

L = overall thermal lossiness* of the house (Btu/°F hr or kW/°C);

T_i = inside temperature (°F or °C);

T = outside temperature (°F or °C);

H = heat supplied by other sources ("free heat") (Btu/hr or kW).

The subscripted plus sign means "if positive, otherwise zero." That is:

$$[x]_+ = \begin{matrix} x \text{ if } x > 0 \\ 0 \text{ if } x \leq 0 \end{matrix}$$

---

*I have borrowed the slightly slangy but vivid term "lossy" from electrical engineering, where it is applied to components that dissipate energy. I use it here to encompass all forms of unwanted heat transfer from the house, including that due to air exchange as well as conduction and radiation.

Equation (2.1) describes the performance of the house's shell. To get actual fuel consumed, G, one must also take account of furnace efficiency:

$$G = \frac{F}{e} \qquad (2.2)$$

where

G = heat content of fuel consumed (Btu/hr or kW);

e = furnace efficiency (heat output/heat content of fuel).

In Figure 2–1, equation (2.1) is plotted to show heat consumption F as a function of outside temperature T with L, T_i, and H treated as fixed parameters. For a particular house, the triplet of numbers (L, T_i, H) provides a simple but often adequate characterization of the house's thermal performance.

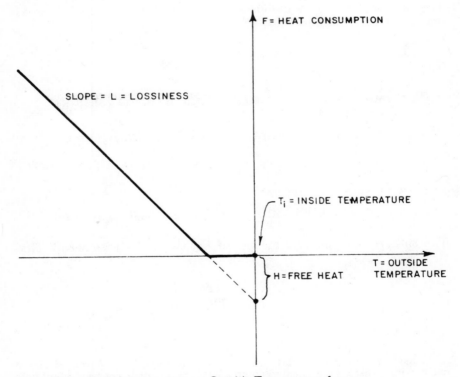

Figure 2–1. Heat Consumption vs. Outside Temperature for an Idealized House

Each of the parameters is the resultant of a number of contributing components. Contributing to lossiness L are the conductances of window glass, walls, roof, and floor, as well as air leaks through cracks, crevices, flues, open doors, and so forth. Contributing to free heat, H, are the warming effects of lights, appliances, and people, as well as sun shining through windows. The inside temperature, T_i, is an average value representing the whole distribution of temperature, which may vary from place to place within the house and from time to time. More refined models take account of individual contributions separately. This improves accuracy insofar as these contributions are nonlinear, as is the case, for example, with air exchange loss, which has a weakly quadratic dependence on inside-outside temperature difference. More refined models also explicitly recognize weather components other than temperature, such as sun and wind, and take account of the house's thermal inertia. In this chapter we will use only the simple model of equation (2.1).

By combining given values of L, T_i, and H with outside temperature data, one can estimate with reasonable accuracy the house's yearly heat requirement. The temperature data are most conveniently given in the form of a histogram:

$h(T)dT$ = number of hours out of the year during which the
temperature lies between T and $T + dT$.

It follows that

$$\int_{-\infty}^{\infty} h(T)dT = 8{,}766, \qquad (2.3)$$

the number of hours in a year. The distribution $h(T)$ depends, of course, on the locality. For central New Jersey, $h(T)$ is approximated by the bar chart in Figure 2−2. The areas of the individual bars show the number of hours in which the temperature lay within successive 5°F (2.8°C) intervals. The chart is based on averaged data from three years.

To obtain the fuel heat F_{yr} required for a year, the information in Figures 2−1 and 2−2 is combined by the formula:

$$F_{yr} = \int_{-\infty}^{\infty} F(T) h(T)dT, \qquad (2.4)$$

or, more explicitly,

$$F_{yr}(L, T_i, H) = \int_{-\infty}^{\infty} [L(T_i - T) - H]_+ h(T)dT. \qquad (2.5)$$

F_{yr} has the units kilowatt hours per year or Btu per year.

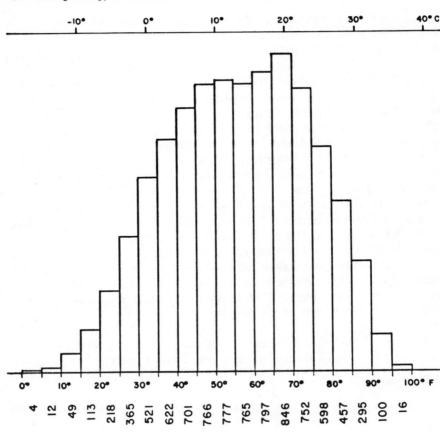

Figure 2−2. Temperature Histogram for Central New Jersey. The Bars and the Sideways Numbers Represent the Number of Hours out of a Year During Which the Temperature Lies Within Successive 5°F Intervals. Based on the Three Year Period Between May 1973 and May 1976

Conservation measures aim to save fuel by altering the parameters L, T_i, and H. In the next paragraphs, therefore, we will look more closely at how yearly fuel consumption F_{yr} depends on these parameters. We will find that the dependence is nonlinear in such a way as to make the economics of conservation more favorable than has sometimes been supposed.

The relationship among L, T_i, H, and F_{yr} can be represented compactly by the single curve of Figure 2−3, which plots two simple parameter combinations against each other. The curve itself depends

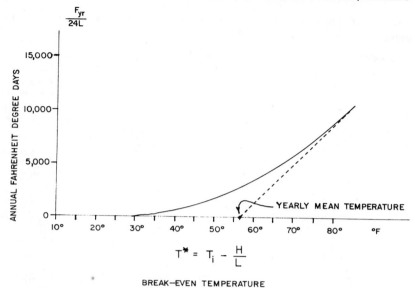

$$T^* = T_i - \frac{H}{L}$$

BREAK–EVEN TEMPERATURE

Figure 2–3. Yearly Space Heat Requirement for Central New Jersey. Given a House's Break-Even Temperature T^* and Lossiness L, the Graph Can be Used to Find the Yearly Heat Requirement F_{yr}. The Number 8766 is the Number of Hours in a Year. A Table of the Curve is Given on the Next Page in both Fahrenheit and Celsius Degrees

only on the histogram $h(T)$ and is therefore characteristic of a locality. That shown in Figure 2–3 is for central New Jersey. The corresponding curve for Minnesota would be higher; for Virginia, lower.

The horizontal axis of Figure 2–3 represents

$$T^* = T_i - \frac{H}{L}, \tag{2.6}$$

the lowest outside temperature at which the house can get along without burning fuel. T^* is often called the "breakeven temperature." In Figure 2–1, it is the point where the slanted line meets the temperature axis. The vertical axis in Figure 2–3 represents

$$\frac{F_{yr}}{24L},$$

whose units are degree days. The curve can be interpreted as giving annual degree days for a locality as a function of the breakeven

Table 2–1. Data for Figure 2–3: Yearly Space Heat Requirement versus Breakeven Temperature.

T^*		$F_{yr}/24L$	
$(^\circ F)$	$(^\circ C)$	$^\circ F$ days	$^\circ C$ days
0	-17.8	0	0
5	-15.0	0.365	0.203
10	-12.2	2.335	1.297
15	- 9.4	10.65	5.917
20	- 6.7	33.87	18.81
25	- 3.9	95.59	52.96
30	- 1.1	216.0	120.2
35	1.7	428.8	238.1
40	4.4	760.8	422.6
45	7.2	1230.	683.7
50	10.0	1853.	1029.
55	12.8	2637.	1465.
60	15.6	3581	1990.
65	18.3	4690.	2604.
70	21.1	5968.	3313.
75	23.9	7411.	4116.
80	26.7	8996.	4997.
85	29.4	10694.	5943.
90	32.2	12465.	6925.
95	35.0	14280.	7933.
100	37.8	16110.	8949.

temperature from which they are measured. Published degree day data conventionally assume the breakeven temperature to be $65^\circ F$ ($18.3^\circ C$). For low loss houses, however, it may be much lower than this. Our retrofitted test house, for example, has a breakeven temperature of about $50^\circ F$ ($10^\circ C$). For such houses the appropriate number of degree days is much less than the published figure, as can be seen from Figure 2–3.

The curve is tangent to the horizontal axis and to a line passing through the yearly mean outside temperature (shown dashed in Figure 2–3). Thus a low mean temperature means a high curve, hence high yearly fuel consumption, as one would expect. The deviation of the curve from its tangents is determined by the spread of the histogram $h(T)$. If there is no spread—that is, if the temperature is the same year round—then the curve coincides with its tangents. As the spread increases—that is, as summers get hotter and winters colder for a given mean—the curve rises away from the tangents. Thus, for a given mean annual temperature, greater seasonal extremes cause greater fuel consumption for space heating, as one would expect.

Although the curve of Figure 2–3 gives all the necessary information for calculating F_{yr} from the house parameters L, T_i, and H, it is somewhat inconvenient for examining the effects on yearly fuel consumption of *changes* in the individual parameters. We have therefore provided a series of plots in Figure 2−4 giving F_{yr} directly as a function of L, T_i, and H. All of these are derived from Figure 2−3.

Of particular interest is F_{yr} as a function of the lossiness L, because most of the conservation measures we will be discussing aim to reduce L. From the plots in Figure 2−4, one can see that a given percentage reduction in L always results in a larger percentage reduction in F_{yr}. It is for this reason that the relatively modest conservation measures reported below were able to achieve such large percentage fuel savings. More generally, this effect means that conservation can be pursued further than might otherwise be thought before diminishing returns render further effort uneconomical.

SIMPLE THEORETICAL ESTIMATES OF LOSSES

Conservation of space heat can be achieved by reducing L or T_i or by increasing H. This study confined itself to measures for reducing L. That does not mean, however, that measures of the other two types are not important. Promising possibilities are mentioned briefly in the concluding section.

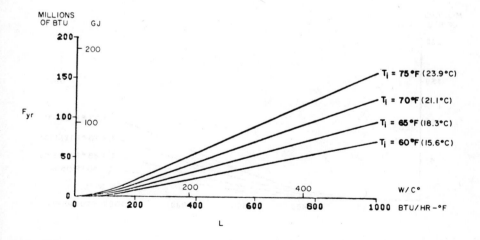

Figure 2−4A. Yearly Heat Requirement F_{yr} (in Millions of Btu) for a House in Central New Jersey as a Function of Lossiness L and Inside Temperature T_i With Free Heat H Fixed

FOR H = 6000 BTU / HR = 1.8 KW

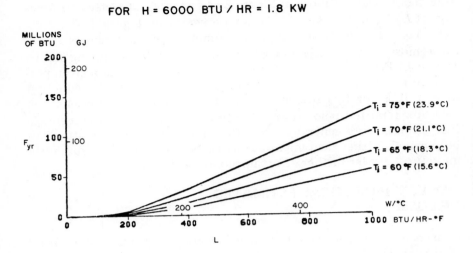

Figure 2–4B. Yearly Heat Requirement F_{yr} (in Millions of Btu) for a House in Central New Jersey as a Function of Lossiness L and Inside Temperature T_i With Free Heat H Fixed

FOR H = 12,000 BTU / HR = 3.5 KW

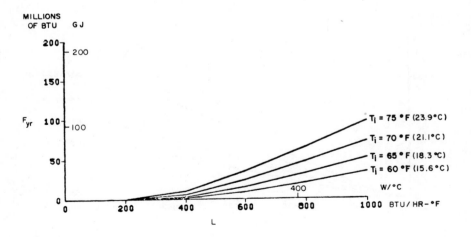

Figure 2–4C. Yearly Heat Requirement F_{yr} (in Millions of Btu) for a House in Central New Jersey as a Function of Lossiness L and Inside Temperature T_i With Free Heat H Fixed

The retrofit experiments discussed below were performed in a rented townhouse in Twin Rivers, New Jersey. Floor plans are given in Figure 2−5. This house is very similar to those used in earlier Twin Rivers studies.

Figure 2−6 gives estimates, based on simple theoretical methods, of the components of heat loss through the shell of the house. Summation of the components gives for L the value $L = 560$ Btu/°F hr (295 W/°C), which as noted below, agrees moderately well with the measured value of L.

A glance at the chart shows that the biggest losses are by conduction through the attic* and the windows and by general air leakage. Previous Twin Rivers experiments had shown attic insulation and moderate sealing of air leaks to be effective. We therefore set as our next targets (1) window losses, (2) remaining air leakage, and (3) basement losses. Our overall aim was to reduce L by about 50 percent.

DESIGN OF RETROFITS

Windows

Windows pose a special problem because of appearance. Unlike attic insulation, which is not seen, window insulation is likely to be highly visible. Aesthetics, therefore, is an inescapable element in design. However, this is an opportunity as well as a problem, because an especially attractive design may reinforce the incentive to conserve energy.

The conventional window insulator, the storm window, is usually placed on the outside. We find, however, that there are definite advantages to working on the inside: no ladders are needed for mounting and removal; materials need not be weatherproof; opening and closing can be handy; and striking decorative effects can be achieved.

To be effective, the insulating layer must be sealed around the edges. Thus conventional curtains, even if made of heavy insulating material, tend to be ineffective because they generally allow the formation of a cold downward convection current between the curtain and the window that communicates with the room. A first problem, then, is to design an insulating layer that can be sealed.

---

*There is a difficulty, however, in treating attic losses, because attic temperatures are too warm to be explained by handbook methods. This problem is dealt with in Chapter 3. Attic losses in Figure 2-6 were estimated before the results presented in Chapter 3 were available. In light of these results, Figure 2-6 attic losses are probably too low.

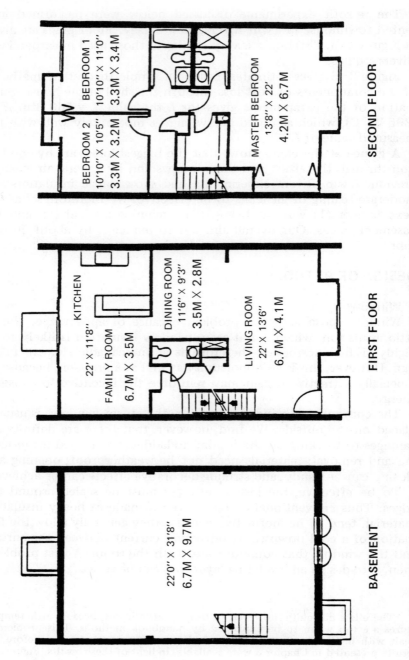

Figure 2–5. Twin Rivers Townhouse. The Plan of the Test House is the Mirror Image of that Shown Here

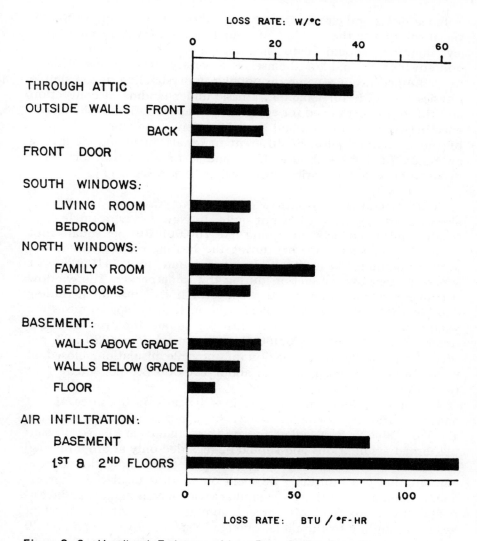

Figure 2−6. Handbook Estimates of Loss Rates Before Retrofit

A second problem concerns translucency. If the insulating layer is to be left in place all the time, then it must be translucent, and at least in part of its area, it should be transparent. These are conditions that should be met in windows that receive little direct sun. In sunny windows, however, it may be best to insulate only at night, so that the solar radiation is undiminished by any extra obstruction. In this case, the insulating layer may be opaque.

Since tastes and circumstances are so variable, there can be no universal solution to the problem of insulating windows. The aim of policy, therefore, should be to encourage designers and do-it-yourself houseowners to find for themselves a variety of solutions. What is needed especially is a common popular understanding of the simple physics involved—for example, a basic understanding of convection and the consequent need for edge seals; an appreciation of the difference between conduction and air infiltration; some quantitative idea of the insulating value of different materials, including air layers; awareness of the greenhouse effect; and so forth. In addition, there needs to be wide familiarity with possible basic designs [1].

South Windows. A south window that is unshaded in winter is almost a solar collector, but not quite. In New Jersey, a single pane south window collects something like 150,000 Btu per square foot (470 kWh per square meter) during the heating season, but it also loses something like 130,000 Btu per square foot (410 kWh per square meter) by conduction during the same period. The window becomes a much more effective collector if it is insulated. Adding another sheet of glass (with at least an inch of air space) raises the window's net gain from 20,000 Btu per square foot (60 kWh per square meter) to about 70,000 Btu per square foot (220 kWh per square meter). Further addition of movable insulation, closed at night, brings the net gain up to about 100,000 Btu per square foot (315 kWh per square meter).

The dollar value of the heat savings depends on the price of fuel and the efficiency of combustion. Some representative figures are given in Table 2−2. Needless to say, these figures are based on simple, broad assumptions and should be regarded only as order of magnitude estimates. Nevertheless, they give some indication of the amount that can profitably be spent on window insulation. For example, spending ten times the annual saving means making an investment with a tax-free, 10 percent annual return. At this level of return, according to the table, one could spend, for example, $4.20 per square foot ($45 per square meter) on night insulation of a south window in an oil-heated house.

A simple way to provide movable insulation is to mount it in the form of interior shutters that fold to the side. This is the method we adopted for the south-facing living room window in the Twin Rivers house (see Figure 2−7). For decoration, we simply mounted the floor length curtains that were already in the window on the shutters so that the overall appearance was little altered: The only difference was that in the open position the curtains hung along the ends of the alcove instead of along the window. Good designers can undoubtedly find ways to design interior shutters so that the shutters themselves are an attractive part of the interior decor. Our shutters are nothing more than 1.5 inch thick masonite-faced panels filled with glass wool and weather stripped around the edges. The materials costs, averaged over the window area, came to about sixty cents per square foot ($6.50 per square meter).

Movable insulation need not take the form of stiff panels. Flexible materials such as quilted curtains can also be used, provided two mechanical problems can be solved: (1) how to gather the material to one side, and (2) how to seal the edges. For edge sealing, sailboat technology may possibly be useful: a rope sewn into the hem slides in a groove. If the bottom edge slides along a smooth horizontal surface, sand in the hem can make an adequate seal. Some basic gathering means and edge seals are shown schematically in Figure 2—8. This is obviously a fertile field for invention and one that manufacturers should be urged to look into.

If the south-facing glass area is very large or the house is very well insulated, then the solar gain in the middle of the day may often be more than the house needs. In that case, it may be worth saving some of the excess heat for the following night. This may be done, for example, by means of a reversible insulating panel that is covered on one side with sealed tubes of eutectic salt. Such salt can absorb large amounts of heat at a fixed temperature. During the day, the panel, which is mounted just inside the glass, is turned so that the salt is facing the sun; at night the panel is reversed so that the stored heat can be released slowly to the room. Simpler heat storage can be accomplished in new construction by exposing massive structural elements such as concrete floors and walls to sun shining through windows.

North Windows. North windows receive only indirect sky radiation in winter, and at the latitude of New Jersey this is never enough to overcome the heat losses. Retrofits, therefore, must compromise among light, view, and heat savings. One way to achieve such a compromise is to divide the area into opaque, translucent, and transparent regions, with corresponding levels of insulation in each. Opaque areas can have very heavy insulation; translucent areas, somewhat less; and transparent areas, least.

A simple type of translucent insulation, used in the main bedroom of our test house, is shown in Figure 2—9.* Bubble plastic of the

---

*This window faces south. The insulation would be more efficient in a north window where the reduction of solar heat would be less important.

Table 2-2.   Typical Seasonal Savings per Square Foot (per Square Meter) Relative to Single Pane Window.[a]

	Heat $Btu/yr-ft^2$ $(kWh/yr-m^2)$	Electricity[b] $\$/yr-ft^2$ $(\$/yr-m^2)$	Oil[c] $\$/yr-ft^2$ $(\$/yr-m^2)$	Gas[d] $\$/yr-ft^2$ $(\$/yr-m^2)$
South Window:				
Double pane (> 1″ air space)	50,000 (158)	0.44 (4.7)	0.30 (3.2)	0.21 (2.3)
Single pane + R8 night insulation	70,000 (220)	0.62 (6.7)	0.42 (4.5)	0.30 (3.2)
Double pane + R8 night insulation	81,000 (255)	0.71 (7.6)	0.49 (5.3)	0.35 (3.8)
North Window:				
Double pane (> 1″ air space)	65,000 (205)	0.57 (6.1)	0.39 (4.2)	0.28 (3.0)
Single pane + R3 translucent insulation	93,000 (293)	0.82 (8.8)	0.56 (6.0)	0.41 (4.4)
East or West Window:				
Double pane (> 1″ air space)	61,000 (192)	0.54 (5.8)	0.37 (4.0)	0.26 (2.8)
Single pane + R3 translucent insulation	65,000 (205)	0.57 (6.1)	0.39 (4.2)	0.28 (3.0)
Single pane + R8 night insulation	70,000 (220)	0.62 (6.7)	0.42 (4.5)	0.30 (3.2)
Double pane + R8 night insulation	92,000 (290)	0.81 (8.7)	0.55 (5.9)	0.39 (4.2)

Notes

[a] Assumes a house with breakeven temperature $T^* = 65°F$ ($18°C$) and overall heat loss $L = 600$ Btu/$°F$ per hour located in central New Jersey. The first column of the table gives the net yearly heat savings relative to single pane. Note that window treatments may affect solar gains as well as conductive losses. The figures do not take account of the reduction in air infiltration that the various window treatments may achieve. Though too variable to estimate in general, this effect may make the true savings substantially larger than those shown.

[b] Assumes \$.03/kWh, heater efficiency of 100 percent.

[c] Assumes \$.49/gallon, furnace efficiency of 60 percent.

[d] Assumes \$.30/therm, furnace efficiency of 70 percent.

Figure 2—7A.   Insulating Shutters in South-Facing Living Room Window.
Curtain was Fastened Directly to Shutters.

kind used to pack fragile objects is mounted behind glass in wooden
frames placed just inside the aluminum windows. This design, using a
very inexpensive material to obtain a pleasing visual effect, is by
Mary Whiteside of New York City. The center panel is hinged for
access to the window. The thermal resistance of these panels (the
"R value") is about 2°F-hr-square-foot per Btu (0.35°C-square-
meter per Watt) or somewhat better than that of two panes of glass.
Combined with the double pane window, the overall resistance is
about 3.8°F-hr-square-foot per Btu (0.66°C-square-meter per Watt).
Materials costs averaged to about $1.60 per square foot ($17 per
square meter), mostly for glass. The cost of the bubble plastic was
negligible.

In the north-facing Twin Rivers family room we installed plexi-
glass panels mounted in wooden frames inside the aluminum sliding

Figure 2–7B. Living Room Shutters All the Way Open and Closed

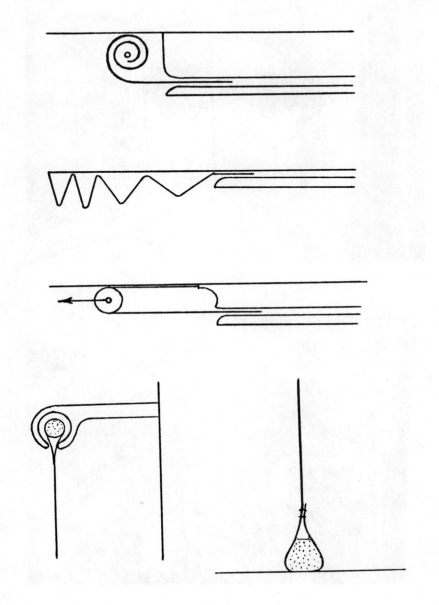

Figure 2—8. Flexible Insulation: Gathering Means and Edge Seals

Figure 2—9. Translucent Insulating Panels Made With Bubble Plastic Behind Glass.

doors. This is shown in Figure 2—10. Figure 2—11 shows the central panel with an experimental pattern of insulating materials of varying opacity designed by Rhoda Roper of Summit, New Jersey. The estimated average R-value of this panel is about $3°$F-hr ft^2/Btu (0.5°C-m^2/W).

Note that these panels overlap the existing door frame and completely cover it. We found this method of mounting to be much simpler than fitting the panels inside the frame as was done in the bedroom (Figure 2—9) because it avoided fussy trimming. The edges are sealed by means of a wide strip of soft plastic foam glued to the back of the panels. This simply presses against the old door frame and conforms automatically to its contours. The panels are held in place by small, removable metal brackets. Materials costs, as before, averaged to about $1.60 per square foot ($17 per square meter).

Figure 2—10. Insulating Panels Inside North-Facing Aluminum Frame Sliding Door

Figure 2−11. Center Panel With a Pattern of Insulating Materials of Varying Opacity Mounted in it

East or West Windows. East and west windows get some sun, but are net losers without insulation. Under the assumptions of Table 2−2, gains and losses are about equal for a single pane plus night insulation. There were no east or west windows in our test house.

The window retrofits included in our experiments are those shown in Figures 2−7, 2−9, and 2−10. These are in no way intended as demonstrations of optimal, ideal, or unique solutions to the window problem, but merely as simple, at most suggestive, designs that seemed suitable to the particular circumstances in our test house. Insulating panels for the windows of the two small bedrooms were also planned, but were not completed in time for the tests. These windows, therefore, were temporarily insulated with glass wool so as to bring the estimated overall reduction in conductive window loss to about 50 percent. The performance of the individual window retrofits was checked by means of simultaneous temperature observations taken inside the room, between the insulation and the window, and outside. Such data triplets give the relative performance of the window and the insulation. Agreement with handbook estimates was generally good. Typical data are given in Table 2−3.

Basement

In many houses, the joint between wood and masonry at the top of the foundation is cold and drafty, and Twin Rivers houses are no exception. A cross-section of the basement wall is shown in Figure 2−12. The thermally thin part of the wall above grade appeared to be an excellent candidate for retrofit, as it is in most houses. We estimated that by sealing the joint and filling the upper space with glass wool we could save about 27 Btu per °F hour (14 W per °C) in conductive losses alone. Extending the insulation all the way to the floor as shown in Figure 2−12, increased the estimated saving to 38 Btu per °F hour (20 W per °C) in conductive losses. The reduction in air infiltration into the basement was probably substantial, though our

Table 2−3. Opaque Shutter Performance (Night).

Typical measured temperatures		
Outside	32° F	(0° C)
Between shutter and window	39° F	(4° C)
Inside	67° F	(19° C)
Thermal resistance		
Window alone (double glass)	1.6 ft.² °F hr/Btu	(0.28 m² °C/W)
Shutter plus window		
Based on temperature data	8.0 ft.² °F hr/Btu	(1.41 m² °C/W)
Based on handbook calculation	8.3 ft.² °F hr/Btu	(1.46 m² °C/W)

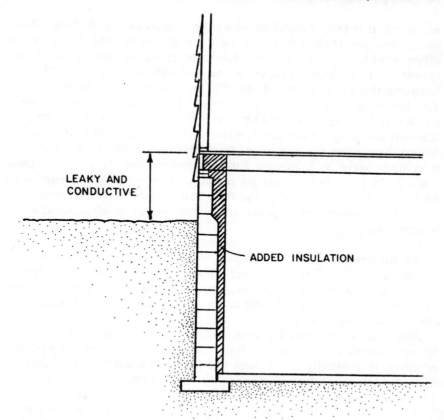

Figure 2–12. Cross-Section of Basement

data do not allow us to separate quantitatively the air infiltration benefits of the separate retrofits.

Attic

Earlier Twin Rivers retrofits included extra insulation on the attic floor to increase its resistance from R–11 to R–30. These retrofits also blocked two large air passages: the open shaft around the metal flue, and a variable gap between the masonry party wall and the wooden structure of the house. All of these measures were also included in the present experiment, but with an important addition: before installing the extra insulation, we pulled up the old insulation and carefully sealed all of the accessible air leaks from the house. These leaks, even aside from the flue shaft and the party wall gap, when taken together constituted a major pathway for air flow. More-over, they are typical not only of Twin Rivers houses, but of most other wooden houses as well. Leaks to the attic are of two main types: (1) holes around pipes, wires, and light fixtures; and (2) gaps between the gypsum board and the two by four partition framing. The latter gaps open a passage from the interior of the partition walls to the attic. Air flows readily into the interior of the partitions through a variety of openings, such as the gaps around heating ducts where they enter the partitions from the basement. Thus, the parti-tion walls serve as highways for infiltration flow. In new construc-tion, a plastic sheet should be installed over ceilings and partitions and under the joists, so that the flow from house to attic is positively blocked. Penetrations of pipes and wires should be eliminated or at least minimized.

Air Infiltration

Our second main target, after windows, was the heat loss due to air exchange between the interior and exterior of the house. As the chart in Figure 2−6 shows, this accounts for more than 35 percent of the heating fuel consumed.

Most houses depend for ventilation on the haphazard infiltration of air through cracks and crevices. Though this varies some with the weather, it is usually more than adequate. The most direct means of conservation, therefore, is simply to tighten up the house until the ventilation is just adequate instead of more than adequate.

The problem with this is deciding how much is enough. Air infil-tration rates are notoriously difficult to determine for both theoret-ical and practical reasons. On the theoretical level, the relationship between infiltration rates and weather variables (wind and tempera-ture) is nonlinear, nonadditive, and dependent on the chance con-figuration of openings in the building's shell (see Chapter 5). This relationship is therefore difficult to capture in a theoretical model that is simple enough to be useful. We can circumvent this difficulty to some extent by turning to practice and relying on tracer gas mea-surements of air infiltration rates rather than theoretical models. But the tracer gas technique, in addition to its high cost, has theoretical complications of its own. For example, it is often necessary to take account of multichamber effects to get any answers at all [2]. The other main measurement technique, pressurization of the house by a blower, has the drawback that it does not load the leaks in the same way as natural forces. Another difficult set of problems concerns the pollutants that the ventilation is supposed to flush out. Relatively little is known about indoor air pollution in houses—how high the concentrations get, how they are distributed in space and time, what chemical reactions occur in the air, and especially, what amounts and patterns of ventilation are really needed to control the pollution.

Under these circumstances, it would seem very difficult to set reasonable standards for air infiltration. A different tack might be better: instead of trying to decide how much haphazard infiltration is enough, it might be better to try to gain control of ventilation—that is, to replace random openings by an ordered ventilation system designed to do the job in the best way. The word "system" need not connote anything elaborate; it can mean nothing more than a set of well-placed openings.

Control has many advantages: it makes measurement, hence standard-setting much easier; it reduces uncertainty about ventilation rate, hence hazard; it allows improvement in the efficiency of the pattern of flow; it allows filtration; and it offers the possibility, at least, of heat recovery. The last item is important because it is the only means by which buildings can be ventilated in a cold climate without incurring a large energy cost.

The first prerequisite of control is the reduction to insignificance of random infiltration. One object of the present experiment, therefore, was to see how low we could make the infiltration rate by sealing leaks.

Earlier Twin Rivers retrofits included caulking around windows and doors and along a number of outside joints. This caulking was also included in the present experiment. In addition, the basement insulation, attic sealing, and window retrofits mentioned above further reduced leakage. Using a blower mounted in the door to depressurize the house and using cigar smoke for a detector, we ferreted out more leaks. Altogether, our sealing efforts amounted to about six person-days.

As Figure 2–13 shows, the infiltration rate was reduced by these methods to between 0.2 and 0.4 air exchanges per hour even in windy weather. This is about as low a rate as one would care to live with without opening a window. Below this level, most houses would be noticeably stuffy. About a third of the remaining air infiltration—the basement's share—is required by the house's gas furnace for combustion and entrainment. For these reasons, any further reduction in air infiltration would have had to be made up by deliberate ventilation. Our experiment, then, achieved about the lowest rate of air exchange heat loss that is feasible without heat recovery.

Summary of Simple Theoretical Estimates

Our theoretical estimates of the savings to be expected from the various retrofits discussed above are summarized in Figure 2–14, which is drawn in the same format as Figure 2–6. By these estimates

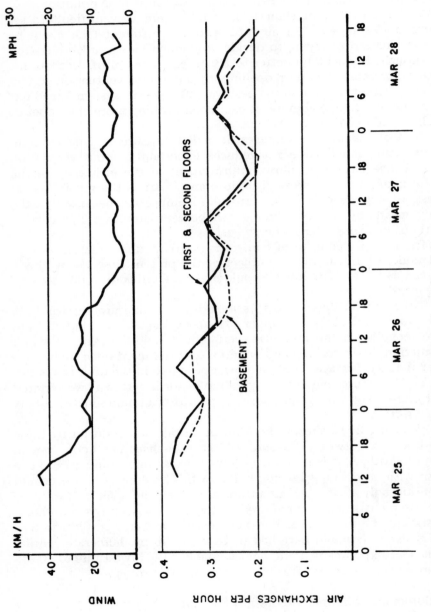

Figure 2—13. Air Infiltration Rate After Retrofit. Based on Tracer Gas Measurements

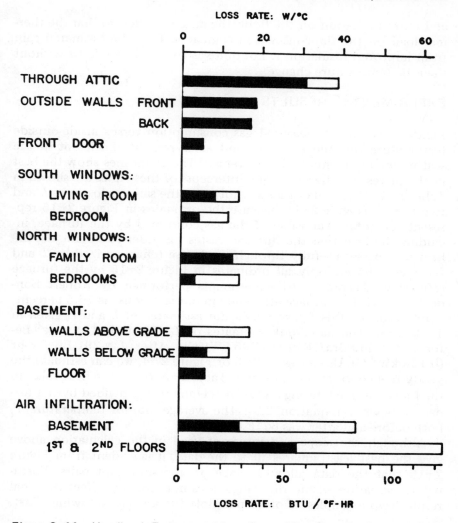

Figure 2–14. Handbook Estimates of Loss Rates After Retrofit. Compare With Figure 2–6

the overall lossiness L should fall to 55 percent of its preretrofit value.

Note that the estimated reduction in heat loss through the attic is relatively small. This is due to an interaction between floor conduction and thermal bypasses around the floor insulation (see Chapter 3). Before retrofit, the attic is considerably warmed by heat leaking up from the house. After retrofit, with the bypasses partially blocked and more insulation on the floor, the attic is colder, so that the thermal load on the floor insulation is greater. Thus the estimated gain from improved insulation is not quite as large as it would be without the attic temperature change.

EXPERIMENTAL RESULTS

Figure 2–15 shows measured gas consumption versus inside-outside temperature difference before and after retrofit. Each dot in the scatterplot represents an hour average. The solid lines show the best least squares fit. The slopes and intercepts of these lines are shown in Table 2–4. These quantities are not quite the same as lossiness L and free heat H (Figure 2–1), because the ordinates in Figure 2–15 represent the total heat value of the gas consumed by the furnace, including the heat that the furnace wastes. In order to obtain just the heat that passes usefully through the house (characterized by L and H), one must multiply all ordinates in Figure 2–15 by the furnace efficiency. According to experiments performed by Robert Sonderegger [3], the furnace efficiency in our test house is 76.5 percent. Application of this figure yields the estimates of L and H given in Table 2–5. The handbook estimates of L (Figure 2–14) were: Before: $L = 560$ Btu/°F-hr (0.295 kW/°C); After: $L = 291$ Btu/°F-hr (0.153 kW/°C). Using Figure 2–3 or Figure 2–4, we can estimate the yearly fuel consumption shown in Table 2–5. G_{yr} is the heat value in the fuel consumed during a year. It is equal to F_{yr} divided by the furnace efficiency (equation 2.2). The average interior temperature T_i both before and after was 67°F (19.4°C).

Although the slope and intercept used in the calculation above give the best least squares fit to the data, it is evident from Figure 2–15 that the data allow a range of slope-intercept pairs. Fortunately, variation within this range does not strongly affect the final result. Two examples of other plausible fits are the following: First,

Table 2–4. Slopes and Intercepts of Regression Lines Before and After Retrofit.

	Slope Btu/°F hr (kW/°C)	Intercept Btu/hr (kW)
Before	878 (0.465)	−10,280 (−3.02)
After	400 (0.210)	− 6,510 (−1.91)

Table 2–5. Parameter Values Based on Experimental Data.

	L $Btu/{}^\circ F\,hr$ $(kW/{}^\circ C)$	H Btu/hr (kW)	T^* ${}^\circ F$ $({}^\circ C)$	$F\,yr$ Btu/yr (kWh/yr)	$G\,yr$ Btu/yr (kWh/yr)	*Percent Saving*
Before	672 (0.35)	7860 (2.3)	55.3 (13)	44×10^6 (12.7×10^3)	57×10^6 (16.7×10^3)	
After	306 (0.16)	4980 (1.5)	50.7 (10)	14×10^6 (4.2×10^3)	19×10^6 (5.5×10^3)	~ 67 percent

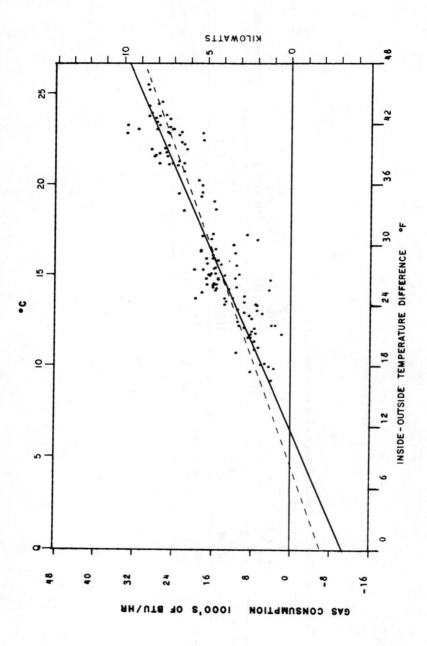

Figure 2–15A. Gas Consumption vs. Outside Temperature Before Retrofit

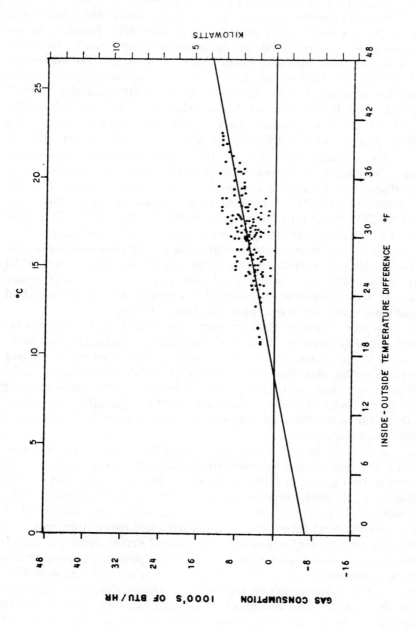

Figure 2—15B. Gas Consumption vs. Outside Temperature After Retrofit

on the basis of direct estimates of the major sources of free heat (the sun, electric appliances, and conduction from the neighboring town-houses), the "before" value of H looks a little large. Possibly, there-fore, the true "before" relationship is better approximated by a line with a higher intercept and lower slope such as the dashed line in Figure 2—15. The dashed line is the best least squares regression line under the constraint that the intercept coincide with the "after" intercept. This line yields for L the value $L = 584$ Btu/°F hr (0.31 kW/°C), which is somewhat closer to the handbook estimate. The resulting yearly gas consumption is $G_{yr} = 60 \times 10^6$ Btu/yr (17.6 × 10^3 kWh/yr), which is not greatly different from the tabulated value. Second, independent estimates made in connection with the attic study discussed in Chapter 3 give for L the "after" value $L = 382$ Btu/°F hr (0.20 kW/°C). The best least squares line with this slope has $H = 7,500$ Btu/hr (2.2 kW) and yields $G_{yr} = 18.3 \times 10^6$ Btu/yr (5.3 × 10^3 kWh/yr), which again is close to the tabulated value.

A circumstance that tends to make the results conservative is that the rented house in which the experiments were carried out was, to begin with, somewhat better than the average Twin Rivers town-house. It was somewhat tighter than average, and it already had double glass everywhere except in the family room.

An estimate of the retrofit investment justified by the savings re-ported above is given in Table 2—6 for different fuels. The fuel actu-ally used in the Twin Rivers house is gas. Estimated costs for our retrofits are: for materials (at retail prices) $425 and for labor $820 ($40 per day), giving a total of $1,245. This, of course, assumes hand work. Some parts of the job, window retrofits especially, could ben-efit from the economies of large-scale production, and all of it could benefit from experience.

The savings tabulated above apply only to winter, but the same retrofits also reduce the summer air conditioning load. Summer sav-ings are of two kinds: (1) the savings in electricity (kWh), and (2) the savings in peak load capacity needed by the power company (kW). The second kind, which can be figured at something like $500 of capital per kilowatt saved, can be quite high and often dominates the electricity savings. Unfortunately, the capital saving does not accrue to the householder under customary pricing policies; hence, an im-portant incentive to conserve is lost. This is a market imperfection, which, as the economists say, results in a misallocation of resources— too little conservation, too much peak load capacity. Incentives are corrected by means of peak hour pricing, which has the effect of passing the capital savings achieved by conservation back to the householder.

Table 2-6. Justified Investment to Secure Observed Energy Savings

	Electricity	Oil	Gas
Assumed current price	3¢/kWh	49¢gal[a]	30¢therm[a]
Assumed furnace efficiency (percent)	100	60	76.5
Yearly saving	$290	$197	$129
Justified investment at 10% tax-free return { current prices:	$2,900	$1,970	$1,290
3%/yr price rise:	$4,144	$2,821	$1,849

[a]One gallon equals 3.8 liters; one therm equals 10^5 Btu or 29.3 kWh.

In addition to the simple reduction in unwanted heat transfer achieved by the retrofits, there is a second effect that is helpful in summer, namely, the slowing of the house's response to changes in outside temperature. This is related to the ratio of the thermal mass to the lossiness: reducing the lossiness lengthens the response time. A long response time helps the house to coast through the summer afternoon consumption peak: The air conditioner can be turned on in the morning to get the house cool, then turned off in the early afternoon before the peak load hours. Both retrofits and peak hour pricing would encourage this strategy. Unfortunately, our tests did not extend into the summer, so we have no quantitative data on summer savings.

FURTHER CONSERVATION MEASURES

Although the conservation measures in our experiment reduced lossiness L by 50 percent and yearly space heat requirements by 67 percent, they by no means exhausted all economic possibilities for space heat conservation. For one thing, we attacked only one of the parameters in the model represented by equations (2.1) and (2.2). Means exist for improving the value of each of the other parameters T_i, H, and e as well. Some of these are discussed briefly below.

Inside Temperature T_i

Beyond simply lowering the temperature uniformly, there is much to be gained by matching temperatures to real needs in both space and time. Parts of the house not in use can be kept cool, and the whole house can be allowed to cool off when no one is home. The potential savings are large: possibly 20 percent for a family with average habits. Technically, this is largely a control problem. The challenge is to design controls that are very simple, inexpensive, automatic, and foolproof. This is not an easy challenge, but we doubt that it is an impossible one.

Free Heat H

A large untapped source of free heat is the waste hot water that goes down the drain. An average family uses seventy gallons (265 liters) per day heated to $135°F$ ($57°C$). This averages to 1,460 Btu's per hour (0.43 kW) relative to room temperature. Recovery of half of this as an addition to free heat H would reduce heating fuel requirements in our retrofitted house by about 17 percent. (Such recovery could be accomplished by means of a stratified holding tank that would allow the water to give up its heat before being released to the sewer.) Much more heat can be recovered from hot water, however, if it is used not for space heat but for preheating the cold water on its way to the water heater. There are two reasons for this: (1) the temperature difference available for heat exchange is that between hot and cold water (typically 80°F [44°C]) rather than between hot water and room temperature (typically 65°F [36°C]), and (2) the recovery can be beneficial all year rather than just in the heating season.

The largest source of free heat is, of course, the sun. In addition to south windows, one can use regular solar collectors. In its retrofitted state, our test house would need only about 220 square feet (20 square meters) of collector to meet 90 percent of the remaining space heat requirement. This could be provided either in the form of conventional flat plate collectors or in some other form, such as an attached, heat-storing greenhouse.

Improvement in the efficiency of appliances, especially refrigerators, tends to reduce the free heat. This is nevertheless beneficial because generation of electricity uses two or three times as much fuel to produce a unit of heat as the furnace would use. Thus, the reduction in free heat at the house due to an appliance improvement is more than made up by the savings at the power plant. Moreover, waste heat that is helpful in winter is a burden in summer.

An important means for reducing the free heat burden in summer is shading sunny windows, preferably on the outside. If the experiment had been extended to summer, this would have been at the top of our retrofit list.

Furnace Efficiency *e*

As noted above, the gas furnace in the test house delivered as useful heat only about three-quarters of the chemical energy in the fuel. Most of the other quarter went up the flue or was consumed without much heating benefit by the pilot light. A simple retrofit is to replace the pilot light with an electronic starter. Year round savings are estimated to be about 8 percent of the gas consumption in an unretrofitted Twin Rivers house or 25 percent of the remaining gas consumption in our test house. Some of the heat lost up the flue can also be recovered (heat exchangers designed for the purpose exist), but not all of it, because excessive cooling of the exhaust allows corrosive condensation in the flue pipe and may spoil the draft. However, so-called sealed combustion furnaces, which do not depend on a convective draft, promise to yield efficiencies above 90 percent.

Even a 100 percent efficient furnace, however, is not the end of the story. Letting energy run all the way down the temperature scale from the temperature of the flame to the temperature of the house without doing anything on the way is inefficient by the second law of thermodynamics. In principle, part of the energy in the flame could run a heat pump and in the end supply more space heat for a given amount of fuel than even a 100 percent efficient furnace.

SUMMARY AND CONCLUSION

Going beyond earlier Twin Rivers experiments, which tested simple retrofits in groups of similar houses, we installed a more extensive set of retrofits in a single house, in order to get some idea of how far space heat conservation could economically be carried. Though more extensive than earlier ones, the retrofits in this experiment were still simple and straightforward. They made no pretense of being optimal or unique. In addition to the attic insulation and caulking that had been included in the earlier retrofits, we installed interior window insulators of various kinds and basement wall insulation. We also did further caulking, especially in the attic, where many passages through the interiors of partitions were found to be open.

These measures reduced the lossiness of the house shell by about half and the estimated yearly fuel consumption for space heating by about two-thirds (i.e., to one-third of its previous value). Overall, these measures appeared to be economical at a return of 10 percent tax-free on investment. If the heating plant had been oil-fired or electric instead of gas, the return would have been significantly higher. Other conservation measures not included in the experiment could have contributed substantial further savings.

Our results join a growing body of evidence that large amounts of space heat can be economically saved by means of many small, low technology measures. In addition, some higher technology measures may be able to save more. It does not appear to be impossible, in fact, that under present technology and economic conditions, space heat in houses could be a minor rather than a major consumer of fuel.

REFERENCES

1. S.R. Hastings and R.W. Crenshaw, Window design strategies to conserve energy. June 1977. *National Bureau of Standards, Building Science Series 104.*
2. Sinden, F.W. 1978. Multi-chamber theory of air infiltration. *Building and Environment* 13:21–28.
3. Sonderegger, R.C. 1977. Modeling residential heat load from experimental data: the equivalent thermal parameters of a house. *Proceedings of the International Conference on Energy Use Management* (Tucson, Arisona; October 1977), eds. R.A. Fazzolare and C.B. Smith. II, 183–94. New York: Pergamon.

REFERENCES

Chapter 3

Critical Significance of Attics and Basements in the Energy Balance of Twin Rivers Townhouses*

Jan Beyea
Gautam Dutt
Thomas Woteki

Center for Environmental Studies
Princeton University

Abstract

Approximately 35 percent of winter energy loss in Twin Rivers townhouses is associated with the attic, despite the presence of nine centimeters of fiberglass insulation. Unexpected heat transfer mechanisms bypass the attic insulation, joining the attic, basement, and house. As a result, a three zone model is required for static heat load calculations and the prediction of retrofit savings.

Magnitudes of the unexpected heat transfer rates can be inferred from attic and basement temperatures and from knowledge of furnace inefficiencies. The model predicts the benefits to be gained by various retrofit strategies. Effectiveness of retrofits may be considerably enhanced by blocking heat transfer bypass paths to the attic.

INTRODUCTION

The thermal performance of attics and basements plays an important role in determining the use of energy in residential structures. The heat transfer from living space to attic frequently represents a significant energy loss. Radiative heat from the furnace in an unused basement leads to further waste.

Several ways have been suggested for reducing energy use by altering the characteristics of the attic: attic insulation, reduction of attic

---

*We have benefited from extensive discussions with Robert Socolow and David Harrje. Most important, we have drawn upon the cumulative body of knowledge obtained by the Twin Rivers group.

ventilation by closing vents, and use of attic fans. Recommendation of attic insulation, at least, has become an accepted part of government policy. This policy has largely been based on attic thermal models that, in predicting savings to be obtained by adding attic insulation [1–3], only consider conduction through the attic floor and roof (and sometimes include ventilation). However, when these standard models are applied to attics in Twin Rivers townhouses, predicted attic temperatures in winter are consistently much lower than the actual measured values [4]. The high measured attic temperatures imply that the attic heat losses are much higher than predicted by standard models. In fact, it is our conclusion that the heat loss through an average Twin Rivers attic is about five times as great as the theoretically predicted value and accounts for 35 percent of the energy leaving the house in winter—even though the attic usually contains nine centimeters (R–11) of fiberglass insulation.

Two major reasons for the ineffectiveness of the attic insulation are (1) air flow into the attic from other parts of the house, and (2) heat transfer into the attic by way of the party walls between adjacent houses.* These heat transfer mechanisms bypass the installed fiberglass attic insulation. If these bypass mechanisms had been eliminated at the time of construction, considerable savings would have resulted. Experiments have shown that similar savings can be expected from retrofitting existing Twin Rivers attics.

The Twin Rivers attic discrepancy should serve as a warning that a better understanding of the thermal performance of attics is essential before the results of attic retrofits can be accurately predicted nationwide. If bypass mechanisms are a common attic phenomenon, then improving the thermal performance of attics is more complicated than currently presumed. On the other hand, the Twin Rivers discrepancy also indicates that on a nationwide basis, the potential energy savings to be obtained from the attic may be larger than previously estimated.

Our analysis of the bypass mechanisms at Twin Rivers shows that the attic is strongly coupled both to living space and to the basement. As a result, a three zone model is required for even a static heat load calculation. The attic and basement cannot be treated separately in predicting total energy use.

In the opening section of this chapter, we review the discrepancies found in Twin Rivers attics and our resolution of the problem. In

---

*While party walls are only found in attached housing, similar large air flow losses through the attic are probably also common in pre–1940 U.S. detached houses where "balloon frame" construction was the rule.

the second section, we deal with attic losses in the context of total energy leaving the house. The three zone model for energy flow is developed, and a procedure is outlined for obtaining net furnace efficiency. We also discuss the theoretical justification for a simple diagnostic test for rating attic performance—namely, the two resistance model test.

THE WARM ATTIC DISCREPANCY

Visual examination of Twin Rivers attics suggests some causes for the warm attics. The furnace flue passes through the attic and is surrounded by an open shaft to isolate the flue from other building materials.* Warm air enters the attic not only through the shaft but also through cracks between the attic floor and the party walls that separate adjacent attics.

As part of an experiment to measure savings in gas use in a number of Twin Rivers houses, the shaft surrounding the furnace flue was sealed (D retrofit), additional insulation was added to the attic floor, and cracks between the house and the party wall were sealed in the attic (A retrofit).** These improvements led to a cooling of the attic, but after retrofits the attic was still warmer than expected. The remaining discrepancy was not eliminated until batts of fiberglass insulation were glued to the attic party walls, isolating the party wall from the attic.

The attic thermal discrepancies may be expressed in terms of a fit to an approximate physical model that is equivalent to a static heat load calculation with variable parameters. As we shall see, the discrepancy is so great that it dwarfs all the approximations in the model. This model assumes that

1. The house interior, the attic, and the outside may each be represented by a single temperature (T_H, T_A, and T_O, respectively). We include basement and neighboring houses as part of our definition of house interior.***

---

*Building codes often require this for fire safety reasons. We have verified that there are ways to block the furnace shaft with fire resistant materials.

**Details of the "ABCD" retrofits referred to in this chapter can be found in Chapter 4.

***Twin Rivers basements typically have roughly the same temperature as the living space. Similarly, neighbor temperatures can be considered the same, to first approximation. In any case, as shown in the appendix to this chapter, an effective two resistance model should hold even if the basement and neighbors are at different temperatures.

2. The heat flux between adjacent regions is proportional to the temperature difference between them; these proportionality constants are referred to as effective conductances and are identified by W_{HA} and W_{AO} for house-to-attic and attic-to-outside heat flow, respectively.
3. There are no internal "sources" of energy in the attic.
4. The thermal storage effects of the attic are negligible during measurement periods.
5. The effects of solar radiation on the roof exterior are negligible.

The physical content of the model may then be stated as an equality of two heat flows:

$$W_{HA} (T_H - T_A) = W_{AO} (T_A - T_O) \qquad (3.1)$$

The instantaneous heat transfer rate from house to attic must equal that from attic to outside. It is convenient to rewrite this equation and to define a temperature ratio, λ:

$$\lambda = \frac{W_{AO}}{W_{HA}} = \frac{T_H - T_A}{T_A - T_O} \qquad (3.2)$$

If both the conductances, W_{AO} and W_{HA}, are constant over time, the attic temperature will keep the same relative position between the inside and outside temperatures. We call either equation (3.1) or equation (3.2) the "two resistance model."

In traditional attic energy loss calculations, W_{HA} is the linearized "UA" value for heat transfer through the attic floor and W_{AO} includes heat transfer through the roof and attic ventilation. For a typical Twin Rivers attic before retrofits, using standard handbook thermal properties and standard attic ventilation rate, we find W_{AO} = 290 Watts/°C and W_{HA} = 33 Watts/°C; hence the value of the ratio λ in equation (3.2) is predicted to be about nine.*

In a statistical analysis of the temperature ratio, the temperature data were restricted to six-hour nighttime averages from midnight to

---

*We use nominal conductivities for the fiberglass and the attic structural materials and make a correction for the geometry of joists (see Appendix A, p. 280). We have confirmed the conductive heat flow by direct measurements at attic floor and roof. For ventilation rates (not measured) we use the value 0.039 m³/s, using the model in Hinrichs and Wolfert [5] and assuming a wind speed of 3m/s. We refer to the results of these calculations as "handbook values" of the conductances W_{HA} and W_{AO}.

6:00 A.M. to increase the validity of assumptions (4) and (5) of the model.* The analysis showed that the average value of λ for the houses in the sample, measured over a period of eighty-three days, was one, and not the predicted value of nine [6].

The first question to answer about the factor of nine discrepancy is whether it could be due to well-known inadequacies in the model. Detailed analyses show that effects included in complex computer programs such as NBSLD, but left out of the elementary static calculation (such as storage and radiation heat transfer), could not possibly explain such a large discrepancy. Furthermore, direct and indirect heat flux measurements ruled out the possibility that the discrepancy was the result of inaccurate estimates of the thermal resistances of attic floor or roof [7,8]. Yet a statistical analysis showed that, late at night, the attic temperature did remain in fixed proportion (with a standard deviation of 1°C) between the house and outside temperatures, suggesting that a two resistance model was empirically valid provided that the conductances took on nonhandbook values. This suggests that a mechanism for additional heat transfer from house to attic exists, characterized by a conductance (W_P) in parallel with the conductance through the attic floor. We decided to use measured attic temperature and the two-resistance model as a diagnostic tool to search for the missing parallel heat path. We modified the attic in various ways and kept checking the temperature ratios statistically to see how closely the measured value approached the predicted value.

Air flow directly into the attic was an obvious candidate for an additional conductance. However, A and D retrofits previously referred to were sufficient to block most air flow into the attic, as shown by tracer gas air infiltration measurements. Thus, if air flow were the only significant bypass mechanism, one would expect agreement between the postretrofit value of the temperature ratio λ observed in the field and the value calculated from the thermal properties of the materials in the retrofitted attic. This agreement was not found. To be sure, the attic became cooler after retrofits, but a large discrepancy still remained: A calculation for retrofitted attics (with additional attic insulation) using handbook thermal properties led to a prediction of λ = 23. The experimental value for the ratio, averaged over thirteen townhouses, was much smaller, equal to 2.5 [6]. This discrepancy suggests that additional heat transfer paths exist in addition to air flow directly into the attic.

---

*Storage effects are minimal when temperatures change slowly with time. This occurs in the early morning hours before sunrise.

We have narrowed this remaining discrepancy to heat transfer within the wall of cinder blocks (the party wall) that divides adjacent townhouses from each other. The cinder blocks are twenty centimeters thick, and the wall extends from the basement to the attic. In the two inhabited floors, each wall is faced with gypsum board, which is separated from the cinder blocks by an air space. In the attic and basement, the cinder blocks are generally uncovered.

Cinder blocks are so constructed as to leave large holes in them. In the wall, they are stacked up in such a manner that the holes in the cinder blocks are vertical, although not necessarily well aligned. Heat flow through the wall in the vertical direction takes place both by conduction through the solid portions of the wall and by air movement through the vertically connected holes. Theoretical estimates suggest that the conductive component of heat transfer is small but that a significant amount of heat may reach the attic by convection within the cinder block cavities.

These theoretical estimates were supplemented by an experiment to measure the extent of attic heating from the party walls [8]. Batts of R-11 fiberglass insulation were cut to shape and attached to both party walls in the attic of the experimental townhouse. The attic had already received the A and D retrofits, that is, it had R-30 insulation on the floor, and all cracks along the party wall, as well as the furnace shaft, were sealed. Following the installation of the insulation on the party walls, the measured value of λ for the first time approached the value predicted by traditional methods. The attic was at last as cold as it was supposed to be.

As a result, we conclude that the party wall thermally bypasses the attic insulation and represents the main source of discrepancy remaining after air flow is blocked. We can estimate the magnitudes of the unexpected conductances (associated with air flow and party wall heat transfer) using another representation of the two resistance model, shown in Figure 3-1. W_{AO} is the conductance due to conduction through the roof and attic ventilation. The conductance between house interior and attic (W_{HA} in the two resistance model) is made up of a set of parallel conductance paths resulting from conduction through the attic insulation (C), by air flow from house to attic (AF), and through the party wall (PW). For convenience, any remaining discrepancy between the two resistance model predictions and experimentally measured attic temperatures is expressed in terms of another parallel conductance between house and attic (DISC). These conductances are shown in Table 3-1.

The principal result indicated in Table 3-1 is that the attic discrepancy is the result of large heat bypass paths between house and

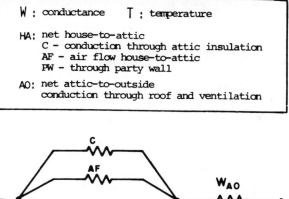

W : conductance   T : temperature

HA: net house-to-attic
    C - conduction through attic insulation
    AF - air flow house-to-attic
    PW - through party wall

AO: net attic-to-outside
    conduction through roof and ventilation

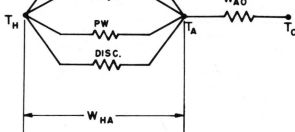

Figure 3-1. Two Resistance Attic Model with Parallel Paths.

attic (by air flow and through the party wall) before the retrofits. The retrofits reduce the conductances through the attic insulation and by air flow but the party wall bypass conductance remains dominant. This has a major impact on the cost-effectiveness of conservation strategies at Twin Rivers.

The discrepancies that remain in Table 3-1 cannot be considered serious, given the accuracy of our measurements and the approximate nature of the two resistance model. We conclude that attic temperatures (and consequently attic heat fluxes) can be predicted reasonably accurately in Twin Rivers houses if the two insulation bypass mechanisms (air flow and party wall) are taken into account. Of course there are other effects not included in our discussion (all of which we considered in unraveling the discrepancy) that play a smaller role in determining attic temperatures at night, but that may be important at other times or for other types of attics. These effects are:

1. Thermal lag introduced by the thermal capacity of the attic materials (this has been shown to be negligible for the time period con-

Table 3—1. Estimated House-to-Attic Conductances for an Average
Townhouse[a] *(Watts/°C).*

	Preretrofit	*Post-ABCD-Retrofit*
Attic insulation	33	13
Air flow bypass through furnace shaft and cracks between building and party wall[b]	160[c]	5[d]
Party wall bypass conductance[e]	74	80
Remaining discrepancy	23	20
TOTAL = W_{HA}	290[f]	116

[a]"House" includes basement and neighbors.

[b]Includes air flow from basement, as well as convection from air spaces that connect to attic.

[c]Derived from change in missing conductance following ABCD retrofit.

[d]Result of SF_6 tracer gas measurements in the experimental townhouse (which was made especially tight).

[e]Includes any contribution from neighbors.

[f]Because attic temperatures lie midway between inside and outside temperatures, this number must equal the total roof conductance (measured experimentally to lie within ± 20 percent of 290 W/°C).

    sidered experimentally, but would be important at times when the attic temperature is changing rapidly).

2. Spatial inhomogeneity of temperature in attics.
3. Variations in the wind and the radiation environment of the exterior (including sun and night sky cooling).
4. Details of radiation heat transfer, for example, from roof to wall to floor.
5. Heat gain in the attic due to the furnace flue and from other metal penetrations into the attic. (Although this effect is relatively small at Twin Rivers, the heat flux from the furnace flue might be important in making an economically optimal decision about insulation thickness in other attics.)

    Some of these effects are already included in modern-day heat load computer codes. However, even a complex computer code, if it does not include attic bypass mechanisms adequately, is no more useful for attics than an old-fashioned handbook estimate. How best to modify existing codes to take into account attic bypass mechanisms (if supporting measurements are unavailable) may become clear as familiarity is gained with a variety of attic types.

HOUSE ENERGY USE

The fact that the party wall is responsible for a large conductance bypass into the attic suggests that the basement is probably also thermally coupled to the attic, since the party walls are bare in the basement and capable of absorbing substantial basement heat. If the basement-attic coupling is large, then an energy balance equation for the basement will reveal the same coupling.

A simple steady state heat flow circuit with three zones is shown in Figure 3-2. This is an extension of the two resistance attic model described earlier, and assumptions analogous to (1), (2), (4), and (5) for the two resistance model are made.

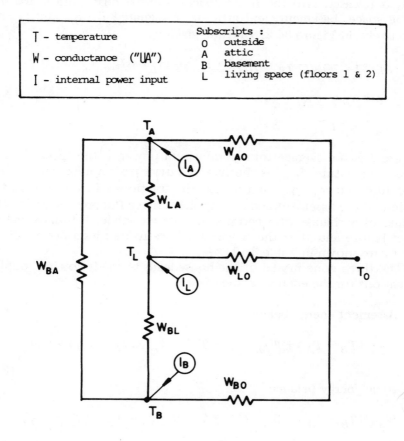

T - temperature	Subscripts :
	O outside
W - conductance ("UA")	A attic
	B basement
I - internal power input	L living space (floors 1 & 2)

Figure 3-2. Three Zone Model—Equivalent Circuit.

This model does not include any thermal capacities and thus neglects the effects of thermal storage. Storage effects become important if the house warms up above the thermostat setting for part of the day, as happens in mild weather, or if very short time periods are modeled. However, the average power (averaged over periods of a day or more) passing through a thermal circuit is insensitive to storage effects, provided the house temperature remains roughly constant.

In the present model, it is assumed that constant fractions of the furnace combustion power are deposited in the attic and the basement and are exhausted at the top of the flue. The remainder of the furnace power, together with power from appliances, people, and sun, is released into the living space. Internal heat sources for the living space, basement, and attic are designated I_L, I_B, and I_A, respectively, in Figure 3-2. They are given by:

$$I_L = (1 - \gamma_A - \gamma_B - \gamma_C) I + I_{\text{free}} = \gamma_L I + I_{\text{free}}$$

$$I_B = \gamma_B I \qquad\qquad (3.3)$$

$$I_A = \gamma_A I$$

where I is the average total combustion power at the specified outside temperature; I_{free} is the average power from appliances, people, and sun; and γ_A, γ_B, and γ_C are the fractions of I dumped in the attic and the basement and leaving the furnace flue, respectively. The values of γ change after certain retrofits are made. Estimated values of γ before and after the ABCD set of retrofits (described in Chapter 4) are shown in Table 3-2.

The three zone model of the house leads to the following coupled equations for the energy balance:

1. Basement energy balance:

$$W_{BA} (T_B - T_A) + W_{BL} (T_B - T_L) + W_{BO} (T_B - T_O) = \gamma_B I$$

$$(3.4)$$

2. Attic energy balance:

$$W_{BA} (T_B - T_A) + W_{LA} (T_L - T_A) + \gamma_A I = W_{AO} (T_A - T_O)$$

$$(3.5)$$

Table 3-2.   Allocation of Furnace Heat Between Attic, Basement, Flue, and Living Area

		Preretrofit *(percent)*	*Post-ABCD-Retrofit* *(percent)*	*Source*
Attic	γ_A	4	1	estimate
Basement	γ_B	26	13	[9]
Flue	γ_C	16	18	[9]
Living area	γ_L	54	68	$\gamma_L = 1 - \gamma_A - \gamma_B - \gamma_C$

3. Living space energy balance:

$$W_{LO}\,(T_L - T_O) + W_{LA}\,(T_L - T_A) = \gamma_L I + I_{\text{free}} + W_{BL}\,(T_B - T_L)$$

(3.6)

The set of coupled energy balance equations can be solved for the furnace combustion rate necessary to keep the living space temperature, T_L, constant for a given outside temperature, T_O. A definition of the furnace system efficiency, ϵ, may be introduced:

$$\epsilon = [\,W_{\text{net}}\,(T_L - T_O) - I_{\text{free}}\,]\,/I$$

(3.7)

where W_{net} is an overall conductance of the living space and is determined by the values of Ws;* ϵ is the efficiency of the furnace relative to a loss-free heat source within the living space and depends on the Ws as well as the γ s.

The same set of simultaneous equations determines the attic and basement temperatures. As shown in the appendix of this chapter, the equation for the attic temperature retains an approximate two resistance form—an explanation of why we found attic temperature data behaving so regularly.

Reliable estimates of I_{free} and the γ values are available from earlier work at Twin Rivers. Estimates of W_{BL}, W_{LO}, W_{BO}, and W_{AO} can be obtained from handbook values of materials properties (see Appendix A) and measured air infiltration data.

The unknown bypass conductances, W_{BA} and W_{LA}, must be determined from measured temperature data, using equations (3.4) and (3.5). A feature of Twin Rivers townhouses is that prior to retrofits, their basements are at a temperature close to the living space. As a result, although the solutions of equations (3.4) and (3.5) for W_{BA} and W_{LA} are sensitive to changes in estimates of the remaining Ws,

* $$W_{\text{net}} = W_{LO} + \frac{1}{W_{BA}}\;\frac{pq - mn}{p + q + m + n}$$

(3.8)

$$\text{where}\quad p = W_{BA}\,(W_{LB} + W_{LA}) + W_{LA}\,W_{LB}$$

$$q = W_{BO}\,W_{AO} + W_{BA}\,(W_{AO} + W_{BO})$$

$$m = W_{LB}\,W_{AO}$$

$$n = W_{LA}\,W_{BO}$$

the sum of W_{BA} and W_{LA} is relatively insensitive. The sum of W_{BA} and W_{LA} turns out to approximate the total bypass conductance determined from the two resistance model. To obtain individual values for W_{BA} and W_{LA}, we have used nighttime furnace and temperature data from five townhouses—those without modifications to their basements. Since W_{LA} does not appear in equation (3.4) (the basement energy balance equation), this equation can be used to solve for W_{BA} in terms of known quantities. W_{LA} can then be determined from equation (3.5).

All the conductances thus obtained are shown in the first four columns of Table 3—3 for typical Twin Rivers townhouses as built and after various retrofits. Equation (3.8) may be used, along with these conductances, to determine the overall conductance (W_{net}) and furnace efficiency (ϵ) as defined by equation (3.7). The values of W_{net} indicate that considerable reduction in a house's overall heat loss can be made if an appropriate party wall retrofit is added to the ABCD or the superretrofit package. Modest increments in effective furnace efficiency (ϵ) are also predicted.

These conductances may also be used to calculate the heat loss rate from the house, attic, and basement for any $T_L - T_O$. The heat loss rate I_{total} is given by

$$I_{total} = I + I_{free} \tag{3.9}$$

and includes furnace inefficiency as a heat loss. Typical heat loss rates as a percentage of the value for an unretrofitted Twin Rivers townhouse are shown in Table 3—4, assuming $T_L - T_O = 20°C$ and $I_{free} = 1.7$ kW (based on regression analysis of consumption data [10]). Perhaps the most interesting result is that 35 percent of the house heat loss occurs through the attic, prior to any retrofits. Table 3—4 also indicates the savings in heat loss rate—19 percent and 37 percent of the "as built" townhouse value after ABCD retrofits and ABCD plus party wall retrofits. Another useful measure is savings in furnace input power, I, which turns out to be 23 percent and 45 percent, respectively, when $T_L - T_O = 20°C$. The additional apparent savings occurs because I_{free} (assumed unchanged) is more effective in house heating after retrofits (see Chapter 2). The gas savings of 23 percent following ABCD retrofits agrees well with measured values for a number of townhouses in cold weather [10]. Gas savings following the party wall retrofit have not been verified yet.

It should be recalled that the model was developed using the steady state assumption. The steady state assumption implies that

Table 3–3. Conductances in the Three Zone Model *(Watts/°C).*

$W_{AO} = 290$, $W_{BL} = 330$ (handbook estimates)

	$W_{LO}{}^a$	$W_{BO}{}^a$	W_{BA}	W_{LA}	W_{net}	ϵ
As built	174	53	105	171	343	0.75
Plus ABCD retrofits[b]	174	53	40	80	294	0.79
Plus hypothetical party wall retrofit[c] (estimated)	174	53	0	16	234	0.79
Superretrofit[d]	84	32	40	80	190	0.79
Plus hypothetical party wall retrofit (estimated)	84	32	0	16	128	0.80

[a] Air infiltration rates were included using typical measured air exchange rates.
[b] See Chapter 4.
[c] A retrofit, such as insulating both sides of each party wall, that reduces party wall heat transfer into attic to a minimal value.
[d] See Chapter 2.

Table 3—4. Heat Loss Rates in the Three Zone Model.[a]
(percent of as built townhouse)

| House Condition | Heat Loss (percent)[b] | | | | Savings by Retrofit |
	$L \to O^c$	$A \to O^c$	$B \to O^c$	Stack[d]	
As built	40	35	12	13	0
Plus ABCD retrofits[e]	40[f]	19	11	11	19
Plus hypothetical party wall retrofit	40[f]	4	11	8	37

[a] Assumes $T_L - T_O = 20°C$, $I_{free} = 1.7kW$; includes stack losses.
[b] Direct heat loss to outside as defined by W_{LO} ($T_L - T_O$), etc.
[c] $L \to O$ means living space to outside; $A \to O$, attic to outside; $B \to O$, basement to outside.
[d] Stack losses at exit from house.
[e] See Chapter 4.
[f] The retrofits are assumed not to affect this heat flow.

the model may lead to inaccurate predictions during the "edges" of the heating season. However, the furnace power during these periods is usually small.

Thus we see that a three zone model for the house, including basement-to-attic and house-to-attic thermal bypass conductances and furnace inefficiencies, is consistent with measured attic and basement temperatures and predicts gas savings from retrofits accurately. Of course, we could not have made these predictions without first having obtained temperature and furnace data from a sample of houses. However, because of our experiments, we are now in a position to make economically optimal suggestions for retrofitting the remaining 3,000 Twin Rivers residences. Our final recommendations await a decision on the optimal way to block party wall heat transfer.

CONCLUSIONS

We have found that the warm attic discrepancy in Twin Rivers attics implies that a three zone house model is necessary for a complete understanding of thermal energy flow in these houses.

We have concluded that insulation bypass mechanisms are responsible for the loss of about 35 percent of the energy released in a Twin Rivers townhouse during cold months. Fortunately, these bypass mechanisms are correctable.

Furthermore, we have shown that the two resistance model for attic temperatures is theoretically valid even if multiple zones are involved. This model can be used as a diagnostic tool to search out bypass mechanisms in different types of attics. If a discrepancy is found with handbook predictions, a multizone model (together with temperature data) may be used to quantify unidentified heat loss mechanisms and to predict the effectiveness of any corrective action.

APPENDIX: VALIDITY OF THE TWO RESISTANCE ATTIC MODEL IN LIGHT OF STRONG COUPLING TO THE HOUSE AND BASEMENT

The large attic-to-basement heat transfer rate discussed in the text suggests that a simple two resistance circuit for attic heat balance excluding the basement might be only a rough approximation. However, even an n resistance circuit can be shown to reduce to an effective two resistance attic model if the "free heat" component in the house is neglected. When the free heat component is included in the circuit, the deviations from the two resistance model for the Twin Rivers houses turn out to affect conclusions by only a few percent.

To prove this result, consider a general n element circuit that connects attic, basement, and house. The living space is considered to be at a uniform temperature, T_L, maintained constant by the thermostat setting and the furnace. Furnace heat plus internal sources of free heat are delivered inside the house. Indirect heating resulting from furnace inefficiencies is included as a fixed fraction of the furnace power added to the basement, attic, or any other node in the circuit. A solution of this equivalent circuit for the inside-outside temperature difference, $T_L - T_O$, indicates that it is proportional to some linear combination of all the heat sources in the circuit. However, since all furnace-originated heat sources are proportional to the furnace power, we obtain

$$T_L - T_O = aI + bI_{free} \qquad (3.10)$$

where I is the combustion power of the furnace, and I_{free} is the power delivered by appliances, people, and the sun. The parameters a and b depend upon the resistances in the circuit and the fractions of furnace power deposited at the various nodes.

The furnace power (I) appears in a useful form in equation (3.7):

$$I = \frac{W_{net}(T_L - T_O) - I_{free}}{\epsilon} \qquad (3.11)$$

Thus W_{net} and ϵ are alternative parameters equivalent to a and b.

We now make a similar analysis with $T_A - T_O$ (attic-to-outside temperature differences) as a variable. Since the network is linear, $T_A - T_O$ can only depend upon a linear combination of $T_L - T_O$ and the heat sources in the circuit. Thus,

$$T_A - T_O = A(T_L - T_O) + BI + KI_{free} \qquad (3.12)$$

where A, B, and K are constants.

Substituting for I, from equation (3.11), we obtain

$$T_A - T_O = (A + \frac{BW_{net}}{\epsilon})(T_L - T_O) + (K - \frac{B}{\epsilon})I_{free} \qquad (3.13)$$

Thus we see that when I_{free} is zero, $T_A - T_O$ is proportional to $T_L - T_O$, and equation (3.13) is equivalent to a two resistance attic model. A similar analysis can be made for the basement temperature, indicating that it too satisfies the proportionality requirement for a two resistance model.

To examine the significance of the I_{free} term, we have solved the three zone circuit of Figure 3–2. The coefficient of I_{free} turns out to be small enough so that inclusion of this term amounts to a small correction to the two resistance model during the colder winter months. Of course, in the warmer months, at the "edges" of the heating season, the I_{free} term may not be negligible.

The key assumption in our argument involves the fixed proportionality between furnace combustion energy and energy dumped into the various zones or nodes of the circuit. The furnace energy deposited in the living space and into the basement (by duct losses) must be roughly proportional to the furnace power. Additional heat added to the basement and attic by radiation from the furnace and the flue are also approximately proportional to the furnace power, provided the hot surfaces are much warmer than the ambient air, as is usually the case. Thus the assumption of constant fractions of furnace energy being deposited in the various nodes appears reasonable.

REFERENCES

1. Department of Housing and Urban Development. 1975. *In the Bank . . . Or up the Chimney? A Dollars and Cents Guide to Energy-Saving Home Improvements.* Washington, D.C.
2. Peterson, S.R. 1974. Retrofitting existing housing for energy conservation: an economic analysis. Washington, D.C.: National Bureau of Standards Building Science Series 64.
3. Jacobs, M., and Peterson, S.R. 1975. Making the most of your energy dollars in home heating and cooling. Washington, D.C.: National Bureau of Standards Consumer Information Series 8.
4. Pollack, A.K. 1976. Modeling attic temperatures in three highly instrumented townhouses in Twin Rivers, N.J. Princeton, N.J.: Princeton University Center for Environmental Studies Report No. 28.
5. Hinrichs, H.S., and Wolfert, C.K. 1974. Fundamentals of residential attic ventilation. Princeville, Ill.: H.C. Products Co.
6. Woteki, T.H.; Dutt, G.S.; and Beyea, J. The two-resistance model for attic heat flow: implications for conservation policy. *Energy—The International Journal* (in press).
7. Dutt, G.S., and Harrje, D.T. 1977. Influence of attics on residential energy conservation—a summary progress report. Princeton, N.J.: Princeton University Center for Environmental Studies Working Paper No. 33.
8. Dutt, G.S., and Beyea, J. 1977. Attic thermal performance: a study of townhouses at Twin Rivers. Princeton, N.J.: Princeton University Center for Environmental Studies Report No. 53.
9. Harrje, D.T.; Socolow, R.H.; Sonderegger, R.C. 1977. Residential energy conservation—the Twin Rivers project. *ASHRAE Transactions* 83, pt. 1.
10. Woteki, T.H. 1976. The Princeton Omnibus experiment: some effects of retrofits on space heating requirements. Princeton University Center for Environmental Studies Report No. 43.

Chapter 4

Details of the First Round Retrofits at Twin Rivers*

David T. Harrje
*Center for Environmental Studies
and Department of Aerospace and
Mechanical Sciences
Princeton University*

Abstract

The first round retrofits at Twin Rivers were directed to isolating the attic from the living area and basement, reducing air flow around windows and doors, and reducing heat flow from the forced air distribution system to the basement. Details of materials used and their placement are presented. The design of the first experiment is also given. These retrofits were grouped into four packages and were deployed in phases over a single winter in twenty-four instrumented townhouses of identical floor plan.

INTRODUCTION

Preliminary models of the energy balance in a Twin Rivers townhouse led to estimates of savings from a variety of retrofits, and consultations with contractors led to corresponding estimates of costs. We decided to group those retrofits that appeared cost-effective into four packages (labeled A, B, C, D) to be discussed in detail below. In the period from January to March 1976, we performed the retrofits in twenty-four nearly identical townhouses (and in the following months we added six more townhouses). Several months before the

*The retrofit procedures depended upon assistance from a number of sources. Kenneth Gadsby and Roy Crosby worked to perfect solutions to many of the sealing problems encountered at Twin Rivers. Representatives from Owens Corning Fiberglas and Certainteed assisted us in sealing a variety of openings in the attic and in achieving solutions to duct wrapping problems and water heater retrofitting.

time of retrofitting, the "Omnibus" instrumentation package (see Chapter 7) was placed in each townhouse to permit before and after comparisons.

The implementation of the retrofits was phased to permit comparison across houses in different stages of retrofit, and packages were implemented in variable sequence. The design of the 1976 winter retrofit experiment is displayed as a schedule in Table 4–1.

Detailed results have been presented elsewhere [1, 2] (see also Chapter 1). Moreover, data reduction and evaluation are still in progress. We have found the winter gas consumption to be reduced between 20 and 30 percent by the full package of retrofits, and we have clear evidence that the attic retrofit packages (A and D) led to the largest savings. Moreover, the retrofits appeared to make the townhouses more comfortable, by reducing temperature differentials between downstairs (warm) and upstairs (cold) [3].

The remainder of this chapter presents the details of the four retrofit packages. Most of these details can be expected to have applicability in a broad spectrum of buildings, including many altogether different from the Twin Rivers townhouses.

RETROFIT A (ATTIC)

The final specifications to the contractors for Retrofit A (the attic retrofit) included: (1) Roll unbacked fiberglass, and stuff openings that exist between the outer attic floor joists (two by fours) and the masonry firewall. For an interior townhouse unit, this involved two walls between the front and rear of each dwelling. (2) Cover the hatch door to the attic space with eight inches (twenty centimeters) of fiberglass insulation, stapling or gluing it in place. (3) Protect against blown insulation moving into the soffit areas or through the attic hatch opening by using unbacked insulation around the hatchway and along the front and rear portions of the attic floor that are adjacent to the soffit areas. In the case of the blown cellulose, this barrier was formed by fire retardant corrugated cardboard walls stapled into place. (4) Install either cellulose or fiberglass insulation by blowing into place (blowing avoided the problems of the many cross braces supporting the roof) to achieve a total value of thermal resistance of at least R–30. This has meant that, in addition to the initial value of R–11 for the three and one-half inch (nine centimeters) vapor-barrier-backed fiberglass, a value of R–19 of additional insulation must be added. For cellulose, with an R value of 3.7 per inch, we have called for five and one-half inches. With fiberglass, with an R value of 2.3 per inch, we have called for eight and three-quarter inches.* The area covered is 720 square feet (67 square meters). The cost for this retrofit during the winter of 1976 was between $155 and $225 depending upon the choice of insulation.

RETROFIT D (SHAFT TO ATTIC)

The purpose of retrofit D was to eliminate a noticeable channel for air flow between basement and attic. In conjunction with retrofit A, it placed a "thermal lid" on the house, but even without retrofit A it was designed to reduce markedly the heat loss due to circulation between attic and basement. A plug of unbacked fiberglass was used to seal, at the attic floor, the shaft that surrounds the furnace flue. The cross-section of the shaft was approximately sixteen inches (forty centimeters) square. The temperature of the surface of the flue at this elevation was measured to be less than 130°F (54°C). Since fiberglass has a char temperature greater than 800°F (430°C), this retrofit presented no local danger of fire whatsoever, and in fact would inhibit the spread of fire from a basement conflagration. (Indeed the temperatures are greater on the ducting in the basement— see Retrofit C.) To perform this sealing operation, a four foot (1.2 meter) section of six-inch (15 centimeter) unbacked fiberglass insulation was wrapped around the flue and pressed into the shaft opening. The elimination of any vertical air movement up the shaft was readily detected by using one's hand as a probe after the seal had been completed. The cost of this item is included in Retrofit A.

RETROFIT B (BASIC LIVING SPACE AND OTHER GAPS AND CRACKS)

The object of this retrofit is to limit the amount of air infiltration resulting from crack openings, especially around windows and doors. The leakage around windows has been traced to three causes: (1) The lack of squareness of the window frames, leading to open spaces even with the windows shut. Either these frames were installed as a parallelogram (see Figure 4–1) or the house had settled after the window installation. (2) The poor condition of the seal between the glass and aluminum frame. (3) Air channels past the molding surrounding the window. Leakage around the patio door was found to have similar

---

*In metric units, we added either fourteen centimeters of cellulose (rated at 0.26 m² °C/W/cm) or twenty-two centimeters of fiberglass (rated at 0.16 m² °C/W/cm) to the existing nine centimeters of floor insulation whose nominal thermal resistance was 1.9 m² °C/W (R–11), to raise the nominal thermal resistance of the floor insulation above the target of 5.3 m² °C/W (R–30).

Table 4–1. Schedule Followed in Retrofitting (1976)

Omnibus*	January 19–23	January 26–30	February 16–20	February 23–27	March 15–19
1			ABCD		
2			AD		⁺B outside
3	ACD		B		
4	ACD		B		
5			C		
6				BD	A
7	ABCD				
8	C	BD	A		
9			ABCD		B outside
10	C	BD	A		
11	ACD	B			
12				BD	A
13	ABD				
14	ABD				
16			C	BD	
**17			BD	A	
**18			C	BD	
19			AD		
**21			CAD	B	

HIT*	December 15–19, 22–26		January 12–16, 19–23		March 15–19
1	B	C	D	AB	B outside
2	AD	C		B	
3	ABD				C partial

*Omnibus and HIT refer to instrumentation packages (see Chapter 7).

**Quad III townhouse—gas appliances.

+Outside caulking on batten board siding homes.

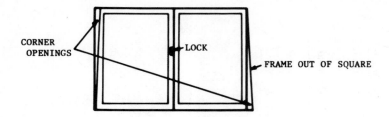

Figure 4—1.   Poor Fit of Window in its Frame

origins. Leakage around the front door was found to be the result of poor alignment at the threshold and the poor condition of the magnetic seal strips on the sides and top of the door.

The windows were improved in the following manner: The normal seal on the sliding window, which relies on a stiff fuzz strip, was augmented by the use of closed cell vinyl foam strips (3/16″ × 3/8″ or 0.5 cm × 1.0 cm cross-section) attached to the sliding windows (see Figure 4—2). The lock mechanism was also adjusted to force the windows into the frame. Where the metal frames were attached to the wood frame, where the glass was attached to the metal frame, and where the wood molding was attached to the wallboard, a fillet of silicone caulking was placed on any suspicious areas. This material is clear, long-lasting (ten year guarantee), and almost invisible, thus matching any decor. This same material was used on the panels of the patio door and in the overhanging closets of the rear upstairs bedrooms wherever air leakage was present. The patio door received a more substantial foam strip (1/2″ × 3/4″ or 1.3 cm × 1.9 cm) to aid in sealing.

The front door sill was adjusted in height to meet the original seal surface on the lower portion of the door. When this alone was inadequate, an additional strip of vinyl with aluminum backing was

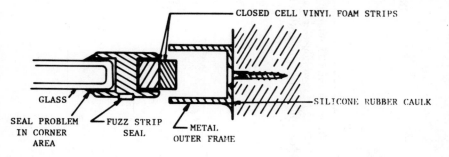

Figure 4—2.   Window Seals

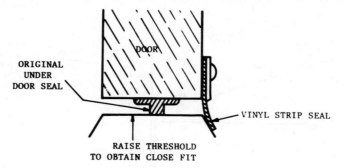

Figure 4—3. Door Seals—Bottom

screwed to the door (see Figure 4—3). The magnetic seals on the sides and top of the door opening were repaired where problems, particularly corner gaps, were found. In a few cases an additional lip seal was added (see Figure 4—4). The attic hatch cover also received a rim made from the foam vinyl strips to seal against vertical air flow.

Exterior caulking was used around the patio door frame and the closet overhang. When the vertical joint between masonry and frame was inspected, it was found that the principal cause for infiltration (as first suggested by the infrared photographs) was warping of the batten in the batten board homes (see Figure 4—5). In these homes a caulking joint was made, using the appropriate color polysulfide synthetic rubber sealant or clear silicon rubber sealant.

The last item under Retrofit B was the sealing of openings in the basement. The openings between the basement ceiling joists (2″ × 8″ or 5 cm × 20 cm) and the fire wall were addressed. As in item (1)

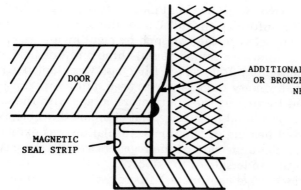

Figure 4—4. Door Seals—Sides

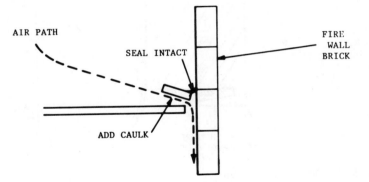

Figure 4–5. Passage for Outside Air at Edge of Facade

of Retrofit A, fiberglass was forced into the openings. Among other basement openings that required sealing were gaps at the corners and spaces around the piping to the kitchen, the dryer exhaust, and the service wiring. Caulking was used along the sill joint and for smaller wall openings. Costs for materials for Retrofit B was approximately $28.

RETROFIT C (CELLAR)

This retrofit concentrated exclusively on the cellar (or basement) and included (1) insulating the furnace and its warm air distribution system, (2) wrapping the water heater, and (3) packing the overhang area under the living room window, which includes two ducts.

The furnace plenum, the main left and right supply ducts, and the nine individual five inch (thirteen centimeter) diameter room ducts were wrapped with two inch (five centimeter) fiberglass backed by aluminum foil with reinforcing thread. Where the five inch (thirteen centimeter) ducts ran between the two inch by eight inch (five centimeter by twenty centimeter) ceiling joists, three and one-half inch (nine centimeter) aluminum-foil-backed fiberglass was stapled across the beams. At first, ordinary duct tape was used, but a superior product was discovered by one of the contractors, a tape with the same reinforcing thread plus a bonding surface that eliminated problems of peeling with repeated heating of the ducts. Insulation was extended to cover completely the underside of the registers as well; the insulation was stapled to the underside of the floor.

The same two inch (five centimeter) fiberglass* was used on the

---

*Where three and one-half inch (nine centimeter) fiberglass can fit, the additional heat resistance (R–11 versus R–7) is worthwhile.

water heaters, again using the new tape. On gas water heaters, care must be taken to use the insulation only on the sides of the tank, staying away from the air inlet on the bottom, the exhaust at the top, and the controls.

The last cellar item was the overhang under the front living room window. Here two ducts extend between the beams to the registers, and the insulation was either marginal or missing. The retrofit included blowing cellulose or fiberglass into the openings or (where blowing equipment wasn't available) hand packing fiberglass insulation into these cavities. Gaps to the outside are a particular problem in this location, which was difficult for the builder to complete properly (since it is only one foot above ground level).

The cost for Retrofit C ranged from $124 to $145 depending on the contractor performing these tasks.

REFERENCES

1. Harrje, D.T. 1976, Retrofitting: plan, action, and early results using the townhouses at Twin Rivers. Report No. 29. Princeton, N.J.: Princeton University.
2. Woteki, T. 1976. The Princeton Omnibus experiment: some effects of retrofits on space heating requirements. CES Report No. 43. Princeton, N.J.: Princeton University.
3. Woteki, T. 1977. Some effects of retrofits on interior temperatures in a sample of houses. CES Working Paper No. 31. Princeton, N.J.: Princeton University.

Chapter 5

Wind, Temperature, and Natural Ventilation— Theoretical Considerations

Frank W. Sinden
Princeton University

Abstract

The weather drives air infiltration by two separate physical mechanisms: (1) wind and (2) convection induced by a temperature difference between indoors and outdoors. These two mechanisms have complex interactions that are sensitive to the location of cracks in a building. The nature of the interaction of the two effects is displayed pictorially for several idealized examples. In an appendix to this chapter, the subadditivity of the effects for a wide class of situations is proven mathematically: the combined effect of wind and temperature is never greater than one would estimate by simple addition of the independent effects.

INTRODUCTION

In temperate zone houses, air leakage through cracks and crevices typically accounts for a third or more of the winter heat load and a somewhat smaller fraction of the summer air conditioning load. How this leakage is linked to the weather is the subject of this chapter.

The weather drives the leakage flow by two separate physical mechanisms: (1) wind and (2) temperature-induced convection. Unfortunately, these do not act independently; that is, their effects cannot be simply superimposed. Rather, they interact in a complex way that depends on the pattern in which cracks and crevices happen to be distributed over the surface of the house. For some patterns, the effects of wind and temperature tend to cancel each other; for other patterns, they tend to add. In fact, for a given fixed pattern of cracks and crevices, the nature of the interaction may vary with the wind and temperature themselves, canceling in some ranges and adding in others. Simple examples given below illustrate these effects.

The complexity of the wind-temperature interaction, though discussed here in theoretical terms, has important implications for practice. It is, for example, bad news for computer modelers, since it appears unlikely that any simple general formula exists that universally represents natural ventilation in buildings. This conclusion is reinforced by field observations. Linear regressions of measured air infiltration against wind and temperature do in fact show erratic results: sometimes the fit is good and sometimes it is not (see Chapter 6). This is exactly what one would expect on the basis of the considerations given below.

Fortunately, achieving the goal of saving energy by rationalizing ventilation does not depend crucially on having a satisfactory computer model. An alternative approach is to develop a practical set of techniques and instruments that can be used in the field to obtain the information necessary to specify and test conservation measures for particular buildings.

Let:

A = rate of air infiltration for a particular building (m^3/s). (Equals rate of air exfiltration.)

W = wind velocity (m/s)

$\triangle T$ = inside minus outside temperature ($^\circ$C).

If the effects of wind and temperature were additive, then the function $A(W, \triangle T)$ could be written in the form:

$$A(W, \triangle T) = A(W, O) + A(O, \triangle T). \qquad (5.1)$$

It will be shown below that this, in general, is not possible. Failing this, one might hope that $A(W, \triangle T)$ would at least be monotonic, that is, that an increase in either wind (W) or temperature difference ($\triangle T$) would always result in increased air flow:

$$\frac{\partial A}{\partial W} > 0, \frac{\partial A}{\partial \triangle T} > 0 \quad \text{for all } W, \triangle T. \qquad (5.2)$$

But it will be shown that even this is not true in general.

It is true, however, that under quite general conditions, $A(W, \Delta T)$ is subadditive:

$$A(W, \Delta T) \leqslant A(W, O) + A(O, \Delta T). \qquad (5.3)$$

This means that the combined effect of wind and temperature is never greater than one would estimate by simple addition of the independent effects. (The proof of this inequality is presented in the appendix to this chapter.)

The first section of this article reviews briefly the flow of air through a single opening. The second section, through a series of simple examples, attempts to give an intuitive picture of the interaction between wind and temperature-induced convection, and in particular to make plausible the results cited above. The last section gives a general mathematical formulation and a formal proof of the subadditivity of $A(W, \Delta T)$.

FLOW THROUGH A SINGLE CRACK

Let p_o, p_i = pressure outside and inside respectively, as in Figure 5–1.

$$\Delta p = p_o - p_i$$

OUTSIDE

INSIDE

p_o

p_i

A

Figure 5–1. Pressure Difference Drives Flow Through a Crack

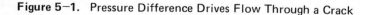

The air flow A as a function of the pressure difference Δp can generally be approximated by

$$A = K(\Delta p)^{\alpha},$$ (5.4)

where the constants K and α are determined by the shape and size of the opening. The exponent α varies with the flow regime as follows [1]:

laminar	$\alpha = 1$
turbulent	$\alpha = 4/7$
entrance, exit effects	$\alpha = 1/2$

Unfortunately, the dimensions and velocities found under ordinary circumstances are such that any or all of the three regimes may occur. The most that can be said in general is that $A(\Delta p)$ is a concave function that can be approximated by the form given above with some compromise α between $1/2$ and 1.

SIMPLE EXAMPLES OF WIND-TEMPERATURE INTERACTION

Consider first a building (for simplicity a rectangular box) that is tightly sealed, and let $\Delta p(z)$ be the outside-inside pressure difference at the point z on the building's shell. We consider in this section what the pressure difference distribution $\Delta p(z)$ looks like under various conditions.

Suppose, for example, that the air is less dense inside than outside, as would be true for a heated building on a cold day. Then as the point z moves downward, the static pressure increases less rapidly inside than outside, and the pressure difference Δp therefore increases. If we arbitrarily assume that Δp is zero at midheight, then the distribution of Δp over the vertical walls is as shown in Figure 5–2. If the density difference is greater (due, e.g., to a greater temperature difference) then the pressure difference variation is more pronounced, as shown in Figure 5–3.

Now suppose that a wind is blowing from left to right, and for simplicity suppose that the effect of the wind is to increase the pressure uniformly on the windward side and to decrease it uniformly by a like amount on the leeward side. Then the distribution of Δp on the vertical sides is shifted, as shown in Figure 5–4. If the wind is blowing harder, then the distribution is shifted further, as shown in

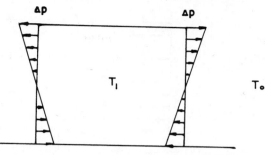

Figure 5–2. Pressure Difference on Walls: Mild Day, No Wind

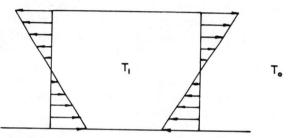

Figure 5–3. Pressure Difference on Walls: Cold Day, No Wind

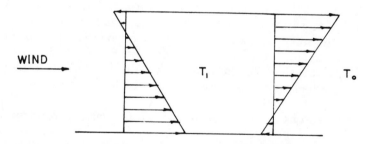

Figure 5–4. Pressure Difference on Walls: Cold Day, Slight Wind

Figure 5–5. Since the density difference is very nearly proportional to the temperature difference,* Figures 5–2 through 5–5 show essentially how the pressure difference distribution, $\Delta p(z)$, varies with wind, W, and temperature difference, ΔT, under the simple assumptions we have made.

---

*The density difference is exactly proportional to $\dfrac{1}{T_o} - \dfrac{1}{T_i}$ where T_o and T_i are the absolute outside and inside temperatures, but this expression is very nearly proportional to ΔT.

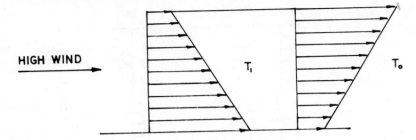

Figure 5–5.   Pressure Difference on Walls: Cold Day, High Wind

Suppose now that the sides of the building are not impervious, but rather are uniformly porous, and for the sake of simplicity of exposition, suppose that the pores are such that the coefficient α in equation (4.4) is equal to 1. Then the rate of air flow through the wall is just proportional to Δp and the arrows in Figures 5–2 through 5–5 can be reinterpreted as air flow vectors. The figures have been drawn so that total inflow equals total outflow. The inside pressure always adjusts itself so that this is the case.

The infiltration rate is obtained by summing the inward flow vectors. Representing this sum by A, one can see by inspection of the figures that A is not a separable function of wind W and temperature difference ΔT as expressed by equation (5.1). In Figure 5–5, for example, one can see that changing ΔT slightly has no effect whatever on A, since it changes only the slant of the distribution of inward arrow lengths, but not their sum. In Figure 5–2, however, changing ΔT (the slant of the distribution) has a definite effect on A. Thus, the effect of temperature difference is not independent of wind.

Figure 5–6 shows a plot of A versus ΔT for various wind speeds.

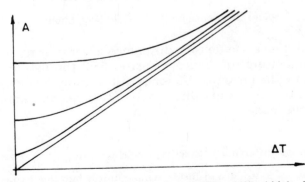

Figure 5–6.   *A* as a Function of ΔT for Various Fixed Wind Velocities in the Case of Uniformly Porous Walls

The interdependence is clear. The case shown in Figure 5−6, however, is relatively benign. A more striking case is shown in Figure 5−7. Here, the uniformly porous walls have been replaced by solid walls with just two small openings—one at the top of the windward wall and the other at the bottom of the leeward wall. As the wind increases from zero, the air infiltration rate actually decreases, as the wind progressively cancels out more and more of the temperature-induced flow. At a certain wind velocity, the effects cancel each other totally; and for higher wind velocities, the flow reverses and increases in magnitude with increasing wind. Plots of A versus W for various fixed temperature differences are shown in Figure 5−8. This is a case in which $A(W, \triangle T)$ is not only inseparable, but is not even monotonic.

Of course, these examples do not prove that $A(W, \triangle T)$ is always inseparable or nonmonotonic, and indeed this is not true. Figure 5−9 shows an example in which (under our simple assumptions) the infiltration rate A is entirely independent of wind, and Figure 5−10 shows a companion example in which A is entirely independent of temperature difference. In these cases $A(W, \triangle T)$ is both separable (trivially) and monotonic.

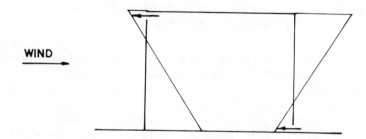

WIND

Figure 5−7. With Openings Arranged as Shown, the Wind and Temperature Effects Tend to Cancel

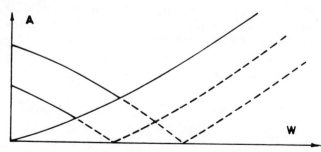

Figure 5−8. *A* as a Function of *W* for Various Fixed Temperature Differences When the Openings are Located as Shown in Figure 5−7

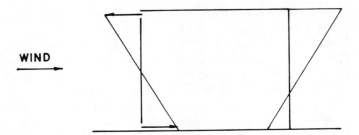

Figure 5—9. Infiltration Rate *A* is Independent of Wind Under the Simple Assumptions Given in Text

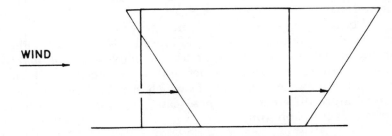

Figure 5—10. Infiltration Rate *A* is Independent of Temperature Difference Under the Simple Assumptions Given in Text

These examples, of course, are based on simple assumptions. Real air flow is much more complex. In practice, the function $A(W, \triangle T)$ is affected not only by the location of openings but also by the aerodynamic idiosyncracies of individual buildings and by irregularities in the air flow itself. Atmospheric turbulence, for example, can cause appreciable air exchange through openings even at low wind speed, so that $A(O, O)$ may not really be zero as assumed above (see [2] for a study of this effect).

In conclusion, then, it is not surprising that the air infiltration response of different individual buildings to wind and temperature is often puzzling and seemingly erratic.

APPENDIX: GENERAL CHARACTERISTICS
OF THE FUNCTION $A(W, \triangle T)$

In the absence of information about a building's details, it would seem that little could be said about the function $A(W, \triangle T)$. We know that it is not necessarily linear or even separable or monotonic. Nevertheless, it does have one useful property under quite general conditions, namely, the property of subadditivity as expressed in equation (5.3). This is stated and proved more precisely below.

Let:

z = a location on the building's shell.

$a(z, \triangle p)$ = air flow through the shell at point z in response to the local pressure difference $\triangle p$.

The function $a(z, \triangle p)$ will be assumed to have the following simple properties:

1. $a(z, \triangle p)$ always has the same sign as $\triangle p$ and $a(z, O) = 0$.
2. $a(z, \triangle p)$ is monotonic with respect to $\triangle p$: $\triangle p_1 > \triangle p_2$ implies that $a(z, \triangle p_1) > a(z, \triangle p_2)$.
3. $a(z, \triangle p)$ is subadditive* with respect to $\triangle p$:
   $$a(z, \triangle p_1 + \triangle p_2) \leqslant a(z, \triangle p_1) + a(z, \triangle p_2)$$

Note that the special form given in Equation (5.4) has all of these properties.

Let:

$\triangle p_W(W, z)$ = pressure difference at point z due to wind W when $\triangle T = 0$.

$\triangle p_T(\triangle T, z)$ = pressure difference at point z due to temperature difference $\triangle T$ when $W = 0$.

The overall pressure difference when both W and $\triangle T$ are acting is

$$\triangle p = \triangle p_W + \triangle p_T + \triangle p_o, \tag{5.5}$$

where $\triangle p_o$ is a constant that adjusts itself so that total flow in equals total flow out, that is, so that

$$\int_S a(z, \triangle p) dz = 0,$$

---

*In particular, any concave function is subadditive.

where S = whole surface. For fixed W, ΔT, consider the subsets of S defined as follows:

$$S_W \quad = \text{set of } z \text{ such that } \Delta p_W \geqslant 0$$
$$S_T \quad = \text{set of } z \text{ such that } \Delta p_T \geqslant 0$$
$$S_{\Delta p} = \text{set of } z \text{ such that } \Delta p \geqslant 0$$

A bar over a set designation will indicate the complement—that is, $\overline{S}_W$ is the set of z such that $\Delta p_W < 0$.

The infiltration rate with both W and ΔT acting is

$$A(W, \Delta T) = \int_{S_{\Delta p}} a(z, \Delta p)\,dz. \qquad (5.6)$$

With wind acting alone the infiltration rate is

$$A(W, 0) = \int_{S_W} a(z, \Delta p_W)\,dz, \qquad (5.7)$$

and with temperature acting alone it is

$$A(0, \Delta T) = \int_{S_T} a(z, \Delta p_T)\,dz. \qquad (5.8)$$

Theorem: If $a(z, \Delta p)$ has the three properties listed above, then

$$A(W, \Delta T) \leqslant A(W, 0) + A(0, \Delta T).$$

Proof: For a fixed W, ΔT, suppose that the constant Δp_o, which equates inward and outward flow, is nonpositive:

$$\Delta p_o \leqslant 0.$$

It follows from equation (5.5) and the definitions of the subsets of S that

$$S_{\Delta p} \subset S_W \cap S_T + S_W \cap \overline{S}_T + \overline{S}_W \cap S_T.$$

Hence:

$$S_{\Delta p} = S_{\Delta p} \cap S_W \cap S_T + S_{\Delta p} \cap S_W \cap \overline{S}_T + S_{\Delta p} \cap \overline{S}_W \cap S_T \qquad (5.9)$$

$$A(W, \Delta T) = \int_{S_{\Delta p}} a(z, \Delta p)\, dz$$

$$= \int_{S_{\Delta p} \cap S_W \cap S_T} a(z, \Delta p_w + \Delta p_T + \Delta p_o)\, dz + \int_{S_{\Delta p} \cap S_W \cap \bar{S}_T} a(z, \Delta p_w + \Delta p_T + \Delta p_o)\, dz + \int_{S_{\Delta p} \cap \bar{S}_W \cap S_T} a(z, \Delta p_w + \Delta p_T + \Delta p_o)\, dz$$

Note (1)
$$\leqslant$$
$$a(z, \Delta p_W + \Delta p_T) \qquad\qquad a(z, \Delta p_W) \qquad\qquad a(z, \Delta p_T)$$

Note (2)
$$\leqslant$$
$$a(z, \Delta p_W) + a(z, \Delta p_T)$$

Note (3)
$$\leqslant$$

$$A(W, 0) = \int_{S_W \cap S_T} a(z, \Delta p_W)\, dz \qquad + \qquad \int_{S_W \cap \bar{S}_T} a(z, \Delta p_W)\, dz$$

Note (3)
$$\leqslant$$

$$A(0, \Delta T) = \int_{S_W \cap S_T} a(z, \Delta p_T)\, dz \qquad + \qquad \int_{\bar{S}_W \cap S_T} a(z, \Delta p_T)\, dz$$

$$\therefore \quad A(W, \Delta T) \leqslant A(W, 0) + A(0, \Delta T) \tag{5.10}$$

(1) By monotonicity of $a(z, \Delta p)$. Terms in Δp that are negative over the domains are dropped. This cannot decrease the integrand.

(2) By subadditivity of $a(z, \Delta p)$.

(3) In each case, the domain of integration is expanded by deleting the symbols $S_{\Delta p} \cap$. Since the integrand in each case is nonnegative over the new domain, this cannot decrease the integral.

To demonstrate the inequality of the theorem, the procedure is to partition the domain of the integral in equation (5.6) into three sub-domains according to equation (5.9), then to apply the properties 1, 2, 3 of $a(z, \triangle p)$ appropriately to the three integrals, and finally to expand the domains. This generates a chain of inequalities linking the two sides of the inequality to be proved. The details of the procedure are displayed in diagrammatic form (equation 5.10). Where a change is only in an integrand with the domain held fixed, the integral sign is omitted to avoid cluttering. The inequalities are to be read downward from one line to the next. The steps are justified in the three notes below the equation.

The proof to this point depends on the assumption $\triangle p_o \leqslant 0$. Under this assumption, it was shown that the infiltration rates satisfy the inequality of the theorem. It follows ex post facto that the exfiltration rates in absolute value also satisfy the inequality, since these are the same. If $\triangle p_o \geqslant 0$, then the proof can simply be turned around, so that it applies directly to exfiltration. Thus the complements $\overline{S}_W$, $\overline{S}_T$, $\overline{S}_{\triangle p}$ replace S_W, S_T, $S_{\triangle p}$, and the sign of $a(z, \triangle p)$ is changed (since the inequality to be proved holds for the absolute value of exfiltration). Thus transformed, the proof goes through as before.

The last point perhaps becomes clearer when one reflects that the symmetry between outside and inside is perfect. There is nothing in the model that allows one to tell which is which except by arbitrary assertion. The difference between $\triangle p_o \leqslant 0$ and $\triangle p_o \geqslant 0$ is simply that in one case, equalization of flow is achieved by adding a constant pressure to the inside and in the other case by adding a constant pressure to the outside. Since outside is indistinguishable from inside, the cases are really the same.

REFERENCES

1. Bailey, F.J. 1958 *An Introduction to Fluid Dynamics.* New York: Inter-science. Pp. 89, 101, 105.
2. Hill, J.E., and T. Kusuda. 1975. Dynamic characteristics of air infiltration, *ASHRAE* 81, pt. I.

Chapter 6

Field Studies of Dependence of Air Infiltration on Outside Temperature and Wind*

Nicholas Malik
Gamze-Korobkin-Caloger, Inc.
Chicago

Abstract

The air infiltration rate, measured in two similar townhouses, depends on wind speed, wind direction, indoor-outdoor temperature difference (DT), average rate of furnace firing, and fraction of time that doors are open. An increase of 0.1 exchange per hour is associated with each of the following: (1) an increase in DT by 12°F (7°C) at low wind speeds; (2) an increase in normally incident wind by two mph (three kilometers per hour) at low DT; (3) ten minutes per hour of increased front door opening; and (4) having the basement door open instead of closed. The wind-temperature interaction is nonlinear, which confounds the modeling. The DT effect is nearly half due to increased furnace firing, which induces an air flow three times larger than that required for stoichiometric combustion.

THE IMPACT OF INFILTRATION ON GAS CONSUMPTION

Simultaneous measurements of rate of air infiltration and rate of energy consumption for space heating have hardly ever been available in field studies of energy use in homes. Accordingly, Figure 6—1

*This chapter is based on an MSE thesis, "Air Infiltration in Homes," accepted by the Aerospace and Mechanical Sciences Department of Princeton University in September 1977.

I gratefully acknowledge the assistance of Roy Crosby, Gautam Dutt, Ken Gadsby, David Harrje, George Mattingly, Andrew Persily, Frank Sinden, and Robert Socolow.

should be of considerable interest. It shows direct evidence that gas consumption is greater, for the same indoor-outdoor temperature difference, when the air infiltration rate is greater.

Figure 6–1 gives quantitative information about the relative significance of heat losses due to air infiltration and due to conductance through the shell. Each data point displayed in Figure 6–1 corresponds to a different night of data taken in the same Twin Rivers townhouse. For each of twenty-six nights, measurements were made of the rate of gas combustion (G), the temperature difference between indoors (downstairs hall) and outdoors (DT), and the air infiltration rate (AI), and averages for each night were computed. When a linear model omitting the air infiltration rate was fitted to the data, $G = -\alpha_1 + \beta_1 \, DT$, the best fit,

$$G = -8{,}200 + (720 \pm 80)\, DT \tag{6.1}$$

had an R^2 of only 0.78 (essentially, left 22 percent of the variation in G unexplained). Here, G is in watts, and DT is in °C. The standard error of the estimate of G for this model is 2,300 watts. However, when a linear model including the air infiltration rate is fitted to the data, $G = -\alpha_2 + \beta_2 \, DT + \gamma_2 \, (AI)(DT)$, the best fit,

$$G = -5{,}600 + (400 \pm 40)\, DT + (250 \pm 20)\, (AI)\,(DT) \tag{6.2}$$

had an R^2 of 0.96 and a standard error of only 950 watts. Again, G is in watts (although originally measured as cubic feet of gas consumed per hour, the gas having an energy content of 1,025 Btu per cubic foot, or 38 MJ per cubic meter), DT is in °C, and AI is in exchanges of air per hour. The straight lines corresponding to equation (6.2) with $AI = 0.5 \, h^{-1}$ and $1.5 \, h^{-1}$ are shown on Figure 6–1, as well as the straight line corresponding to equation (6.1).

The first term in equations (6.1) and (6.2) contains the heating by appliances and people; a portion of the heat loss to sinks, like the ground, that are warmer than outside air; and a contribution from heat stored in the structure during the day. It has the physically correct negative sign. The second and third terms represent conductive heat losses and losses due to air infiltration, respectively. Accordingly, the ratio of air infiltration heat loss to total heat loss may be written $R = 250 \, AI/(400 + 250 \, AI)$, where AI is in exchanges per hour. For this townhouse, therefore, air infiltration contributes 24, 38, and 48 percent of the heat loss when the air infiltration rate is, respectively, 0.5, 1.0, and 1.5 exchanges per hour. At the "handbook" constant exchange rate for townhouses, 0.75 exchanges per

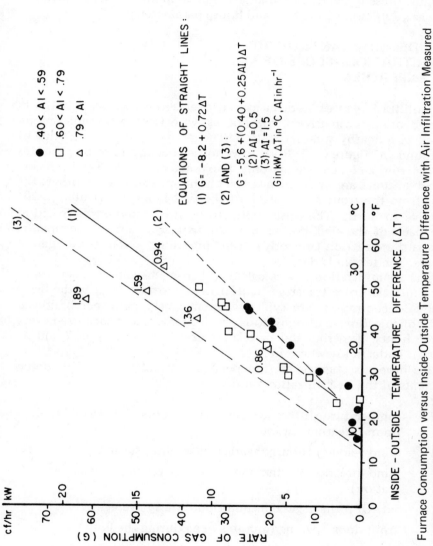

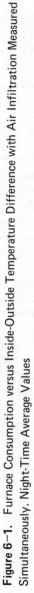

Figure 6–1. Furnace Consumption versus Inside-Outside Temperature Difference with Air Infiltration Measured Simultaneously. Night-Time Average Values

hour, R is 32 percent, in general agreement with the rule of thumb that air infiltration typically accounts for one-third of all heat losses in conventional residential housing. The subsequent sections of this chapter present the results of an attempt to model the air infiltration rate as a function of weather and house parameters.

THE DETERMINANTS OF AIR INFILTRATION—SCOPE OF AN EXPERIMENT

Air infiltration rates were measured over several winter months in two identical Twin Rivers townhouses, with weather variables monitored at a nearby weather station. The geometry of the experiment is found in Figure 6—2. Both townhouses occupy interior positions in the row and hence have only two walls exposed to the outside. The two units are oriented nearly at right angles to one another: the axis from the front to the back of the first house is oriented at $10°$ relative to north. The least shelter from other buildings is found at the back of the first house, and (unfortunately for the occupants) this is the direction (westerly) of the prevailing as well as the highest winds. The terrain is flat.

The air infiltration rate is calculated from the rate of decrease of concentration of a tracer gas (sulfur hexafluoride, SF_6) in the living area. Concentrations are typically about thirty parts per billion at time of injection; and reinjection, in this experiment, occurred every three hours. Experimental details are sketched in Chapter 7 and reported in detail elsewhere [1, 2].

We have investigated six independent variables as possible determinants of the air infiltration rate:

DT = temperature difference between indoors (hallway) and outdoors (weather station).

V = wind velocity (hourly average at weather station).

θ = wind direction (instantaneous hourly reading at weather station).

G = rate of furnace gas consumption (hourly average).

F = front door opening (minutes open during the hour).

B = basement door opening (minutes open during the hour); basement door opens into the living area.

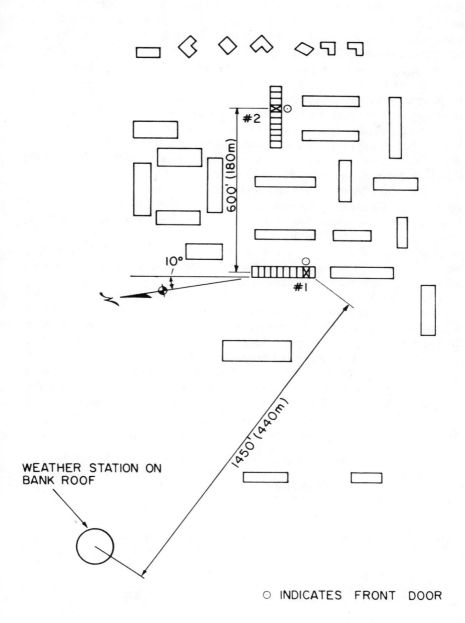

WEATHER STATION ON
BANK ROOF

○ INDICATES FRONT DOOR

Figure 6–2. Plan of Twin Rivers, Showing Location of Experimental Houses
and Weather Station

Results of regression analyses, when particular linear representations of the air infiltration rate were tested, are presented in the next two sections. We use SI units in these expressions; Table 6-1 should facilitate conversion to American units.

On physical grounds, one should expect the air infiltration rate to increase with wind velocity and temperature difference, but complex interference effects may be anticipated from these two sources of pressure difference over the shell of the house (see Chapter 5). One should expect, for these townhouses with only two exposed orientations, that wind incident on the house normal to the front and back door should be more effective in creating air infiltration than wind incident from a direction along the building axis. One should expect air infiltration to be enhanced when the furnace is running, because furnace combustion reduces the pressure in the basement, and combustion air must enter the basement either directly or by way of the living area. The air flow up the flue when the furnace is running is several times that required for combustion, in order to entrain the combustion products, and this flow too must be matched by a corresponding flow into the house from outdoors.

One of course expects the air infiltration rate to be larger the longer the front door is open, assuming it is open equally wide on all occasions, a quantity not measured. We are actually measuring the air infiltration rate for the living area, a volume that excludes the basement, but there is air flow between living area and basement not only through the basement door but also through leaks in basement ducts and through other passages (see Chapter 3). The largest effect of the basement door being open, we would expect, is to increase the "stack effect" pattern of flow, where cold air enters the basement but leaves the house from the living area. There should also be addi-

Table 6-1. Conversion of Units for Variables in Analysis of Air Infiltration

Variable	Units in This Article	Conversion to American Units
AI	exchanges of air in "living area" per hour	—
DT	$^{\circ}$C	1°C = 1.8°F
V	km/h	1 km/h = 0.622 mph
θ	degrees	—
G	kilowatts	1 kW = 3.33 cf/h (gas at 1,025 Btu/cf)
F	minutes per hour	—
B	minutes per hour	—

tional air infiltration in the living area when the furnace is running if the basement door is open. Although these effects suggest models with interaction terms ($DT \cdot B$ and $G \cdot B$), we have tested more elementary models linear in B, still expecting to see increased air infiltration the longer the basement door is open.

All of the effects expected on physical grounds have been found clearly in the data. We have reduced a large number of data sets, each generally associated with a one week "run" in one house. Only a few runs are discussed here; a larger number of runs are discussed elsewhere [2]. We divide the discussion below, somewhat arbitrarily, according to whether the wind speed is low (less than 6 mph = 10 km/h) or high (more than 6 mph = 10 km/h).

A PARAMETRIC FORM FOR THE AIR INFILTRATION RATE AT LOW WIND SPEEDS

Regression Analysis—House 1

When we confine the analysis to cases with wind speeds not exceeding six miles per hour (ten kilometers per hour), here called "low," the effects of wind are minimized. Figure 6−3 shows a scatter plot of the air infiltration rate, AI, against the indoor-outdoor temperature difference, at low wind speeds and with the front door opening restricted to less than two minutes per hour. Each data point is one hour's data. Six data sets are shown, all from the same house (House 1) but in several different months. Three data sets (FEB1, FEB2, and APR1) follow one trend, the other three follow another.

In both cases, AI increases approximately linearly with DT, with roughly the same slope, but one pattern is displaced above the other. The house acts as if it had two different "porosities," the house being tighter in one case relative to the other. The higher pattern corresponds to data taken during generally milder weather. It may be that in mild weather, windows and doors are opened rather frequently and are closed carelessly, whereas in winter, people make sure their windows and doors are closed tight.

The mild weather data sets (APR2, MAY, and SEPT) will not be studied in this chapter.*

---

*A confounding variable for two of these data sets (APR2 and MAY) is the presence of a tree barrier on the windward side of the house [3] (see also Figure 1-10C, p. 34). We had expected the barrier to reduce air infiltration, but the porosity effect appears to have confounded the analysis. Careful data reduction emphasizing angle dependence at high wind speeds shows an effect of the barrier: 0.2 exchange per hour reduction in air infiltration rate for winds that strike the barrier [2].

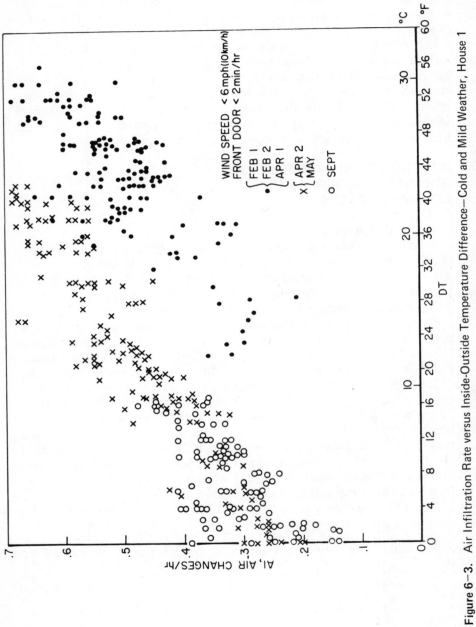

Figure 6–3. Air Infiltration Rate versus Inside-Outside Temperature Difference—Cold and Mild Weather, House 1

The results of a multiple regression analysis applied to an aggregate of the three cold weather data sets (with front door opening unrestricted) is presented in Table 6−2. When only the variable DT has entered the analysis, the equation for the air infiltration rate is:

$$AI = 0.186 + (0.0148 \pm 0.0018)DT. \qquad (6.3)$$

At this stage, four of the five other tested variables are statistically significant. All four survive the significance tests of the multiple regression analysis, which yields:

$$AI = 0.193 + (0.0095 \pm 0.0020)DT + (0.0107) \pm 0.0020)G$$

$$+(0.0016 \pm 0.0003) B + (0.0088 \pm 0.0022)F$$

$$+(0.0074 \pm 0.0020) \mid V \cos (\theta - 280°) \mid . \qquad (6.4)$$

A term linear in V, but angle-independent, is not statistically significant once the angle-dependent velocity is entered in the regression.

Consider the coefficients of the various terms in the above equation. The coefficient of DT is indicative of the magnitude of the

Table 6−2. Regression Statistics for House 1 at Low Wind Speeds.
(242 cases: Files FEB1, FEB2, APR1)

Variable	Mean	Standard Deviation
AI	0.540 exch/hr	0.098 exch/hr
DT	24.1°C (43.4°F)	3.2°C (5.8°F)
V	6.03 km/h (3.75 mph)	2.03 km/h (1.26 mph)
$V \mid \cos (\theta - 280°) \mid$	3.89 km/h (2.42 mph)	2.36 km/h (1.47 mph)
G	6.9 kW (23.0 cf/h)	3.5 kW (11.5 cf/h)
F	0.5 min/hr	2.1 min/hr
B	7.4 min/hr	16.8 min/hr

	Stepwise Statistics			
Variable Entered	Partial F	R^2	Standard Error of AI	Overall F
DT	22.0	0.23	0.086	73
G	32.5	0.35	0.080	63
B	34.2	0.43	0.075	59
F	15.9	0.45	0.073	49
$V \mid \cos (\theta - 280°) \mid$	14.2	0.49	0.071	44

stack effect at low wind speeds. At the mean value of DT ($43°$F or $24°$C), the contribution of the stack effect is approximately 0.2 exchanges per hour, 40 percent of the mean value of the air exchange rate.

The coefficient of G is a measure of the variation of AI with the rate of gas consumption. It indicates that continuous furnace operation (maximum consumption: 75 ft^3 or 2.1 m^3 of natural gas per hour) results in an additional air exchange rate of approximately 0.24 ± 0.05 air changes per hour. When Socolow carried out a similar analysis using data for air infiltration rate and gas consumption taken at five minute intervals over a single night, he found that 0.19 air changes per hour were associated with continuous furnace firing [4]. The two results, therefore, are in agreement. Two reasons for an effect of gas consumption on air infiltration are: (1) air is needed for combustion, and (2) air is entrained with exhaust gases going up the flue. Stoichiometric air required for combustion of methane amounts to 800 cubic feet per hour (23 cubic meters per hour) when the furnace fires continuously. The volume of living space is approximately 10,000 cubic feet (300 cubic meters). This implies that the supply of stoichiometric air is equivalent to 0.08 air exchanges per hour. Comparing this to the values for continuous firing just presented, we see that about one-third of the induced air due to continuous furnace operation is due to stoichiometric air. The other two-thirds can be accounted for by the entrained air.

The coefficients of B and F are definitely significant. There will be an increase in AI of 0.10 air changes per hour if the basement door is kept open the whole hour, and an additional increase that extrapolates to 0.53 air changes per hour if the front door is kept open the whole hour. Put another way, keeping the basement door open for sixty minutes is like keeping the front door open for eleven minutes (the basement door opens into the interior hallway). In another investigation, we found evidence that the effect of the front door opening is significantly enhanced with simultaneous basement door opening. This could be due to reduction in resistance to air flow from the basement to the living space. It should show up in a term like $F \cdot B$ in a regression analysis, but this has not been pursued.

The fact that the variable V does not enter the regression equation once $V \mid \cos(\theta - 280°) \mid$ is included indicates that, at least in the low wind speed condition, the only component of the wind velocity that has a significant effect is the one that is perpendicular to the house row, namely, $V \mid \cos(\theta - 280°) \mid$. However, one has to bear in mind that the value of V is restricted to below six miles per hour (ten kilometers per hour). Moreover, the term $V \mid \cos(\theta - 280°) \mid$ is highly correlated with V. The contribution of the mean value of $V \mid \cos (\theta - 280°) \mid$ to the mean value of AI is found from Table 6−2 to be equal to only 6 percent.

Finally, we note that the constant in equation (6.4), 0.193 exchanges per hour, is significantly greater than zero (the standard error being only 0.071 exchanges per hour). Thus, our data suggest that the air infiltration rate approaches a value greater than zero on a mild, calm day when both DT and V approach zero. Hill and Kusuda have anticipated that this effect should be present and that it is related to residual turbulence [5]. Further experimental work near this limit is required, because the implications for public health in tight houses on mild, calm days are significant.

Regression Analysis—House 2

Figure 6−4 is a scatter plot, analogous to Figure 6−3, but here superimposing four data sets from House 2 on the three data sets from House 1 that have just been studied. The data for House 2 lie above these data for House 1, but not as far above as the "high porosity" data (from data sets SEPT, APR2, and MAY) shown in Figure 6−3.

A regression analysis for House 2 is limited by the absence of instrumentation to detect basement door and front door openings and gas consumption. (For the most part, however, the basement door and the front door were deliberately kept closed during periods of data gathering.) Consequently, only weather variables can be considered. Table 6−3 shows results of a regression analysis at low wind

Table 6−3. Regression Statistics for House 2 at Low Wind Speeds.
(431 cases: Files OCT, NOV1, NOV2, DEC)

Variable	Mean	Standard Deviation
AI	0.48 exch/hr	0.095 exch/hr
DT	17.5°C (31.5°F)	5.1°C (9.2°F)
V	5.23 km/h (3.25 mph)	2.41 km/h (1.50 mph)
$V \mid \cos(\theta - 15°) \mid$	3.73 km/h (2.32 mph)	2.36 km/h (1.47 mph)

	Stepwise Statistics			
Variable Entered	Partial F	R^2	Standard Error of AI	Overall F
DT	464.6	0.48	0.069	396
$V \mid \cos(\theta - 15°) \mid$	74.7	0.56	0.063	269

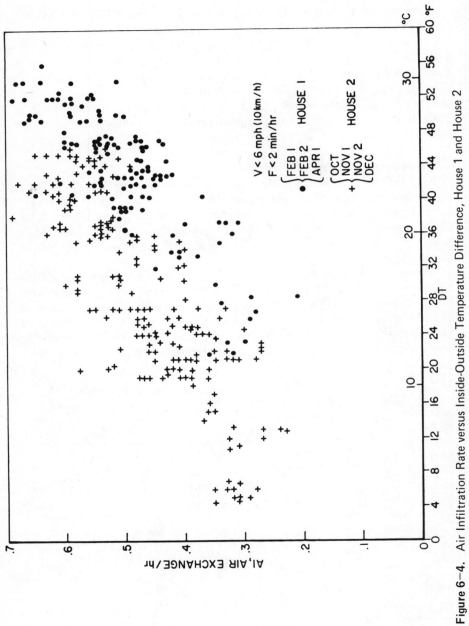

Figure 6–4.   Air Infiltration Rate versus Inside-Outside Temperature Difference, House 1 and House 2

speeds, when the data sets OCT, NOV1, NOV2, and DEC are aggregated. In this case AI can be represented as a function of DT by the following equation:

$$AI = 0.26 + (0.0128 \pm 0.0007)DT \qquad (6.5)$$

Here, as in equation (6.3), the coefficient of DT represents a combination of the stack effect and the furnace effects. The coefficients of DT in the two equations are consistent with one another. This might have been expected, since both houses are of the same type.

When the effect of wind velocity is explored, the data are better explained by a term linear in $\mid V \cos (\theta - 15°) \mid$, essentially the perpendicular component of the velocity, rather than by a term linear in V. The same preference was observed in House 1. The resulting equation is:

$$AI = 0.22 + (0.0128 \pm 0.0005)DT$$
$$+ (0.0111 \pm 0.0013) \; V \mid \cos (\theta - 15°) \mid \qquad (6.6)$$

The coefficient of the V-dependent term is slightly larger than in equation (6.4) for House 1, but to one standard deviation, the coefficients nearly overlap.

A PARAMETRIC FORM FOR THE AIR INFILTRATION RATE AT HIGH WIND SPEEDS

We confine our attention to one data set (APR1), obtained in House 1 over a period of six days (April 1–6, 1975), during which, for three days, there was an exceptionally violent storm. The hourly average wind speed varies between 3.5 miles per hour (5.6 kilometers per hour) and 29.9 miles per hour (48.1 kilometers per hour), and the wind direction spans the whole circle. We divide our data set into three subsets, according to whether the indoor-outdoor temperature difference, DT, lies between 40°F (22°C) and 50°F (28°C); between 30°F (17°C) and 40°F (22°C); or between 18°F (10°C) and 30°F (17°C). By working within narrow bands of DT, we minimize the problems of complex interaction effects between wind and DT.

22°C (40°F) $\leq DT \leq$ 28°C (50°F)

There are sixty-three data points in this subset, and they are shown against wind velocity in Figure 6–5, for several ranges of wind direction. Even though in this particular data set there are no easterly

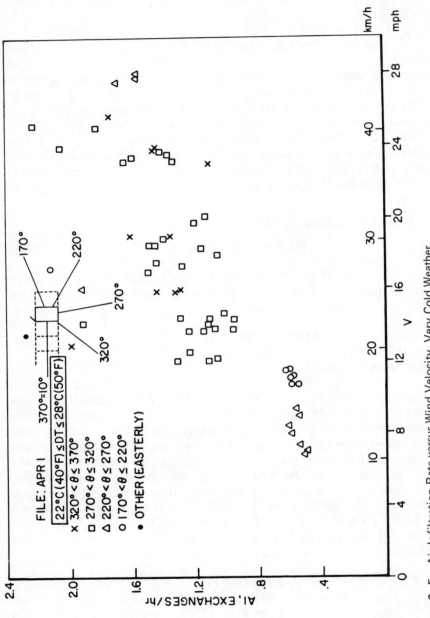

Figure 6–5. Air Infiltration Rate versus Wind Velocity, Very Cold Weather

winds, Figure 6–5 shows clear evidence of the effect of wind direction. For example, at twelve miles per hour (nineteen kilometers per hour) the air infiltration rate is nearly doubled when the wind comes from the rear of the house (data points shown as squares) instead of along a direction parallel to the townhouse row (data points shown as circles).

Ignoring wind direction for a moment, we attempt a fit to the data linear in wind velocity. We obtain:

$$AI = (0.037 \pm 0.003) \, V + 0.21 \tag{6.7}$$

The R^2 is 0.69, and the standard error of estimate is 0.22 exchanges per hour. Using a stepwise regression, we find that a term linear in the gas consumption enters next in the equation, giving:

$$AI = (0.027 \pm 0.003) \, V \; + (0.030 \pm 0.007) \, G + 0.15 \tag{6.8}$$

The R^2 at this step assumes the value of 0.78, and the standard error of estimate is reduced to 0.19 exchanges per hour. We observe that as G is entered in the equation, the coefficient of V is significantly reduced. Some of the wind effect appears to be due to greater gas consumption in higher winds.

In order to study the influence of wind direction, we plot the residuals (Figure 6–6) defined by the difference between the measured value of AI and the value obtained from equation (6.8). Generally speaking, the residuals are positive in the neighborhood of the perpendicular to the row axis ($280°$) and are negative in the neighborhood of the parallel to the row axis. This leads us to approximate the dependence on θ by a sinusoidal function, $V \cos(\theta - \phi)$. The best fit to the data is found for $\phi = 300°$. The fit is significantly better than for $\phi = 280°$, the direction of the perpendicular to the house row axis. (On physical grounds, a term with $\phi = 280°$ was expected to be the more statistically significant. The fact that a term with $\phi = 300°$ has a better fit can either be due to an instrument error or to the complexity of the wind effect.) We obtain:

$$AI = (-0.002 \pm 0.004) \, V + (0.30 \pm 0.003) \, G$$

$$+ (0.027 \pm 0.003) \, V \, | \cos(\theta - 300°) | + 0.31 \tag{6.9}$$

The R^2 increases to 0.91, and the standard error of estimate is reduced to 0.12 exchanges per hour. Comparing equation (6.9) with

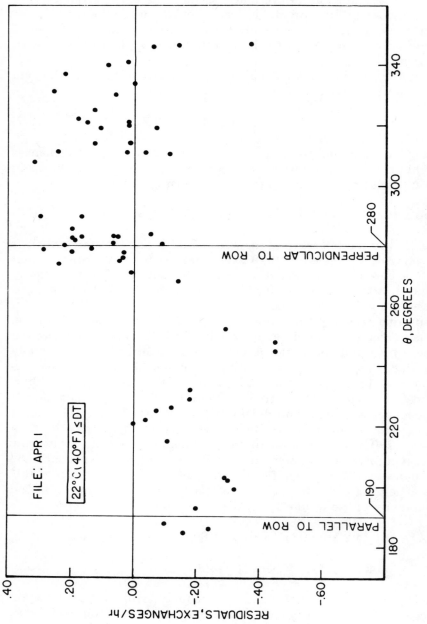

Figure 6–6.   Residuals of a Linear Fit to the Data in Figure 6–5, Plotted Against Wind Direction

equation (6.8), we observe that the coefficient of an angle-independent V term becomes statistically insignificant once an angle-dependent V term is included.

17°C (30°F) $\leq DT \leq$ 22°C (40°F)

As seen in Figure 6−7, there are not as many data points at high wind in this data set compared to the previous data set shown in Figure 6−5. However, the ranges of the variables other than DT are largely overlapping, so that setting parameters independently for this data set forms a check on the previous equations. The present data set contains data for easterly winds (the set of points at the lower left in Figure 6−7) that will be excluded from the analysis. Figure 6−7 shows angle-dependent effects (higher air exchange rates for normally incident wind), for example near eighteen miles per hour (29 kilometers per hour), that are quite similar to those we have observed in Figure 6−5.

When we attempt a one parameter fit to these data, linear in wind velocity, we obtain:

$$AI = (0.032 \pm 0.004)\, V + 0.11 \qquad (6.10)$$

The R^2 is 0.65, and the standard error of estimate is 0.24 exchanges per hour. As the variable G is introduced in the equation, we obtain:

$$AI = (0.026 \pm 0.004)\, V + (0.027 \pm 0.010)\, G + 0.06 \qquad (6.11)$$

The R^2 becomes equal to 0.71, and the standard error of estimate is reduced to 0.19 exchanges per hour. The coefficients in equation (6.11) are essentially the same as those in equation (6.8).

When a term incorporating wind direction is included, $V \cos (\theta - \phi)$, the anomalous preference for $\phi = 300°$ rather than $\phi = 280°$ is again observed. Analogous to equation (6.9), we obtain:

$$AI = (-0.007 \pm 0.004)\, V \pm (0.007 \pm 0.007)\, G$$

$$+ (0.032 \pm 0.004)\, V \mid \cos (\theta - 300°) \mid + 0.44 \qquad (6.12)$$

The R^2 increases to 0.90, and the standard error is reduced to 0.13 exchanges per hour. Again, as in equation (6.9), the angle-independent velocity term has become nearly insignificant.

The term linear in the rate of gas consumption in equations (6.8), (6.9), and (6.11) (but oddly not in equation [6.12]) is more than twice as large as what we found for low wind speeds (see equation

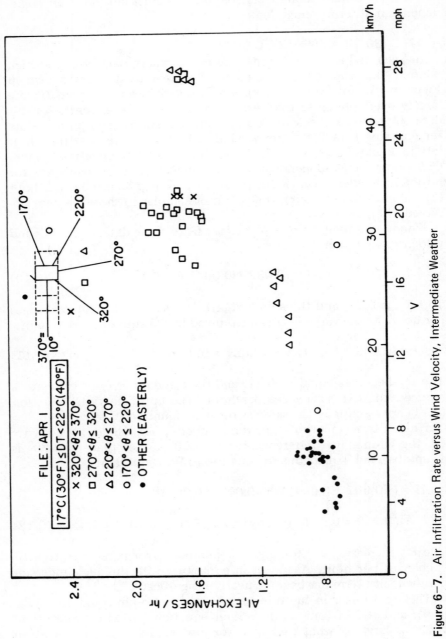

Figure 6—7. Air Infiltration Rate versus Wind Velocity, Intermediate Weather

[6.4]). It is indeed reasonable that the air infiltration associated with a given amount of furnace firing should be larger in windy weather, as wind will increase the entrainment of house air with combustion products on their way out of the flue.

10°C (18°F) $\leq DT \leq$ 17°C (30°F)

This mild weather data set, shown in Figure 6−8, is quite small, but it shows evidence (for example, near 18 mph = 29 km/h) that directional effects of incident wind are less pronounced than in colder weather, an unexpected result that we explore further below. The best fit to this data set analogous to equations (6.9) and (6.12) is:

$$AI = (0.010 \pm 0.003) \, V + (0.030 \pm 0.007) \, G$$

$$+ (0.009 \pm 0.002) \, V \mid \cos (\theta - 280°) \mid + 0.14 \tag{6.13}$$

Here, there are forty-one data points, and the R^2 is 0.95. The standard error of estimate is equal to 0.09 exchanges per hour. The angle-independent wind velocity has become more important relative to the angle-dependent wind velocity. The appearance of the "true" normal to the townhouse, 280°, instead of the value 300° in equations (6.9) and 6.12), emerged from iterating the regression analysis to increase the accuracy of the fit, and it remains unexplained. The constant term in the equation is significantly smaller here.

The Wind-Temperature Interaction

The lack of consistency between equation (6.13) on the one hand and equations (6.9) and (6.12) on the other suggests the existence of a complex interaction between wind and temperature, whose potential existence had been revealed in the theoretical analysis in Chapter 5. To see the nature of this interaction for this particular townhouse, we construct Figure 6−9, in which we replot the data previously shown in Figures 6−5, 6−7, and 6−8, this time against DT, with wind velocity restricted to between ten miles per hour (sixteen kilometers per hour) and twenty miles per hour (thirty-two kilometers per hour) and with easterly winds excluded. We see clearly that the influence of wind direction, θ, on the air infiltration rate is more pronounced the larger the value of the indoor-outdoor temperature difference, DT.

This suggests that we try to model the wind-temperature interaction using some nonlinear terms. When we try a term, $DT \cdot V \cos (\theta - 300°)$, which evidently enhances wind effects in colder

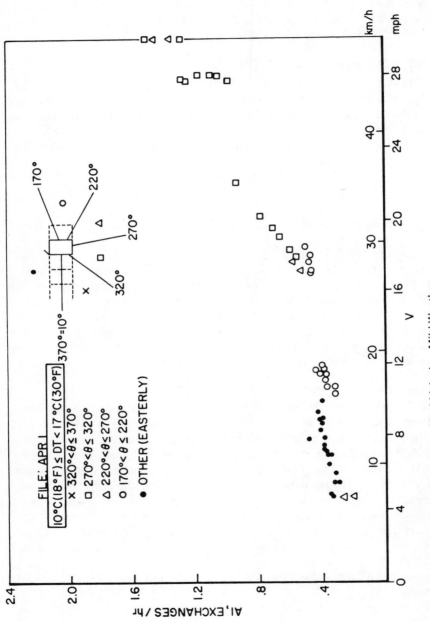

Figure 6—8. Air Infiltration Rate versus Wind Velocity, Mild Weather

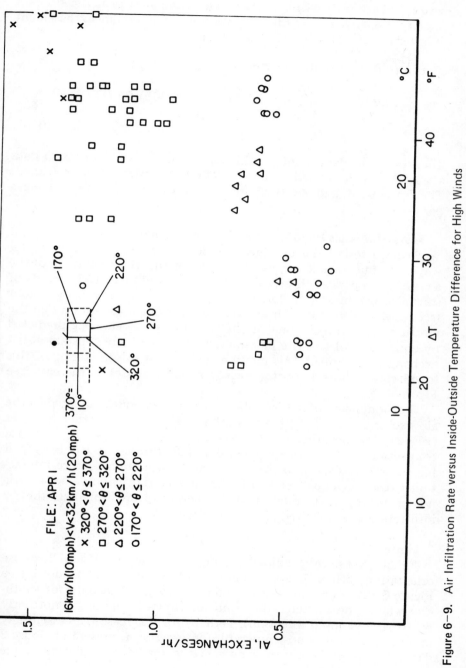

Figure 6—9.   Air Infiltration Rate versus Inside-Outside Temperature Difference for High Winds

weather, we find that this captures all of the statistically significant velocity dependence. With the addition of a nonlinear basement door term and a furnace term, we obtain:

$$AI = (0.0011 \pm 0.0001)DT \cdot V \mid \cos{(\theta - 300°)} \mid$$

$$+ (0.023 \pm 0.003)\,G + (0.00014 \pm 0.00005)\,B \cdot DT$$

$$+ 0.30 \qquad\qquad (6.14)$$

There are 144 data points in this regression—all of the data in data set APR1, with westerly wind direction and with DT unrestricted. The R^2 is 0.93, and the standard error of estimate is 0.12 exchanges per hour.

Tests of Models Beyond Their Original Domain

We have tested the nonlinear model, equation (6.14), in several ways. We find that it comes close to predicting the magnitude of the air infiltration rate observed during periods with easterly winds of six miles per hour (ten kilometers per hour) to ten miles per hour (sixteen kilometers per hour), with the significant exception that the measurements reveal none of the directional dependence predicted by equation (6.14). (The measured rate is essentially constant at 0.4 exchanges per hour.) This may be evidence of the sheltering of this townhouse (House 1) by the nearby rows of houses to the east (see Figure 6−2).

The nonlinear model, equation (6.14), is adequate to predict the air exchange rate for "high" westerly winds in an earlier data set (FEB2). On the other hand, it evidently does not have any smooth connection to the models, equation (6.3) through (6.6), developed for "low" winds. Given that the form of wind-temperature interaction chosen in equation (6.14) vanishes at zero wind velocity, it is not surprising that equation (6.14) seriously underpredicts the air infiltration rate observed at low wind speed.

House 2

Finally, we have examined the high wind data for House 2, whose orientation differs by approximately 90° from that of House 1 (see Figure 6−2). Our data sets contain high wind data only for southerly winds (the sheltered direction for House 2), none for northerly winds (the exposed direction). Perhaps for this reason, an essentially opposite form of wind-temperature interaction is present in House 2 data sets: the influence of wind speed is smaller the higher the value of *DT*. There appears to be a destructive instead of a constructive interaction between pressure difference due to buoyancy (*DT*) and pressure difference due to wind (*V*). As Sinden has shown (see Chapter 5), both kinds of interactions are possible on physical grounds.

A destructive wind-temperature interaction leads to significant energy savings. It is, therefore, well worth pursuing these nonlinear effects in the field and in laboratory experiments, to begin to understand their physical origins. At present, we have only the first glimmerings of ideas about how they might arise.

SUMMARY

The air infiltration rate has been measured in two similar townhouses, using a method based on the detection of a tracer gas (SF_6). The method of measurement yielded reproducible rates of air infiltration within 0.1 air exchanges per hour in any single one-week run, once outside temperature, wind speed, and wind direction were controlled for. At low wind speeds, air infiltration rates were found to increase linearly with decreasing outside temperature, with a slope of approximately 0.008 air exchanges per hour per °F (0.014 exchanges per hour per °C). At high wind speeds, the observed nonlinear wind-temperature interactions had different forms in the two houses. Nonetheless, clear evidence for the effects of wind on air infiltration rate was obtained, including evidence that the effect of wind is enhanced when the wind direction is perpendicular to the house row axis. In linear regression models, coefficients of either wind velocity or the perpendicular component of wind velocity ranged from 0.03 to 0.06 air exchanges per hour per mile per hour of wind velocity (0.02 to 0.04 exchanges per hour per kilometer per hour of wind velocity).

Additional physical effects could be discerned in multiple linear regression analyses, including increased air infiltration rates for fixed outside temperature and wind when (1) furnace on time is increased, (2) front door open time is increased, and (3) basement door open time is increased. The basement door is an interior door, and result (3) calls attention to the significance of separate zones with distinct air infiltration rates within the house.

The equations presented in this article give glimpses of the physical principles at work in determining air exchange rates in a house that so far are poorly understood. Advice cannot now be given to residents concerning which interior doors to keep closed to reduce air infiltration rates, nor concerning when to open windows so that air infiltration rates are not decreased uncomfortably in mild weather with low winds, once houses are tightened for cold weather and high winds. Extensive field experience and laboratory modeling would appear to have high priority to enhance the effectiveness of the world's expanding programs in energy conservation in housing.

REFERENCES

1. Harrje, D.; Hunt C.; Treado, S.; and Malik, N. 1975. Automated instrumentation for building air infiltration measurements. CES Report No. 13. Princeton, N.J. Princeton University. Center for Environmental Studies.
2. Malik, N. 1977. Air infiltration in homes. MSE thesis, Department of Aerospace and Mechanical Sciences, Princeton University.
3. Mattingly, G., and Peters, E. 1977. Wind and trees—air infiltration effects on energy in housing. *Journal of Industrial Aerodynamics* 2:1–19.
4. Socolow, R.H. 1976. Energy utilization in a planned community in the United States. In *Energy Conservation in the Built Environment*, ed. R.G. Courtney, pp. 447–57. Proceedings of the CIB Symposium held at the Building Research Establishment, Garston, Watford, April 1976. Hornby, Lancaster, England: The Construction Press.
5. Hill, J.E., and Kusuda, T. 1975. Dynamical characteristics of air infiltration. *ASHRAE Transactions* 81, pt. 1.

Chapter 7

Instrumentation for Monitoring Energy Usage in Buildings at Twin Rivers*

David T. Harrje
*Center for Environmental Studies
and Department of Aerospace and
Mechanical Sciences
Princeton University*

Richard A. Grot
*Center for Building Technology
National Bureau of Standards*

Abstract

The measurement systems used at Twin Rivers for determining energy usage are described. These include a weather station, three different systems for the measurement of temperatures and energy-related events in a house, automated devices to measure the air infiltration rate, and infrared thermography. Each of these systems played a role in assessing the actual usage of energy in individual buildings, in identifying the factors that determine energy consumption, and in checking the accuracy of theoretical models for predicting the energy performance of dwellings.

INTRODUCTION

Early in the project at Twin Rivers it became evident that there was little actual data on many of the important factors that affect the energy consumption of an occupied dwelling. Though it was well recognized that air infiltration was one of the major sources of heat losses in buildings, very little actual measurement of air infiltration had been made, and the instrumentation to make this measurement in a nonobtrusive manner such that normal dwelling usage could continue during the test did not exist at the beginning of the project.

*The authors wish to acknowledge the contributions of Kenneth Gadsby and Jack Cooper in the development and field evaluation of the instrumentation systems. The calibration and early field studies with the infiltration units were aided by the efforts of Nicholas Malik at Princeton and of Max Hunt at the National Bureau of Standards.

Within a house, there had been few studies of the actions of the occupant, such as opening doors and windows, turning on vent fans, adjusting the thermostat, and operating appliances, that can significantly affect the energy requirements of the dwelling.

The performance of the heating and cooling system is usually given by laboratory tests at steady state conditions, and there has always been some question as to the actual performance of this equipment, especially under partial loads and transient operation. The assessment of energy conservation strategies, such as increasing the amount of insulation in a dwelling, adding storm windows, caulking, or night setback of the temperature, usually assumes an understanding of the heat loss mechanisms in built dwellings, and very little had been done to verify the nature of the losses and their relative importance.

The systems described in this chapter consist of a remote weather station, a 200-channel data acquisition system with sensors for determining the detailed response of three townhouses, an event-activated rapid scan system for determining the real time response of the dwelling and its mechanical system, a 12-channel data system that was deployed in a sample of thirty-one dwellings in order to obtain a more detailed statistical pattern of the important parameters affecting energy consumption, a tracer-gas-based air infiltration measurement system capable of operating unattended for a period of a week, and infrared thermography for locating heat losses in the building envelope in a rapid, noncontact manner. Typical laboratory instrumentation and field checkout instrumentation were also used. It is to be understood that such instruments as hot wire anemometer probes and heat flux probes added directly to our knowledge of the houses and the systems under investigation, and that special oscilloscopes, counters, and checkout circuits were used to insure that the field equipment was operating properly and to diagnose difficulties when they occurred.

DATA SYSTEMS FOR WEATHER AND FOR HIGHLY INSTRUMENTED TOWNHOUSES

Similar data acquisition systems were used to process data from the weather station and from the first three townhouses instrumented in our program. One basic 20 channel data acquisition system was used for the weather station, and another was expanded to 200 channels to accommodate the large number of channels desired in the three (adjacent) townhouses. Data from both systems were sent over telephone lines to our Energy Utilization Laboratory at Princeton

University and were recorded on a magnetic tape recorder and a teletypewriter. The taped data were batch processed by computer, while the teletypewriter output was manually scanned several times a day for quality control. The importance of quick scanning cannot be overemphasized; without it one is certain to lose considerable data from local power interruption or other system malfunction.

The channels monitored in the weather station are listed in Table 7–1, and those monitored in the highly instrumented townhouses (HIT) are listed in Table 7–2. When both data systems were on line, the townhouse data were logged every twenty minutes, the weather station once an hour. When weather data alone were transmitted, a twenty minute interval was chosen to give further detail.

The data acquisition system provides channel sensitivity of either 0.1, 1.0, or 10 millivolts, with a range equal to about 2,000 times the sensitivity. Thus, considerable latitude was possible in choosing individual sensors. Several sensors are shown in Figure 7–1.

In both the weather system and the HIT system, temperatures were measured with linearly compensated thermistors, which were chosen because they give the desired voltage output and are small, accurate, and relatively inexpensive. (Figure 7–1 shows a mounted model.) In both systems, humidity was measured via dual bobbin moisture sensors. This approach to measuring temperature and humidity required a well-regulated voltage source, whose level was also recorded.

Table 7–1. Channels Monitored in the Weather Station.
(data recorded hourly)

Outside humidity—dewpoint
Outside temperature
Wind speed averaged
Wind speed instantaneous
Wind direction
Solar flux—total
Solar flux—shaded
*Solar flux—west
*Solar flux—east
Rainfall
*Ground temperature
Barometric pressure
System voltages

---

*Obtained for limited time periods.

Table 7−2. Sixty-Three Channels Monitored in the Three Highly Instrumented Townhouses.* *(scan every twenty minutes onto magnetic tape in Energy Laboratory at Princeton)*

1	Thermostat setting
2	Basement temperature
3	First floor temperatures—6 total
4a	Second floor temperatures—3 total
4b	Attic temperature
5a	Furnace gas consumption or air conditioner electricity consumption
5b	Furnace fan on time
5c	Duct flow rates—9 total
5d	Supply and return flow rates—4 total
5e	Register temperatures—9 total
5f	Supply and return temperatures—4 total
5g	Supply and return humidity—2 total
6a	Water heater electricity consumption
6b	Electric range electricity consumption
6c	Electric dryer on time
6d	Electric refrigerator on time
7a	Front door open time
7b	Front living room window open time
7c	Front bedroom window open time
8a	Back door open time
8b	Back bedroom #1 window open time
8c	Back bedroom #2 window open time
8d	Basement door open time
8e	Bathroom vent fans on time—3 total
9a	Total electricity consumption from lighting and 110 volt appliances
9b	Voltage level, townhouse and system—4 total
10	Hot and cold water temperatures

*Numbering system conforms to Table 7–3 and indicates roughly how we have "collapsed" channels in the Omnibus houses.

Other approaches to measurement were closely parallel in the HIT system and the weather system. Both the average rate of air flow in ducts and the average wind velocity were measured using digital counters and digital-to-analog converters. The rotations of a cup anemometer were added over the counting interval, as were the rotations of a spinning disk mounted in the duct that chopped a light beam in an optical switch. This addition resulted in a proportional build-up of voltage on a counter card, with recycling each time the level reached ten volts. Similarly, both instantaneous flow rates in ducts and instantaneous wind velocity were measured by reading the anemometer output as a pulse rate on three-to-a-card tachometers. The instantaneous wind velocity (useful for detection of gusting) was obtained by having a three-cup anemometer drive a direct current generator. The methods of recording thermostat setting and wind direction were also closely related. An internal linear potentiometer was built into a standard home thermostat (see Figure 7−1), so that output voltage

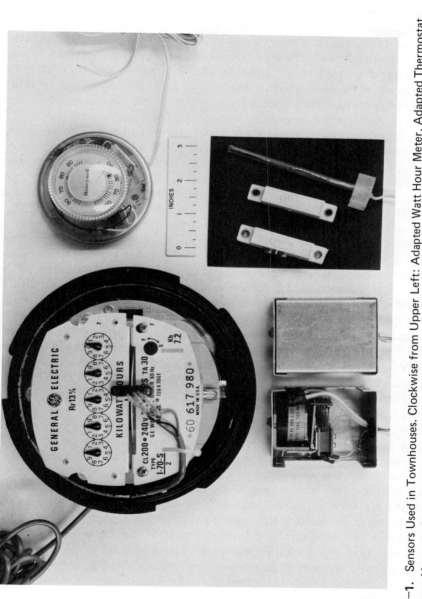

Figure 7–1. Sensors Used in Townhouses. Clockwise from Upper Left: Adapted Watt Hour Meter, Adapted Thermostat, Thermistor, Magnetic Switches, Dual Water Heater Relays.

was linearly related to temperature setting. The wind direction, similarly, determined a potentiometer setting through the rotation of a weathervane.

The remaining weather sensors were (1) a rain gauge of the tipping bucket type, which sent a record of each tip to the counter card (the same approach was also used to measure air conditioner condensate); (2) solar flux meters for both total and shaded solar flux (either a temperature-compensated solarimeter or a pyranometer) whose millivolt output was stored over time on a digital volt time integrator; and (3) a transducer for measuring barometric pressure.

A large number of sensors for the highly instrumented townhouses measured the duration of specific events. To measure the "on time" of appliances such as refrigerators and clothes dryers, switches were inserted at the power supply that were activated at a set level of current. (For example, the current demanded by the compressor was monitored at the refrigerator.) The switch energized a small synchronous motor within the instrument package, which turned a potentiometer at a constant rate so that voltage increased linearly with on time. The potential difference from one reading to the next provided an accurate measure of appliance energy consumption in the interval for those appliances whose energy use is dominated by a mode of operation that draws power at a constant level. This simple and inexpensive technique was trouble-free when care was taken to assure good contact at the wiper of the potentiometer. To measure the "open time" of windows and doors, standard burglar alarm switches were used to energize motors similar to those used for the constant power output appliances (see Figure 7-1).

To measure the energy consumption of appliances, like the range, that operate at variable power output, standard watt hour meters were used, modified so that a switch was tripped as the Airy disk spun inside the meter. Optical switching was found to be preferable to mechanical switching, the latter becoming unreliable after many contact closures (see Figure 7-1). Counting and digital-to-analog conversion were accomplished by methods similar to those used to record air flow rates. A bank of five standard watt hour meters in each house permitted the monitoring of four appliances plus the total electric consumption for the house. A similar modification of the standard gas meter provided the measurement of gas consumption by the furnace. Here a small arm was attached to the 0.5 cu. ft. dial of the gas meter such that the rotation of the dial opened and closed a microswitch.

Further details of these systems are found in early reports from our program [1, 2].

DATA SYSTEM FOR FAST READOUT IN HIGHLY INSTRUMENTED TOWNHOUSES (RAPIDSCAN)

A second data acquisition system ("Rapidscan") was installed in one of the three highly instrumented townhouses (and, subsequently, in ten other townhouses), which had two additional capabilities not present in the system described in the previous section. First, it was much faster, capable of sampling twenty data points per second; its 100 channel capacity was matched to the sixty-three sensors in the highly instrumented townhouse (see Table 7−2) and could therefore acquire a complete townhouse profile in about five seconds.

Second, the signal-conditioning package allowed data collection in both an event-activated mode and at a definite interval. Up to sixteen distinct events were able to activate a readout from all of the townhouse sensors; events used at Twin Rivers included changes in front door position (open or closed), changes in refrigerator operation (compressor on or off), and changes in furnace operation (main gas valve open or closed). The event was identified through dedication of two, eight bit channels and binary encoding. A record of the day, hour, minute, and second was also stored. The interval for standard data acquisition was adjustable from five seconds to one hour, but it was normally set at one minute. Output was recorded on seven track magnetic tape in the townhouse.

A fast readout system has been particularly useful in understanding the furnace operation, which is characterized by a firing cycle ranging from ten minutes on and ten minutes off in cold weather to three minutes on and forty minutes off in mild weather. The cycles of duct temperatures and room air temperatures are remarkably stable over time, until one either changes the mode of furnace operation (for example, from intermittent to continuous fan), or adds insulation to the ducts, or otherwise retrofits the house (see Chapter 1, Figures 1−18a and 1−18b).

DATA SYSTEM FOR LIGHTLY INSTRUMENTED (OMNIBUS) TOWNHOUSES

A less sophisticated data acquisition system was required, when it was decided to monitor a larger number of townhouses before and after retrofitting. The "Omnibus" instrumentation packages shown in Figure 7−2 were developed to meet this need, based on a few sensors

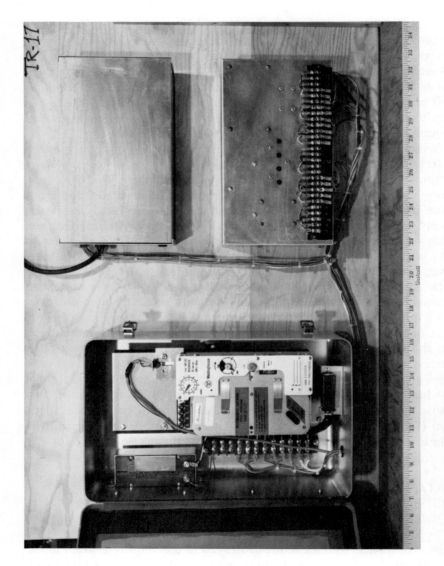

Figure 7–2. Omnibus Instrumentation Package

similar to those deployed in the highly instrumented townhouses discussed above, but recording output as pulses on a slowly moving magnetic tape. The recorder was the four channel Westinghouse WR−4C demand meter widely used by utilities, one channel of which is used to mark fifteen minute intervals. The data-processing facilities of Public Service Electric and Gas Company were used to count the pulses on the three data channels contained in every fifteen minute interval, with output (number of counts) recorded on magnetic tape.

Confronted with the requirement of twelve pieces of data per hour, we multiplexed the three data channels so that four different sensors could be read every hour. The channels monitored, listed in Table 7−3 and located spatially in Figure 7−3, reflected a variety of considerations and compromises; one temperature measurement per floor was judged sufficient, based on readings in the highly instrumented townhouses. Duct temperatures, duct flow rates, and appliance usage rates were abandoned as of secondary importance—except for the water heater, whose direct and indirect role in total energy use stands out dramatically. Total "open time" of doors and thermostat setting were retained in recognition of their interest to those studying resident behavior.

Outputs of the sensors that are shown in Figure 7−1 were transformed into pulses through resistance-controlled oscillators contained in integrated circuit chips. Temperatures from basement to attic were measured using uncompensated thermistors whose resistance varies with temperature. Door "open times" were recorded

Table 7−3. Channels Monitored in the Lightly Instrumented ("Omnibus") Townhouses.

1.	Thermostat setting
2.	Basement temperature
3.	First floor temperature
4.	Second floor temperature
5.	Furnace on time or air conditioner on time
6.	Electric water heater on time
[a]7.	Front door or front window open time
[a]8.	Back door or back window open time
[b]9.	Total electricity consumption

Channels 1−8 are recorded hourly, and Channel 9 is recorded at fifteen-minute intervals.

[a]The measurements of Channels 7 and 8 were combined to Channel 7, and the free Channel 8 was assigned to attic temperature just prior to the 1976 winter.

[b] As the study progressed, the need for additional attic temperatures and/or flow measurements became evident in certain homes. By multiplexing these sensors, four measurements then replaced the total electric consumption channel.

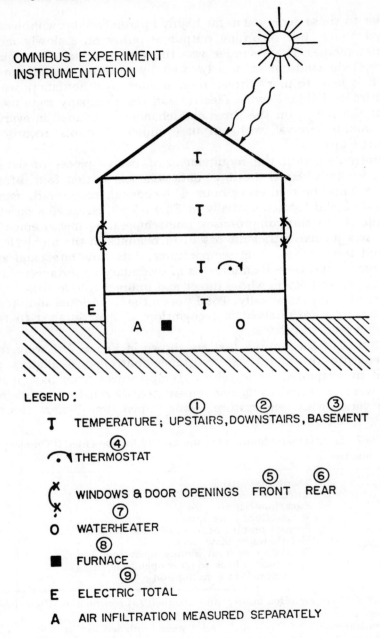

OMNIBUS EXPERIMENT
INSTRUMENTATION

LEGEND :

T   TEMPERATURE ; UPSTAIRS, DOWNSTAIRS, BASEMENT
         ①   ②   ③

⌒   THERMOSTAT
         ④

x
⌒   WINDOWS & DOOR OPENINGS FRONT   REAR
x   ⑤   ⑥
         ⑦

O   WATERHEATER
         ⑧

■   FURNACE
         ⑨

E   ELECTRIC TOTAL

A   AIR INFILTRATION MEASURED SEPARATELY

Figure 7−3. Location of Omnibus Instrumentation

using the motor-potentiometer arrangement described previously. The energy consumption of furnace, water heater, and air conditioner was also recorded as an "on time," thus departing from the approach of using modified utility meters adopted in the highly instrumented townhouses and described above. The measurement of "on time" of the electric water heater was based on a relay (shown in Figure 7-1) that closed when power was consumed; for the gas water heater, a thermal switch that activated with heating was placed in the flue; for the gas furnace and electric air conditioner, the switch responded to a signal from the control transformer. The temperature setting on the thermostat was monitored using the built-in potentiometer described above.

Further details of the Omnibus data acquisition system are found in an earlier report by Hall and Harrje [2].

MEASUREMENT OF AIR INFILTRATION

An automated unit for the measurement of the air infiltration rate in houses has been brought through successive stages of development. The device is based on standard methods of leak detection. A tracer gas (sulfur hexafluoride, SF_6) is injected into the house and its concentration is sampled periodically. The detection method is based on the electron absorption properties of SF_6, and a gas chromatographic column is located upstream from the electron absorption measurement to separate SF_6 from oxygen, which is also an electron absorber. The output, therefore, is two temporally separated sharp dips (negative spikes) in current across the absorber; the dip due to oxygen saturates the system but the device is calibrated so that the falling SF_6 concentration shows up as dips of steadily decreasing magnitude over time. Between samplings, the device is continuously flushed with argon.

Initial concentrations of SF_6 of about thirty parts per billion are achieved through the injection of roughly 10cc of SF_6 into a central duct of the forced air distribution system of the house. The concentration within the house becomes uniform after not more than fifteen minutes. Average house concentrations are measured by sampling from the return duct of the forced air system, with the fan kept in the mode of continuous operation throughout the experiment. Typical air exchange rates, λ, for a house range from 0.5 to 1.0 exchange per hour, where λ is defined by $dC/dt = -\lambda C$, C being the concentration at time t. A house exchanging air at $\lambda = 1.0$ exchange per hour, therefore, loses 95 percent of its SF_6 in three hours (0.95 = $1 - e^{-3}$). Reinjection of SF_6 every three hours has been a standard mode of operation.

The Mark II device [3] is shown in Figure $7-4$. A mechanically activated timer accomplishes sampling every fifteen minutes and injection every three hours. Output current is recorded on a roll of paper on a chart recorder. The Mark III device, in operation since 1975, has solid state timing, permitting both the injection interval and the sampling interval to be varied [4]. The output of the Mark III device is digitized and recorded on a magnetic tape cassette. The

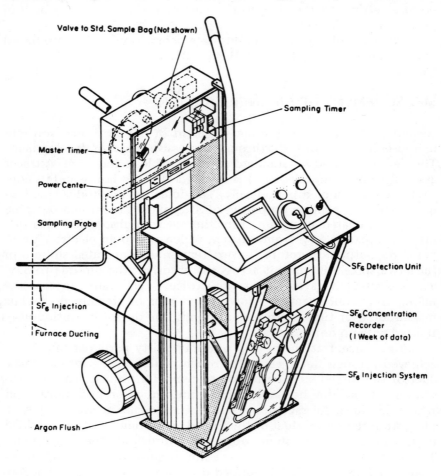

Figure 7–4. Automated Air Infiltration Unit—Mark II

digital data are also displayed, permitting immediate data reduction in the field.

Both the Mark II and the Mark III devices normally operate for an entire week without attention. At the end of the week, the SF_6 and the argon are replenished and the cassette or chart paper is replaced. At such low SF_6 concentrations, accidental discharge of an entire week's supply of SF_6 presents no health hazard.

INFRARED THERMOGRAPHY

An infrared thermographic system owned by the National Bureau of Standards (see Chapter 1, Figures 1–5A, 1–9A) has been used frequently both inside and outside the houses at Twin Rivers. The thermographic system has a twenty-five degree angle lens and both a black and white and a ten color monitor. When surfaces of uniform infrared emissivity are examined, the monitor gives immediate qualitative evidence of structural defects through its vivid display of cold and hot surfaces. Used in conjunction with contact probes of surface temperature, infrared thermography is on its way to becoming a quantitative tool as well.

Among the defects identified by infrared thermography have been missing or poorly installed insulation and problems at corners, around windows and doors, around closets, and at the points between framing and masonry. Infrared thermography has also given useful information about heat losses from ducts in walls and from vents and flue, and about the degree of penetration of outside air into the space between the sheetrock side walls of the living area and the masonry fire wall between adjacent units. Some photographs in black and white are found in Chapter 1, Figures 1–5B, 1–9B, 1–9C. Color photographs that document the changes associated with retrofit in several townhouses are found in a report by Grot, Harrje, and Johnston [5].

REFERENCES

1. Fox, J.; Fraker, H., Jr.; Grot, R.; Harrje, D.; Schorske, E.; and Socolow, R.H. 1973. Energy conservation in housing: first annual progress report (1973). CES Report No. 6. Princeton, N.J.: Princeton University.
2. Hall, S., and Harrje, D. 1975. Instrumentation for the Omnibus experiment. CES Report No. 21. Princeton, N.J.: Princeton University.
3. Harrje, D.; Hunt, C.; Treado, S.; and Malik, N. 1975. Automated instrumentation for building air infiltration measurements. CES Report No. 13. Princeton, N.J.: Princeton University.

4. Harrje, D., and Grot, R. 1977. Automated air infiltration measurements and implications for energy conservation. In *Proceedings of the International Conference on Energy Use Management* (Tucson, Arizona; October 1977), eds. R.A. Fazzolare and C.B. Smith, I. 457–64. New York: Pergamon.
5. Grot, R.; Harrje, D.; and Johnston, L. 1976. Application of thermography for evaluating effectiveness of retrofit measures. In *Third Biennial Infrared Information Exchange*. St. Louis, Mo.: AGA Corporation.

Chapter 8

Modeling Residential Demand for Natural Gas as a Function of the Coldness of the Month*

Lawrence S. Mayer
Yoav Benjamini
Center for Environmental Studies
Department of Statistics
Princeton University

Abstract

A simple two parameter model of the monthly demand for natural gas for space heating is developed. First a simple indicator of the coldness of the month labeled "modified degree days" is presented. Both aggregate monthly demand and monthly demand for a single unit are modeled as a function of this indicator. The model has two parameters: a reference temperature that reflects the internal temperature and free heat contribution, and a slope parameter that reflects the thermal behavior of the dwelling. Variation in these two parameters is related to characteristics of the dwelling. Finally, the effect of the onset of the energy crisis on the two parameters is assessed.

INTRODUCTION

Simple statistical analysis can be a useful tool for developing, testing, and monitoring policy programs designed to reduce the residential demand for energy. Such analysis may also be useful for monitoring the effects of changing demographic patterns or the effects of an acute temporary energy shortage on residential demand. The most simple statistical experiment would consist of measuring total energy demand at the monthly level on a sample of residential units before and after the implementation of a conservation program. The before

*The authors gratefully acknowledge the aid of Martin Pensak and Thomas Schrader in the development of our ideas; and the aid of Gautam Dutt, Frank Sinden, and Robert Socolow in the preparation of this chapter.

and after demands would be compared in order to see whether the program had been effective in reducing demand. Unfortunately, the analysis is complicated by the fact that the fuel required for space conditioning is a major portion of the residential demand for energy and the temperature distribution over the month is a major determinant of this portion of the demand. Since the weather is not under the statistician's control, some attempt must be made to adjust the monthly demand for the coldness or warmness of the month prior to making a before-after comparison. Because the anticipated effects of many of the suggested conservation programs are small, albeit important, it is crucial that the adjustment of demand for weather be as accurate as possible. Otherwise the error introduced by a faulty adjustment may distort the assessment of the effects of the program.

Among the mechanisms that are possible candidates for affecting residential demand are (1) increases in the price of various fuels and the associated reliance on the market to induce the "rational" consumer to use less energy; (2) changes in building codes designed to make new housing more energy-efficient; (3) tax incentives for the homeowner to retrofit the structure of the dwelling; (4) laws that would force, in the legal sense, the homeowner to use less energy; (5) laws that would supply residential consumers with more information regarding their level of consumption, on the theory that knowledgeable consumers already have enough incentive to conserve energy; (6) changes in social institutions, such as school programs that try to develop a strong conservation ethic in American youth; and (7) more incentives for both academic and private commercial research programs to develop and produce new building materials, more efficient appliances, and more efficient housing designs. Most of these mechanisms will initially affect demand by only a few percent. To detect such effects statistically, it is necessary to have valid, reliable models of weather effects; otherwise, the policy effect is lost in the weather noise.

Two problems arise in trying to adjust for the effects of the coldness or warmness of the month: first, an indicator of the coldness or warmness of the month must be chosen, and second, the relationship between this measure and demand must be modeled. Subsidiary considerations stemming from these problems are the focus of this chapter. We concentrate on the problem of measuring the coldness of the month and of developing a model of the monthly demand for natural gas.

The most widely used indicator of the coldness of a month, a measure labeled "degree days," will be reviewed in the next section. The indicator we develop is presented as an alternative to the conventional degree days measure.

Our analysis leads to a simple measure of the coldness of the month that we label "modified degree days" and a simple two parameter model that accurately predicts both the aggregate demand for natural gas and the demand for a single dwelling as a function of the number of modified degree days in the month.

We test these ideas by considering the demand for natural gas in a sample of 401 almost identical owner-occupied townhouses located in Twin Rivers, New Jersey. The units considered are two, three, and four bedroom units located within a subset of the general planned community, the subset known as "Quad II." In this quad, natural gas is used almost exclusively for space heating, and a few homeowners have also installed gas lawn lights. The units are of masonry bearing wall construction with wood ceilings and floors and are typical of contemporary two floor townhouse design found in the northeastern United States.

The major conclusions of our analysis are:

1. The modified degree day is a simple measure of the coldness of a month that has a stronger theoretical foundation than does the conventional degree day measure. The former is obtained by considering a model that is a simple first order approximation of the response of a residential space heating system to outside temperature.

2. For our sample, the modified degree day is an excellent predictor of both aggregate monthly demand for natural gas and monthly demand for natural gas for a single unit. It is, in fact, a better predictor of demand than the conventional degree day.

3. The reference temperature parameter and the slope parameter contained in the two parameter demand model have simple physical interpretations. The reference temperature is a crude reflection of the temperature at which the furnace "comes on," and the slope parameter is a rough indicator of the additional amount of natural gas added to hourly demand by a decrease of one degree in the outside temperature.

4. The two parameters are significantly related to design characteristics of the dwelling, including whether the unit is an interior or end unit, the number of bedrooms or size of the unit, the orientation of the unit, and the presence of optional double glass windows and double glass patio door.

5. The two parameters themselves are almost uncorrelated.

6. The onset of the energy crisis and the consequent reduction in the demand for natural gas is reflected in changes in the two parameters. Surprisingly, the crisis appears to have affected the slope more than the reference temperature.

As a consequence of the last finding, we suggest that models of the type developed may be excellent tools for assessing the effects of various policies on residential energy demand.

In the next section we review conventional degree days, develop modified degree days, and then compare the two. In the third section we model natural gas consumption (both monthly aggregate demand and monthly demand for a single unit) as a simple linear function of modified degree days. In the fourth section we consider the variation in the parameters of the simple demand model. In the final section we use the model to assess the form of the residential consumer's response to the onset of the energy crisis as indicated by the Arab oil embargo of 1973.

A PARAMETER-DEPENDENT MEASURE OF THE COLDNESS OF A MONTH

Before developing the "modified degree days," we review the original "degree days" measure—a measure that is found throughout the energy policy, engineering, and energy-forecasting literature. It is a simple and convenient measure that is used by utilities to assess the coldness of a heating season; it is even reported by some newspapers and television weatherpersons as a cumulative indicator of the coldness of a heating season. Remarks such as "this has been an extremely cold winter in that we have accumulated 150 more degree days than normal" are becoming a common part of our "weather chat."

Conventional degree days in the United States are computed as follows. Consider a particular month and let $\overline{T}_j$ be the maximum temperature for the jth day in the month, and $\underline{T}_j$ be the minimum temperature for the jth day in the month; then the degree day component for the jth day is

$$D_j = \max \left\{ 65°F - 1/2 \, (\overline{T}_j + \underline{T}_j), 0 \right\} \tag{8.1}$$

where the value 65°F is referred to as the reference temperature.*

---

*In the United States, Fahrenheit degree days are always reported. Practices in other countries are exact analogs, although choice of the reference temperature varies from country to country.

The number of degree days or, simply, degree days for the month is obtained by summing the degree day components over the days in the month. Formally, $DD = \sum_j D_j$, where the sum is over the days in the month. The statistic $T = 1/2\,(\overline{T}_j + \underline{T}_j)$ is called the midrange of the daily temperature, and thus equation (8.1) indicates that any day with a midrange over 65°F contributes nothing to the coldness of the day or the month as indicated by the degree day measure.

The number of conventional degree days is a reasonable measure of the coldness of a month in the sense that the demand for energy for residential space heating is approximately linear in degree days for the cold winter months. The approximation is particularly good when a large aggregate of dwellings is considered. Our experience has indicated that the correlation between demand for natural gas for space heating and degree days is often as high as 0.94 for an aggregate of fifty similar dwellings.

We feel that in spite of this high correlation, the conventional degree day has several deficiencies as an indicator of the coldness of the weather for monitoring conservation efforts. First, although a good predictor of aggregate demand, it can easily be improved upon as a predictor of the demand for individual dwellings. Second, although the conventional degree day is a statistic computed from data, it does not have a firm statistical foundation in the sense that it is not derived from a statistical analysis of the space heating process. Third, although the conventional degree day is a good predictor of aggregate demand for energy for space heating for the cold winter months, it is not as good a predictor of such demand for the marginal months. This statement is not surprising, since the degree day component of a day with midrange of 65°F or higher is zero regardless of how low the minimum temperature for the day is. Fourth, although the degree day measure works well for conventional houses whose reference temperatures are around 65°F, it does not work well for low loss houses, whose reference temperatures are much lower.

At the cost of introducing a free parameter into the indicator of the coldness of a month, we developed a measure that suffers none of the above deficiencies.

In order to develop an alternative measure of the coldness of a month that leads to a simple model of the demand for natural gas for our sample, we considered a simple idealized model of hourly behavior of the response of the space heating system of a Twin Rivers unit to outside temperature and then integrated that behavior over hours to approximate the monthly response of the system to parameters that summarize the distribution of temperatures for the month.

This integration leads to a measure that includes two parameters, both of which are interpretable in terms of the hourly behavior of the system.

A reasonable first order model of the response of the Twin Rivers space heating system to outside temperatures is defined by the following conditions:

1. Furnace consumption per hour is proportional to the positive part of the difference between a reference temperature (R) and the outside temperature (T).
2. The outside temperature (T) is almost constant over the hour.
3. Natural gas is used solely at the furnace.

The reference temperature is assumed to be a function of the interior temperature, the solar heat gain by the house, and the presence of other heat sources in the house such as appliances and people.

Assuming the units in our study approximately satisfy these conditions, we obtain an indicator of the coldness of the month by aggregating the hourly behavior of the space heating system described in the model. In order to do so we define the following terms:

C_{ij} = The amount of energy consumed by the furnace during the ith hour of the jth day.

T_{ij} = The outside temperature during the ith hour of the jth day (a constant due to condition 3).

Then under assumptions 1, 2, and 3:

$$C_{ij} = \rho \max \left\{ R - T_{ij}, 0 \right\} \qquad (8.2)$$

Summing over the hours of the day gives the fuel consumption for day j:

$$C_j = \rho \sum_i \max \left\{ R - T_{ij}, 0 \right\} . \qquad (8.3)$$

We will call the sum on the right (to which consumption is proportional) the modified degree day component for day j:

$$MD_j (R) = \sum_i \max \left\{ R - T_{ij}, 0 \right\} . \qquad (8.4)$$

Summing this over some set of days such as a month or year gives modified degree days for that period;

$$MDD\,(R) = \sum_j MD_j\,(R)\,. \tag{8.5}$$

Fuel consumption (C) for the period is proportional to modified degree days:

$$C = \rho\,MDD\,(R)\,. \tag{8.6}$$

Note that we leave the reference temperature (R) unspecified. Thus *MDD* for a given period is not a single number but is a function of R. This allows us to fit different values of R to different houses.

The above derivation assumes that hourly temperature data T_{ij} are available. This may, however, not be the case. Very frequently, only daily maximum and minimum temperatures are recorded. The following paragraphs show how $MDD\,(R)$ may be estimated using such data. To a rough approximation, the temperature at Twin Rivers varies in such a way that approximately the same amount of time is spent each day at all temperatures between the minimum and the maximum temperature. We state this formally as a fourth condition of our model.

4. Each day's temperature profile is equivalent to a sequence of hourly temperatures that rise or fall linearly between the day's minimum and the day's maximum temperature.

Hourly data from Twin Rivers have been used to test this condition, as follows:

Let $S_{ij} = (T_{ij} - \underline{T}_j)\,/\,(\overline{T}_j - \underline{T}_j)$ be the standardized temperature for the ith hour of the jth day. Then under condition 4, the distribution of S_{ij} over the hours in the day is uniform. In Figure 8–1 we display a distribution of the standardized temperature for fifty-five winter days. Figure 8–1 is nearly flat, indicating that the linear model of hourly temperature is a reasonable approximation.

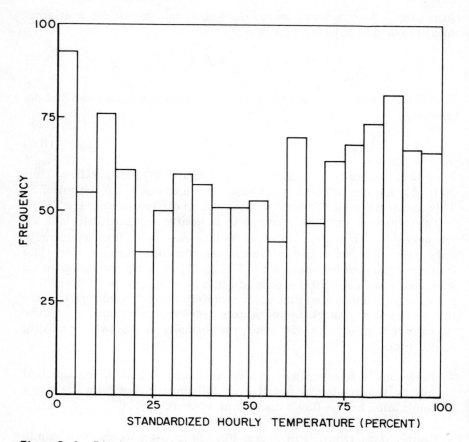

Figure 8–1. Distribution of Standardized Hourly Temperatures (Measured as Percent of "Distance" from Daily Minimum to Daily Maximum), for Fifty-five Winter Days.

If the distribution of temperature is uniform over the day, then the proportion of the day colder than the reference temperature can be expressed as

$$
P_j = \begin{cases} 0 & \text{if } R < \underline{T}_j \\ (R - \underline{T}_j) / (\bar{T}_j - \underline{T}_j) & \text{if } \underline{T}_j \leqslant R \leqslant \bar{T}_j \\ 1 & \text{if } \bar{T}_j < R \end{cases} \tag{8.7}
$$

and the mean temperature deficit over the proportion of the day colder than the reference temperature can be expressed as

$$\left[\int_{\underline{T}_j}^{R} (R - \theta) / (\overline{T}_j - \underline{T}_j) \ d\theta \right] P_j^{-1} \tag{8.8}$$

This yields the following form for the modified degree day component of the jth day;

$$MD_j = \begin{cases} 0 & \text{if } R < \underline{T}_j \\ (R - \underline{T}_j)^2 \ / \ 2 \ (\overline{T}_j - \underline{T}_j) & \text{if } \underline{T}_j < R < \overline{T}_j \\ R - (\underline{T}_j + \overline{T}_j) \ / \ 2 & \text{if } \overline{T}_j \leqslant R \end{cases} \tag{8.9}$$

The number of modified degree days for the month, then, is:

$$MDD = \Sigma \ (R - T_j)^2 \ / 2 \ (\overline{T}_j - \underline{T}_j) + \Sigma \left[R - (\underline{T}_j + \overline{T}_j)/2 \right] \tag{8.10}$$

where the first summand is over the days that satisfy $\underline{T}_j < R < \overline{T}_j$ and the second summand is over the days that satisfy $\overline{T}_j < R$.

To summarize, modified degree days differ from conventional degree days in two ways. First, the 65°F reference temperature in conventional degree days is replaced by a reference temperature parameter R that is fitted to the data; and second, the distribution of temperatures over a typical day is taken into consideration in modified degree days but not in conventional degree days. Our data exploration shows that the addition of a variable reference parameter is decidedly the more important difference between the modified and conventional measures.

Note that the modified degree component for the jth day, if the jth day satisfies both $\overline{T}_j < R$ and $\overline{T}_j < 65°F$ is the same as the conventional degree component except for an added constant. Also note that if conditions 1 through 4 are adopted, then the computation of modified degree days, like the computation of degree days, requires only the daily minimum and maximum temperatures as input. We feel this is a distinct advantage over more elaborate measures that would require hourly data.

We complete this section by comparing the two measures. The number of conventional degree days and the number of modified degree days for each of the months in our study are displayed in Figure 8–2. The modified degree days are computed with $R = 62.3°F$ (16.8°C), a value that we justify in the next section. Note

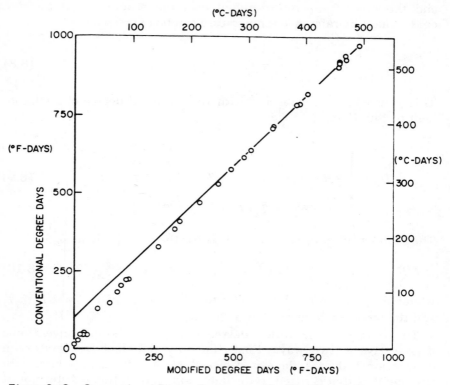

Figure 8—2.   Conventional Degree Days versus Modified Degree Days

that if every day in a month has a maximum temperature of less than 62.3°F (16.8°C), then the number of modified (Fahrenheit) degree days for the month is equal to the number of conventional (Fahrenheit) degree days minus 2.7 times the number of days in the month.

MODELING THE DEMAND FOR NATURAL GAS

Aggregate Demand

To compare the use of conventional degree days and modified degree days as predictors of aggregate monthly demand for natural gas, we used a sample of 401 Quad II townhouses and consumption statistics obtained from the local utility for the period from May 1971 to April 1974. Since gas is used almost solely for space heating in these townhouses, data for July and August of each year were dropped from the analysis.

We consider the models $(C - k) = \beta(MDD)$ and $(C - k) = \beta DD$, where C is the aggregate demand for natural gas for the month and k is a small constant that allows for the natural gas, approximately 600 cubic feet (650 MJ) per month, used by the furnace pilot light.

For the first model, the slope parameter and the reference temperature parameter that is contained in modified degree days are fitted to the data by an iterative least squares procedure. Note that the model is highly nonlinear in the reference temperature. The values obtained for the slope and reference temperature are 18.8 cubic feet per $^\circ$F day (424 W/$^\circ$C) and 62.3°F (16.8°C), respectively. It is interesting to note that this value of R, combined with the assumption that the average interior temperature is 70°F (21°C), indicates that the average free heat contribution to the house is about 8°F (4°C), a value that agrees fairly well both with our theoretical calculations and with our other empirical studies of the house. For the second model, the slope parameter is fitted by least squares, yielding a value of 17.0 cubic feet per $^\circ$F day (383 W/$^\circ$C).

In order to compare the forecasts generated by the two models, we considered a typical cold thirty-one day winter month that has 900 conventional degree days, no days with $\overline{T}_j > 62.3^\circ$F, and therefore, 816.3 modified degree days. The modified degree day model predicts $(18.8 \times 816.3) + 600 = 15{,}950$ cubic feet (17.24 GJ) for average demand, and the conventional degree day model predicts $(17.0 \times 900) + 600 = 15{,}900$ cubic feet (17.19 GJ) for average demand. Thus the models yield very similar predictions for such cold months.

In Figures 8−3 and 8−4 we display the relationship between the two indicators of the coldness of the month and the aggregate demand for natural gas. (The 600 cubic feet [650 MJ] attributable to the pilot light can be seen in the data for mild months.) Note that in Figure 8−4 the display is a function of the fitting, since the number of modified degree days cannot be computed until the parameter R is estimated.

As suggested, for the cold months (around 900°F days or 500°C days), the two measures are equally good predictors of energy demand. However, the modified degree day is a better predictor of demand in the mild months. To see this, the mild weather corners of Figures 8−3 and 8−4 are enlarged in Figures 8−5 and 8−6. For the very mild months—less than 50°F days or 30°C days—the modified degree day is clearly a better predictor of demand than is the conventional degree day.

Suppose that the space conditioning units and temperature distribution in a community conformed to our idealized model and

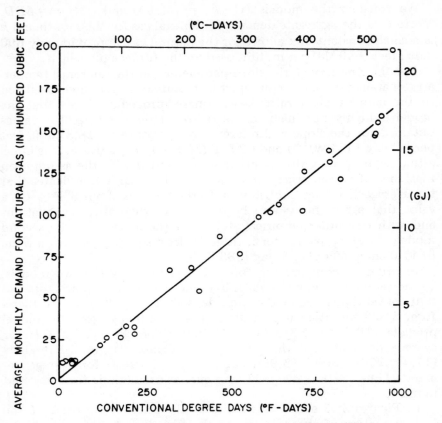

Figure 8–3. Aggregate Demand for Natural Gas versus Conventional Degree Days

thus that aggregate monthly demand was linearly related to modified degree days. Furthermore, suppose that degree days and simple regression are used, perhaps by the local utility, to forecast aggregate demand. It is interesting to ask whether the forecasts using conventional degree days would be systematically biased with regard to actual demand. In Figure 8–7 we display the relationship between the forecasted demand at Twin Rivers using conventional degree days and the actual demand assuming our model.

As expected, the model using conventional degree days systematically overestimates demand in the mild months. For example, if the actual average demand were 1,574 cubic feet (1.70GJ), the conventional degree day model predicts 2,691 cubic feet (2.91GJ)—an error

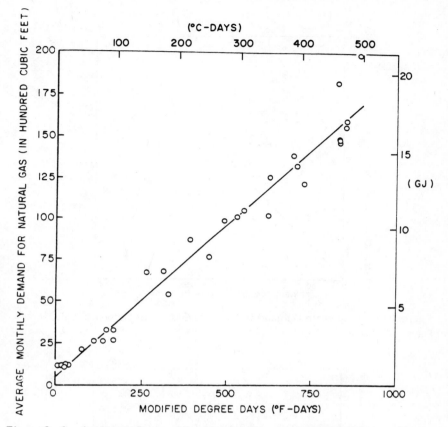

Figure 8–4. Aggregate Demand for Natural Gas versus Modified Degree Days

of over 70 percent. Although the demand in the mild months is small, it is by no means unimportant. It may be that this demand is the most responsive to public policy or the market, since in some sense, people are less dependent on space heating in these months. Furthermore, a second bias appears: assuming our model holds, there is a tendency for a model based on conventional degree days to underestimate the demand in the very cold months. This result is slightly surprising because for the very cold months, the number of degree days and the number of modified degree days have a simple additive relationship; however, it is the best linear relationship between degree days and demand that is used to forecast demand. The regression line is biased upward for the mild months and thus, by the nonlinearity between degree days and modified degree days, is biased downward for the very cold months.

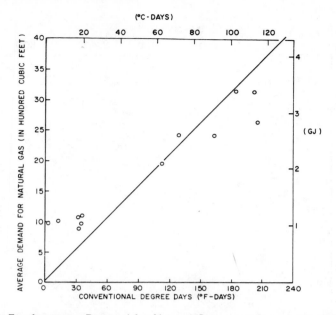

Figure 8–5. Aggregate Demand for Natural Gas versus Conventional Degree Days—Mild Months

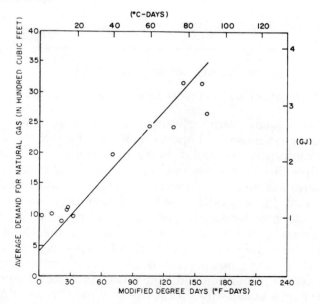

Figure 8–6. Aggregate Demand for Natural Gas versus Modified Degree Days— Mild Months

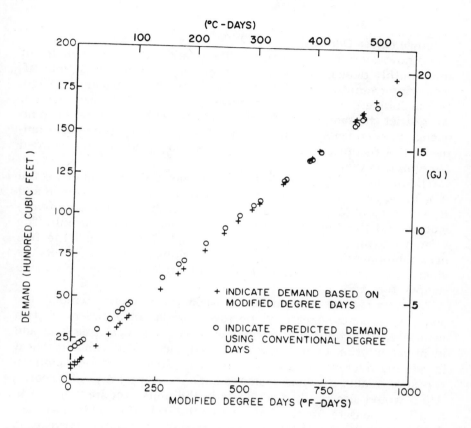

Figure 8–7. Aggregate Demand for Natural Gas Predicted from Models Based on Conventional and Modified Degree Days

For a month with 1300°F days (720°C days)—January 1977 was such a month—our model yields average monthly demand of 23,100 cubic feet (25.0GJ), while the conventional degree day model forecast is 22,000 cubic feet (23.8GJ), an error of 5 percent.

Of course, overestimates become underestimates, and vice versa, whenever the reference temperature embedded in the model of modified degree days is found to have a value higher than the conventional reference temperature.

Single House Demand

We now consider the use of modified degree days as a predictor of the monthly demand for single housing units. We use data from fifteen winter months, running from November 1973 to January 1976, and including the months from November to April for each season. We restrict the sample to fifty-two units for which there has been no change in occupants over the period of observation, which have complete data records, and which displayed no obviously misrecorded consumption values.*

The model $C = \beta(MDD) + k$ is fit for each unit by minimizing the sum of squares residual as a function of the two parameters, β and R, with $k = 650\,MJ$ or 600 cubic feet per month. The reference temperature and the slope parameter are associated with each unit. The reference temperature reflects the thermostat setting and the free heat component of the heat balance. The slope parameter reflects the change in demand for natural gas as a function of changes in outside temperature.**

We consider the relationship between the reference temperature and the slope parameter. A positive correlation between the two would result if houses of varying size with identical free heat and identical interior temperatures were sampled. (The same free heat lowers the reference temperature further below the interior temperature in a smaller dwelling than in a larger dwelling.) A positive correlation would also result if residents in the units that are "hardest to heat" compensate for the leakiness or the lack of insulation of their dwelling by raising the thermostat setting. A negative correlation would result if the "leakier" dwellings in our sample were colder or if the larger houses in our sample were more than proportionately effective in retaining free heat.

The cross-plot of the two parameters is displayed in Figure 8–8. The observed correlation between the two parameters is − 0.19.

---

*A parallel analysis has been performed by Schrader [1], based on the gas consumption in the same population of Quad II townhouses during the twelve winter months from November 1971 through April 1973. Qualitative conclusions of the two studies are in excellent agreement.

**Schrader [1] presents an extensive discussion of the theoretical underpinnings of the two parameter model (see also Chapter 2).

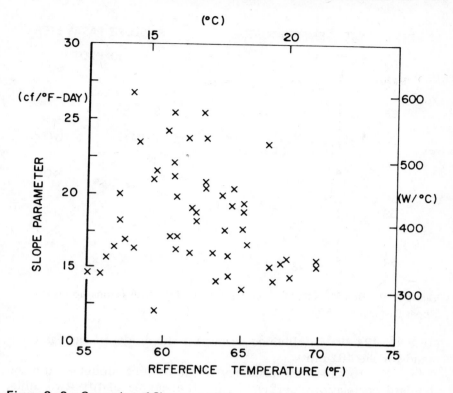

Figure 8–8. Cross-plot of Slopes and Reference Temperatures from Fits to Monthly Consumption of Natural Gas for Individual Townhouses.

In Figure 8–9 we display the quartiles, extremes, and box plots of the reference temperatures and the slope parameters.* Both parameters are distributed very symmetrically. The mean reference temperature is 62.1°F (16.7°C) with a standard deviation of 3.7°F (2.1°C); the mean slope parameter is 18.0 cubic feet per °F day (405 W/°C) with a standard deviation of 3.54 cubic feet per °F day (20 W/°C). The median reference temperature is 62.0°F (16.7°C), and the median slope parameter is 17.5 cubic feet per °F day (395 W/°C). Note that the means and medians over houses are close to the values

---

*A box plot displays (1) the median of a distribution (by an asterisk); (2) the first and third quartiles (by pluses); (3) the highest value less than 1.5 midranges above the median and the lowest value less than 1.5 midranges below the median (by crosses); (4) outliers between 1.5 and 2.0 midranges of the median, if any (by circles); and (5) outliers beyond 2.0 midranges of the median, if any (by asterisks). The middle two quartiles, whose extent is the midrange, are enclosed in a box. See Tukey [2] for further details of box plots.

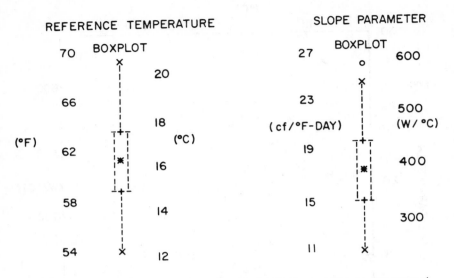

Figure 8—9. Box Plots and Histograms for the Reference Temperatures and Slopes Displayed in Figure 8—8

(16.8°C, 424 W/°C) obtained earlier for the model of aggregate demand for the 401 units.

In order to assess the accuracy of fit for our model we use the standard correlation coefficient. For the sample of fifty-two units, the median correlation between demand for a single unit and modified degree days is 0.97. The correlation became a test for bad data: three units that yielded low correlations were examined and found to have misrecorded demand statistics. When these values were replaced by the correct statistics, the correlations became well within the observed range.

VARIATION IN THE PARAMETERS OF THE DEMAND MODEL

In the preceding section we showed that the monthly demand for natural gas for a single unit could be accurately modeled using a simple two parameter model. One of the parameters, the reference temperature, primarily reflects short-term decisions on the part of the occupants. It is heavily a function of the thermostat setting, and this setting is controlled by the people inside the dwelling. Conversely, the other parameter—the slope—primarily reflects the physical properties of the dwelling, such as the rate of conduction of heat through the shell and the rate of air infiltration through cracks and leaks in the walls.

We must note that it is not strictly true to think of the reference temperature as a behavioral variable and the slope as a physical parameter. The free heat component of the heat balance is a physical factor that has a direct effect on the reference temperature. Conversely, long-term behavioral decisions such as the purchase of storm windows affect the slope parameter as well as the reference temperature.

Although the townhouses under investigation are almost identical, they differ with respect to design variables such as number of bedrooms, number of neighbors, presence of double glass windows, and compass orientation of the unit. In this section we use simple descriptive methods to assess whether these design variables have an effect on the two parameters of the demand model.

In Figure 8-10 we display the comparison box plots for end units and interior units for the two parameters. Being an end unit appears to have a large effect on the slope parameter but a negligible effect on the reference temperature. The end units have additional exposed wall and have been shown to be higher consumers on the average than the interior units [3]. Figure 8-10 gives some indication that the disparity between the demand for gas in end and interior units is likely to be due to the presence of an extra exposed wall, which

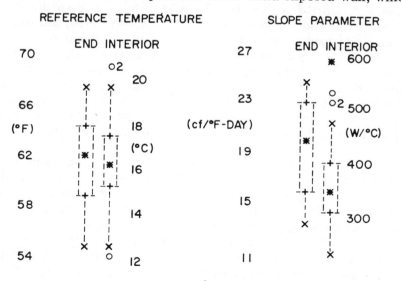

Figure 8-10. Box Plots of Reference Temperature and Slope for the Subsamples of End and Interior Units

primarily affects the slope. To the extent that the reference temperature reflects the thermostat setting, there is no evidence that the occupants of end units set their thermostats at a different level than do occupants of interior units.

In Figure 8—11 we compare those units that were equipped with double glass windows at time of purchase with those units that were equipped with standard single pane windows. The comparison box plot indicates that the units with insulated windows have a lower median and larger spread with respect to the slope parameter than do the other units. The lower median is as expected, but we have no explanation for the larger spread. The presence of double glass windows appears to have no effect on the reference temperature. Thus, there is no support for the theory that people who opt for double glass will also set their thermostats the lowest (a hypothesis that might have been expected to be confirmed since rooms with double glass windows are believed to be comfortable at lower indoor air temperatures than rooms with single glass windows).

In Figure 8—11 we also compare those units that have a double glass patio door with those units that do not. The patio door is at the rear of the house and is forty-five square feet (4.2 square meters) in area. The presence of the insulated door affects the slope parameter as expected and, as with the windows, appears to have no effect on the reference temperature.

In Figure 8—12 we display the relationship between the number of bedrooms and the two parameters. The two, three, and four bedroom units have roughly 1,200, 1,500, and 1,600 square feet (110, 140, and 150 square meters) of living area, respectively. The relationship between the number of bedrooms and the parameters is as expected. First, the larger the unit, the higher the slope parameter. Second, occupants of two bedroom units include couples without children, who probably tend to have lower average interior temperatures (in part, because they leave the house unoccupied more frequently).

The relationship between the orientation of the house and the two parameters is displayed in Figures 8—13 and 8—14. In Figure 8—13 we indicate the orientation of each unit in a plot of the slope parameter against the reference temperature. Note that the units facing north and south appear to tend to lie in the region of the plot characterized by low slope parameter and high reference temperature.

In Figure 8—14 we directly compare the different orientations with respect to the two parameters. When compared to the units facing east and west, the units facing north and south tend to have both smaller slope parameters and higher reference temperatures. This

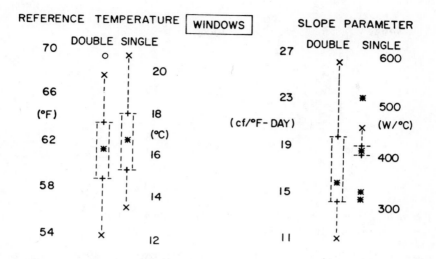

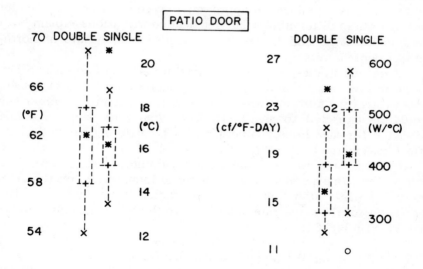

Figure 8–11. Box Plots of Reference Temperature and Slope for the Subsamples with Double Pane and Single Pane Windows and for the Subsamples with Double Pane and Single Pane Patio Doors.

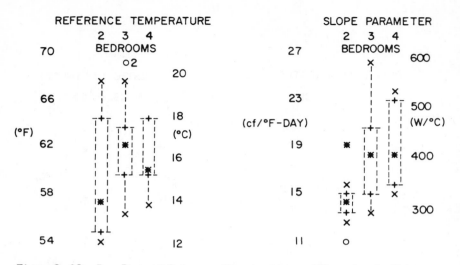

Figure 8—12. Box Plots of Reference Temperature and Slope for the Subsamples with Two, Three, or Four Bedrooms

result is probably a solar effect: The north-south-oriented units have a larger solar heat gain than do the east-west-oriented units in the colder months, but have an approximately equal gain in the milder months. These differential solar free heat contributions explain both the smaller slope and the higher reference temperature of north-south-oriented units.

In previous studies, we have observed no effect of compass orientation in raw data on monthly winter gas consumption over houses. A compass orientation effect from the sun's path in the winter sky would be expected to give a stronger signal when slopes are first extracted for each house, as here, and it is satisfying to see that the effect has emerged.

As a final step we used the standard dummy variable model to regress the slope parameter and reference temperature on the characteristics of the unit that might be expected to be significant. The regression for the slope parameter leads to the following equation for the slope (in W/$^\circ$C):

$$\beta = 262 + 36 \text{ (end)} + 59 \text{ (single pane patio door)}$$
$$\quad (63) \quad (20) \qquad\quad (20)$$

$$+ 79 \text{ (3 bedroom)} + 120 \text{ (4 bedroom)} + 50 \text{ (west)} + 61 \text{ (east)}.$$
$$\quad (20) \qquad\qquad (20) \qquad\qquad (25) \qquad\quad (23)$$

(8.11)

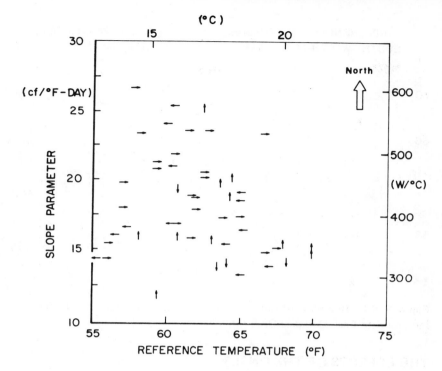

Figure 8–13. Cross-plot of Reference Temperatures and Slopes, Indicating Compass Orientation of Each Townhouse

The constant, 262 W/°C, is the slope for an interior, two bedroom, north- or south-facing unit with double pane patio door. The independent variables on the right hand side are (0, 1) dummy variables. Standard errors are given in parentheses below the coefficients.

The above equation explains 50 percent of the variation in the slope parameter. Thus, the simple design features account for a large proportion of the variation in the response of the unit to a change in the outside temperature. The regression of the reference temperature on the same design features explains less than 20 percent of the variation in the reference temperature. As expected, design features have more effect on the slope parameter than on the reference temperature.

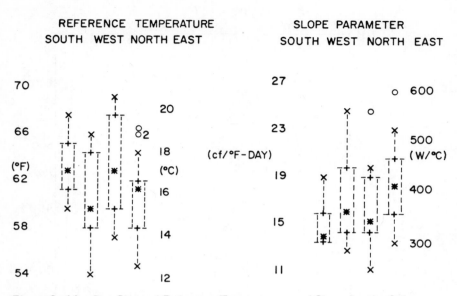

Figure 8-14. Box Plots of Reference Temperature and Slope for the Sub-samples with Each Compass Orientation

THE EFFECTS OF THE ONSET
OF THE ENERGY CRISIS ON
THE TWO PARAMETERS

In other reports, we have shown that the demand for natural gas at Twin Rivers was significantly reduced by the onset of the energy crisis as indicated by the Arab oil embargo [3]. In this section we ask whether the simple two parameter demand model can be used to assess the shape of the effect of the onset of the crisis on demand.

Since we are suggesting the two parameter model as a tool for monitoring the effects of policy interventions or other factors on residential demand, it is crucial that we demonstrate that the effect of the onset of the crisis was reflected in the two parameters of the model, since this onset was a factor known to affect demand significantly.

Our prior conjecture was that the short-term effect of the onset of the crisis would appear as a significant change in the reference temperature, but that there would be no change in the slope parameter. We argued that people who responded quickly to the crisis did so by lowering their thermostat settings and that thus the short-term response should be reflected in the reference temperature.

The models fitted in the last section use data that were recorded after the onset of the crisis, which occurred in October 1973. The models are refitted using twelve months of winter data from the two winters prior to the embargo. The parameter values obtained are summarized in Figure 8–15.

The median reference temperature for the preembargo years is 60.5°F (15.8°C) and for the latter years it is 62.5°F (16.9°C), while the median slope parameter for the preembargo years is 19.6 cf/°F day (442 W/°C) and for the latter years it is 16.6 cf/°F day (375 W/°C). Thus, we find the curious result that the onset of the crisis is reflected in the model but appears to have affected the reference temperature less than the slope parameter.

At first glance, this finding seems to support the position that the residents responded to the embargo by modifying the structure and not by reducing the setting on their thermostat. Our experience at Twin Rivers, however, makes us suspect this position. Instead, we conjecture that the residents may have responded to the embargo differentially in various months. If the residents responded to the onset of the crisis by lowering their thermostat setting more in the colder months than in the milder months, then this effect might be reflected in the slope parameter. More investigation is needed.

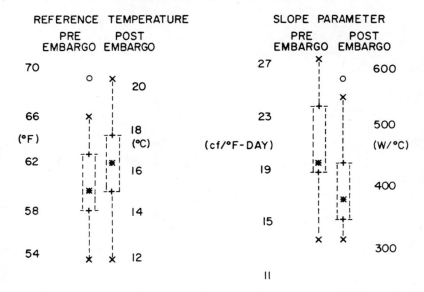

Figure 8–15. Box Plots of Reference Temperature and Slope Derived from the Data After the Arab Embargo (the Data Previously Considered) Compared with Box Plots of Reference Temperature and Slope Derived from Data on Monthly Gas Consumption Before the Arab Embargo in the same Townhouses.

We conclude by remarking that we feel that modified degree days and the related parameter model are concepts worthy of the attention of the energy analyst. We hope they prove to be a powerful tool for analyzing the effect of policy intervention on residential demand.

REFERENCES

1. Schrader, T.F. 1978. A two-parameter model for assessing the determinants of residential space heating. MSE Thesis, Department of Aerospace and Mechanical Sciences, Princeton University.
2. Tukey, J. 1977. *Exploratory Data Analysis*. Reading: Addison-Wesley.
3. Mayer, Lawrence S. 1977. Estimating the effects of the onset of the energy crisis on residential energy demand. *Energy and Resources*, 1 (in press).

Chapter 9

Movers and Stayers: The Resident's Contribution to Variation Across Houses in Energy Consumption for Space Heating*

Robert C. Sonderegger
Energy and Environment Division
Lawrence Berkeley Laboratory

Abstract

A general method is proposed that identifies the contribution of resident-dependent effects to the observed variability of energy consumption in similar houses. The method presumes that in addition to records of energy consumption over time, one has access to information about the date of change of occupants. For Twin Rivers data, the role of resident-dependent effects is seen to dominate the role of effects that depend on structural variations over which the resident has no effective control.

INTRODUCTION

One of the questions central to the Twin Rivers program is why there is so much variation in energy consumption across identical houses. The highest users of energy typically use at least twice as much energy as the lowest users, whether one looks at winter gas consumption (nearly entirely space heating) or summer electric consumption (about one-half air conditioning).

Looking at energy consumption data alone, one cannot distinguish between two alternative hypotheses concerning the observed varia-

*This article is based on a chapter of the Ph.D. thesis, "Dynamic Models of House Heating based on Equivalent Thermal Parameters," submitted to the Aerospace and Mechanical Sciences Department of Princeton University, September 1977. The author wishes to thank Jan Beyea and Robert Socolow for general guidance, and Peter Bloomfield and Lawrence Mayer for spirited discussion of an earlier version of this analysis.

tion in energy consumption: (1) variation is due to occupant behavior, and (2) variation is due to differences in nominally identical structures over which the occupant has no control. In the first category one would place interior temperature setting, opening of windows, deployment of drapes, and level of use of appliances. In the second category one would place missing panels of insulation, cracks in the structure, and defects in appliances.

Should one of the two hypotheses be strongly verified and the other strongly rejected, the significance for public policy is clear. If occupant behavior is dominant, one concentrates attention on the residents, clarifying by research and subsequent publicity the kinds of actions that have energy penalties and savings and their magnitudes. If nominally identical units are structurally far from identical, however, one concentrates one's attention on quality control at the time of construction (on energy performance standards) and on periodic on-site inspections of building performance.

Our data tend to confirm the first hypothesis at Twin Rivers—the resident rather than the structure creates most of the observed variation in consumption. There is little reason to believe that this result generalizes to other communities, however—at least not without considerable further testing. What we put forward here is a method to distinguish between the contribution of resident and of structure—a method that can be applied whenever one has, in addition to data on energy consumption, data about where and when there has been a change of occupant (typically a sale or change of tenant, often coded directly in utility records).

The general strategy is to examine the changes in energy consumption of a sample of houses for which a change in ownership occurs. Such houses play a role similar to identical twins in heredity-environment studies. In practice, this means choosing two winters between which the occupants of a sizable number of houses have changed. If the energy use of this sample, the "movers," correlate well from one winter to another, one would have evidence pointing to the likely role of construction quality in creating variability in energy consumption. However, if the movers' consumption in the first winter does not correlate at all with consumption in the second winter, all variation in energy use would be attributed to the differences among occupants.

Also analyzed in the same way is another sample of houses without change in ownership, the "stayers," a control group of sorts. Correlations performed on this sample show that time-dependent effects play a noticeable role in the variation in energy consumption between houses, and we have tried to model these effects.

It is useful to elaborate on the fundamental idea behind this analysis of movers and stayers, before the description of the actual data manipulation. Consider the energy consumption of nominally identical houses (same floor plans) in two winters with perfectly identical weather conditions. If the energy-related behavior of the occupants in each house were unchanged from one winter to the other (but not identical to one another), we would expect each stayer house to use the exact same amount of heating energy in both winters. The only differences in consumption would occur among houses, not between the two winters.

In the case of the movers, the occupants of each house have changed from one winter to the other, and energy-related behavior is likely to be different. If, nonetheless, each mover house used the same amount of heating in both winters, like the stayers, we would conclude that occupant behavior is not a relevant factor influencing energy consumption. Any variation in energy use among houses would have to be attributed to hidden structural differences between the nominally identical units. If, in turn, high users in the first winter became randomly low, middle, or high users in the winter following the move, with no apparent correlation, we would attribute the cause to the change in occupants and deduce that differences in occupant behavior, not hidden structural differences, are responsible for the observed variation in energy use among nominally identical houses.

The actual data, as can be expected, is more complex than either of these extreme cases. The weather conditions in the two winters under consideration are not identical, and neither are the houses. To complicate matters further, the 1973 oil embargo occurred between the two winters. Even when the data are corrected for these effects, the movers' consumption patterns do not fit precisely either of the two extreme scenarios sketched above. They do, however, resemble more closely the scenario of random change in consumption levels after a move, rather than that of constant consumption levels. This leads to the conclusion of this chapter that variation in occupant behavior is the chief cause for the observed variation in gas consumption among houses. An interesting deviation from the ideal case described earlier is displayed by the stayers: their individual consumption levels do not remain exactly constant; in other words, some "crossover" between houses occurs, indicating that consumption patterns change in time even if both house and occupant remain the same.

The quantitative derivation and subsequent discussion of the above effects and the methods to correct for unequal weather in the two winters and for houses of more than one type are the topics treated in this chapter. The energy consumption data of movers and stayers were previously studied by Lawrence Mayer and Jeffrey Robinson, following the suggestion of Robert Socolow. Mayer and Robinson showed that a significant difference exists between movers and stayers, when comparing the change in individual consumption from one winter to another, in a nonparametric statistical investigation [1]. In this chapter, a parametric approach will be formulated and quantitative results will be derived that assign the causes of the variation in energy consumption between "identical" houses.

DESCRIPTION OF THE DATA

Meter readings of gas and electricity consumption from public utility records have been collected over a period of several years for most houses in the four quads of Twin Rivers. For this analysis, the 248 townhouses located in Quad II have been selected. They are arranged in blocks of up to ten units facing each of the four compass directions. As only the furnace runs on natural gas in these houses, the monthly gas consumption readings* directly indicate the energy used for space heating. The distribution of gas consumption in the six-month winter season (November–April) of 1971–1972 is shown in Figure 9–1 for a sample of 205 townhouses selected for this study.

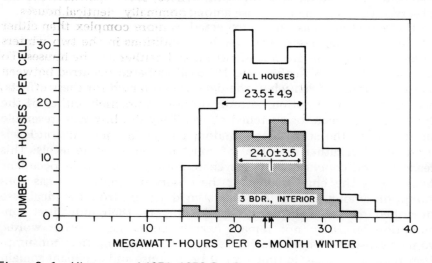

Figure 9–1.   Histogram of 1971–1972 Gas Consumption

*The original readings are in units of hundreds of cubic feet of natural gas, corresponding to 102,500 Btus or 30.04 kWhs or 108.2MJs. The unit chosen in this article is MWhs (1MWh = 3.6GJ).

The rates of consumption of highest and lowest users are more than a factor three apart. The standard deviation is 22 percent of the mean. A sizeable portion of this variation can be ascribed to the different physical features of the house. Aside from the number of bedrooms, by physical features we intend such "obvious" design differences as double pane versus single pane windows and an extra end wall (for end units). Among all physical features tested, these have been shown to be the only statistically significant factors [1].

The first two rows of Table 9–1 display the main statistics of the gas consumption of the full sample of 205 houses and of three subsamples of two, three, or four bedroom interior units with all-insulated glass. The means of the distributions decrease with diminishing number of bedrooms and decrease in the second winter, compared to the first, a consequence of 12 percent conservation and 5 percent milder weather [1]. Conservation and dependence on weather, though interesting topics by themselves, are not the subject of this paper. To eliminate the effect of these factors, the gas consumption in the second winter is adjusted "across the board" by multiplying all 1973–1974 data by the ratio of the means of both winters, 1.182; the results are shown in the bottom row of Table 9–1, in the units implicit to the rest of this chapter—"constant 1971–1972 MWh per six-month winter."

Implied in this correction is the assumption that the variation in gas consumption is proportional to the level of consumption—in other words, that the standard deviation is proportional to the mean. The same assumption will be used in a subsequent section, when correcting for variations caused by differing house features. The proportionality of individual gas consumption to degree days tends to support this assumption: as the weather gets colder, the variation in consumption caused by hidden structural differences among houses (manifest in their individual proportionality constants) increases proportionately. At the same time, larger houses (with larger proportionality constants) have more window frames and wall surfaces to cause variation in consumption than smaller houses. Variations among the occupants (e.g., differences in the thermostat setting or in the frequency of window openings) cause similar variations in gas consumption, though one can argue that they are less than proportional to the level of consumption. The data presented in Table 9–1 lend enough support to the assumption of proportionality of standard deviation to level of consumption to justify its adoption throughout this chapter: the coefficients of variation (standard deviation divided by the mean), though not constant, show no obvious correlation with the

Table 9–1. Gas Consumption Statistics in Two Winters of the Full Sample and of Subsamples with Two, Three, and Four Bedroom Interior Units with Insulated Glass (MWh per six-month winter)

| | | Full Sample (N = 205) | X Bedroom, Interior, Insulated Glass | | |
			X = 2 (N = 32)	X = 3 (N = 45)	X = 4 (N = 16)
1971–1972	Mean	23.46	17.69	23.77	25.49
	Standard Deviation	4.89	2.44	3.84	3.99
	Coefficient of Variation	0.209	0.138	0.161	0.156
1973–1974	Mean	19.85	14.00	20.31	22.56
	Standard Deviation	4.60	2.13	3.29	2.74
	Coefficient of Variation	0.232	0.152	0.162	0.122
1973–1974 adjusted*	Mean	23.46	16.55	24.01	26.67
	Standard Deviation	5.44	2.52	3.89	3.25
	Coefficient of Variation	0.232	0.152	0.162	0.122

*1973–1974 values multiplied by the ratio of the means 23.46/19.85 = 1.182

corresponding means. As one would expect, the coefficients of variation of the full sample, which includes houses of all sizes, are larger than those of the three more narrowly defined subsamples. The standard deviation of the full sample shrinks somewhat less than proportionately to the mean from one winter to the other, a disturbing but not dramatic deviation from our hypothesis.

The assumption of invariance of the coefficient of variation makes the following analyses easier and is more plausible on theoretical grounds than, say, assuming that the standard deviation is an invariant. However, it is not essential to the conclusions of this chapter; the following analyses would have similar results if the data were treated in a fashion consistent with the assumption of a standard deviation invariant with consumption.

THE VARIATION IN ENERGY CONSUMPTION CAUSED BY DESIGN FEATURES OF THE HOUSES

In this section we will eliminate the "obvious" variation due to design features, such as number of bedrooms, by using regression techniques. We have also carried out parallel studies of a more nearly identical set of houses composed of three bedroom, interior units. There are very few movers (twenty-one) among these houses, and the results, therefore, have reduced statistical significance, but they are consistent with what we obtain when including all types of houses.

The relative importance of design features can be assessed from the data through ordinary least squares regressions of the gas consumption of the 205 houses. Regressions performed for the two winters yielded the following estimates of the coefficients:

1971–1972: $GC = 25.14 - 5.98 BR2 + 3.03 BR4 + 3.26 END - 0.95 INS$ (9.1a)
$\qquad R^2 = .523 \quad (.56) \qquad (.75) \qquad (.59) \qquad (.35)$

1973–1974: $GC = 25.88 - 7.06 BR2 + 4.28 BR4 + 2.90 END - 1.39 INS$ (9.1b)
$\qquad R^2 = .565 \quad (.60) \qquad (.79) \qquad (.62) \qquad (.37)$

where GC is the gas consumption in MWhs per six-month winter;

$BR2$ and $BR4$ are variables taking the value of 1 if the unit has two or four bedrooms, respectively, and 0 if otherwise;

END takes the value of 1 for end units, 0 for interior units;

> INS is the area of double glass in houses where such an option was exercised, in tens of square meters (mean $(INS) = 1.21$).
>
> The numbers in parentheses indicate the standard errors of the estimated coefficients.

These regressions essentially repeat the analyses done by Mayer and Robinson [1] and, before them, by Fox [2]. Of main interest to us is that about 54 percent of the total variance* in the gas use of the 205 houses can be attributed to "obvious" design features, represented by the variables $BR2$, $BR4$, END, and INS. The main purpose of this chapter is to find the sources of the remaining 46 percent.

As discussed more fully in the Appendix to this chapter, in selecting the sample of 205 houses from the full set of 248 townhouses, all units for which data were missing in either of the two winters were excluded. Moreover, all houses with a change in ownership in either winter were eliminated, including those with a move in October or May (houses with a move during these extra two months "bracketing" the six-month heating seasons were excluded in order to avoid any interim effects caused by an imminent or a recent move).

Figure 9–2 displays the frequency of moves from the beginning of the first winter to the end of the second. Out of the 205 units, 52 houses were found to have different owners in the two winters 1971–1972 and 1973–1974). Choosing the winters two years apart, rather than one, was necessary to obtain a reasonable size of this subsample.

NORMALIZING THE GAS CONSUMPTION

The next step is to eliminate the variation caused by the "obvious" physical features from the 205 houses. To this purpose, the gas consumption of each house is normalized by the amount it "should" have used, given its physical features, according to the regression equations (9.1a) or (9.1b):

$$GN_i = \frac{G_i}{GC_i} \times 100 \tag{9.2}$$

---

*The variance is estimated by the square of the standard deviation. The figure of 54 percent is an average of the two R^2 values in equations (9.1a) and (9.1b).

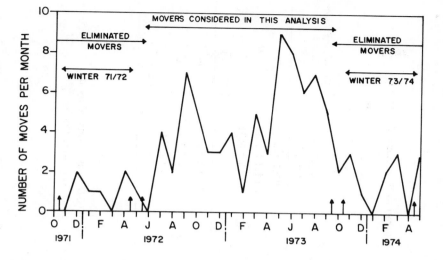

Figure 9−2. Plot of Moves Occurring During a Thirty-two Month Period

where G_i is the measured gas consumption per six-month winter of the ith house:

  GC_i is the gas consumption of the ith house estimated by the regression equations (9.1a) or (9.1b);

  GN_i is the normalized gas consumption (100 = "right on target").

An alternate and more familiar way to eliminate the variation explained by "obvious" physical features would have been to take the residuals, $G_i - GC_i$, as a measure of relatively high or low consumption. Normalized gas consumptions, GN_i, were preferred on the grounds that the residuals are observed to increase with increasing gas consumption levels, G_i. It is easier for a large house to be 2 MWhs "off target" than a small house, while it is roughly equally likely for both to be 10 percent "off target."

Table 9−2 displays the relevant statistics in both winters for both movers and stayers. The first and third columns refer to the normalized consumption, GN_i, of all houses; the second and fourth columns refer to the raw consumption, G_i, of a subsample of three bedroom interior units. If we have been successful in making all houses "identical" by normalizing their gas consumption, their distribution should be the same as for physically identical houses. Specifically, we are interested in comparing the widths of the distributions. Because

Table 9–2.   Normalized Gas Consumption Statistics for Stayers and Movers Compared to Raw Gas Consumption of Three Bedroom Interior Units

		Stayers		Movers[a]	
		Full Sample (N = 153)	Three Bedroom Interior (N = 57)	Full Sample (N = 52)	Three Bedroom Interior (N = 21)
1971–1972	Mean	100.8 ± 1.1[b]	24.5[c]	97.7 ± 2.0[b]	22.7[c]
	Standard Deviation	14.1 ± 0.8[d]	3.6	14.2 ± 1.39	3.0
	Coefficient of Variation	0.140 ± 0.008	0.149	0.145 ± 0.015	0.132
	F value	1.13		1.21	
1973–1974	Mean	100.3 ± 1.2	20.6	99.2 ± 2.29	19.7
	Standard Deviation	15.0 ± 0.9	3.0	16.5 ± 1.62	3.2
	Coefficient of Variation	0.150 ± 0.009	0.143	0.167 ± 0.017	0.164
	F value	1.10		1.04	

[a] A change in ownership occurred in these houses between the two winters.

[b] Units: dimensionless; 100 = estimate by equations (9.1a) or (9.1b).

[c] Units: MWhs per six month winter.

[d] All distributions here assumed to be Gaussian. Thus, the error of the standard deviation (SD) was estimated by $\sigma_{SD} = SD/\sqrt{2N}$, the error of the mean (M) by $\sigma_M = SD/\sqrt{N}$. The error (σ_c) of the coefficient of variation was estimated by $\sigma_c = \sigma_{SD}/M$.

of the different units (dimensionless and MWhs per six-month winter), the coefficients of variation (COV) should be compared. The F values for movers and stayers in both winters are obtained by dividing the square of the larger COV by the square of the smaller COV. None of the F values are significant at a 2×5 percent (two-sided) level of confidence, which is equivalent to saying that the distributions are likely to represent the same variable.

THE EVIDENCE FOR DISCRIMINATING BETWEEN MOVERS AND STAYERS

As we have just seen, the distributions of gas consumption for both movers and stayers, in both winters, are statistically equivalent. The difference between movers and stayers becomes apparent only when we ask how well the consumption level of each individual house is reproduced from one winter to another. A suitable measure of this reproducibility is the "relative consumption":

$$RC_{ii} = \frac{GN_i(t_3)}{GN_i(t_1)} \qquad (9.3)$$

where RC_{ii} is the relative consumption of the ith house;

      t_1 and t_3 indicate the winters 1971–1972 and 1973–1974, respectively.

A value of $RC_{ii} = 1$ means that the ith house has used the same amount of gas in the second winter as it used in the first, after allowing for what a house of its size uses "on average."

    Anticipating later usefulness, the statistics have been calculated for the natural logarithm of relative consumption $LRC_{ii} = ln\,(RC_{ii})$ and are shown in Table 9–3. Since the relative consumption varies relatively little around its mean equal to unity we have $ln\,(RC_{ii}) \simeq RC_{ii} - 1$, and the variance of LRC is not much different from the variance of RC. Figures 9–3A and 9–3B compare the relative consumptions of movers and stayers.

    The small difference in the means is not significant.* On the other hand, the difference in the variances is highly significant.** A change

---

*A t test of the difference between the means yields a value of $t = 0.614$. More than forty, but less than fifty, out of one hundred pairs of random samples of the same variable could be expected to produce the same difference between their means.

**The ratio of the variances gives an F value of 3.11. There is only a 0.1 percent chance for a random F value higher than 1.81.

Table 9–3.   Statistics on the Natural Logarithm of Relative Consumption

Statistics	Stayers (N=153)	Movers (N=52)
Mean	-0.0059 ± 0.0087	0.0112 ± 0.0262
Standard Deviation	0.107 ± 0.006	0.189 ± 0.019
Variance (SD^2)	0.01148 ± 0.00004	0.03576 ± 0.00034

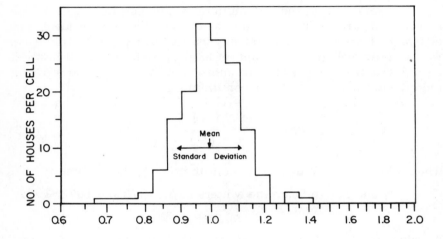

Figure 9–3A.   Relative Consumption of 153 Stayers

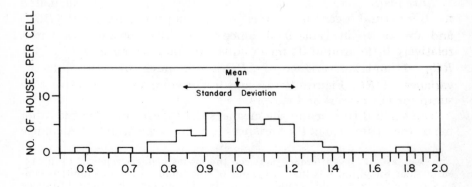

Figure 9–3B.   Relative Consumption of 52 Movers

in ownership greatly disrupts the "traditional" consumption level of an individual house; averaged over a large number of houses, however, disruptions of opposite sign tend to compensate each other.

It is interesting to observe that, if we define relative consumption as the ratio of the raw (instead of normalized) gas consumptions:

$$RCR_{ii} = \frac{G_i(t_3)}{G_i(t_1)} \quad , \tag{9.4}$$

the means and the variances for both winters and for both movers and stayers are very close to the corresponding statistics for RC, as seen in Table 9-4. So why work with normalized gas data rather than with straight raw gas data, when apparently the physical features are "divided out" anyhow by taking relative consumptions? The reason is that we need to compare the variance of the movers' relative consumption to the maximum possible variance. If the consumption level of each house in the second winter were totally unrelated to its own level in the first winter, we would compute a maximum variance for the relative consumption of 0.05011 ± 0.00048. To obtain this result, we add the variances of the logarithms* of the movers' normalized gas consumptions in both winters,

$$\sigma^2 [LGN(t_1)] + \sigma^2 [LGN(t_3)] = (0.145)^2 + (0.171)^2 = 0.05011 \ ,$$

$$\tag{9.5}$$

according to the laws of propagation of variance of uncorrelated factors. Had we used raw gas data, the result in equation (9.5) would have been more than twice as large, because it would have included the variation due to the "obvious" physical features as well.

The difference between the movers' relative consumption, 0.0358, and the maximum possible variance of 0.0501 that we derived suggests that there exists a weak link between the consumption of movers' houses before and after the change in ownership. An F test, however, predicts a better than 5 percent chance that two random samples (of only fifty-two units) of the same variable would have produced the same ratio of the variances.

Thus, over the two year period, the movers' houses "forget" much of their previous consumption levels, while the stayers "remember"

---

*Though not explicitly shown in any table, the variances of the logarithms are nearly identical to the square of the coefficients of variation listed in Table 9-2.

Table 9-4. Natural Logarithm of Relative Consumption from Raw Gas Data, *LRCR*, * and from Normalized Gas Data, *LRC*. *

Statistics	Stayers (N=153)		Movers (N=52)	
	LRCR	*LRC*	*LRCR*	*LRC*
Mean	-0.0112 ± 0.0090	-0.0059 ± 0.0087	0.0116 ± 0.0269	0.0112 ± 0.0262
Standard Deviation	0.111 ± 0.006	0.107 ± 0.006	0.194 ± 0.019	0.189 ± 0.019
Variance (SD^2)	0.01238 ± 0.00004	0.01148 ± 0.00004	0.03767 ± 0.00036	0.03576 ± 0.00034

*As defined in equation (9.4). Numerical values identical to Table 9-3.
**As defined in equation (9.3).

much better, though less than perfectly. The following section is devoted to a quantitative interpretation of these qualitative effects.

A THREE FACTOR MULTIPLICATIVE MODEL FOR GAS CONSUMPTION

The facts of central importance to the following discussion are the differences among the variances of relative consumption, *RC*, for stayers, for movers, and for houses where the consumption level changes at random from year to year.

A three factor model is proposed to interpret the meaning of these differences both qualitatively and quantitatively. The three factors that appear to play a role are (1) nonpersistent consumption patterns of residents and/or house—"change," responsible for the broadening of the relative consumption distribution as time goes by; (2) persistent behavior of the occupants—"lifestyle," manifested in the abrupt change across a move; (3) "quality," establishing a weak link between the consumption patterns of a house before and after a move.

The distinction between persistent and nonpersistent effects is made necessary by observing that the stayers do not reproduce their consumption rankings from year to year perfectly. This observation is the primary evidence of the factor "change."

By "change" we intend (1) changes occurring in the occupants' lives over time: children are born, adults trade domestic life for a job, incomes change, and so forth; (2) changes imposed on the house: the addition of storm windows and storm doors, the paneling of walls in the basement, the purchase of humidifiers and other appliances, and the like; (3) aging of the house: the compression of attic and wall insulation by moisture, cracked wall joints, new leaks around window frames. Experience with these houses suggests that the first two points listed here, changes involving the occupants, are predominant (but our method of analysis cannot tell this).

By "lifestyle" we intend that part of the occupant-related behavior assumed to be persistent in time, including thermal preference, the operation of south facing drapes, and thermostat setbacks.

"Quality" encompasses any built-in invisible differences, persistent in time, between apparently identical houses, possibly caused by variable diligence of different construction crews building the town or by wind exposure, color, and so forth.

Admittedly, some of the distinctions between the three factors may be arbitrary. Compare, for instance, the "persistent" yearly trek to Florida of one family to the "once in a lifetime" voyage to Europe of another. Nor can interactions between the different factors be ruled out. The assumptions made in the model proposed below will be spelled out in detail shortly. The multiplicative model is represented by the following equation:

$$GN_i(t) = 100 \cdot C_i(t) \cdot L_i \cdot Q_i \tag{9.6}$$

where t represents time (t_1 in the first winter of 1971–1972, t_2 in the second (1972–1973), t_3 in the third (1973–1974));

$GN_i(t)$ is the normalized gas consumption of the ith house, as defined by equation (9.2), in the tth six-month winter;

$C_i(t)$ is the time-dependent variable, "change," for the ith house;

L_i is the "lifestyle" for the occupant of the ith house, independent of time;

Q_i is the "quality" of the ith house, also time-independent.

The means of the three variables, C, L, Q, are assumed to be close to unity. The variance of each variable determines the extent to which that variable contributes to the total variation of the normalized gas consumption, GN, among identical houses.

The relative consumption, defined in equation (9.3), of stayers, movers, and random pairs,* "divides out" two, one, or none of the factors of the model:

Definition: RC_{ii} $= \dfrac{GN_i(t_3)}{GN_i(t_1)}$ (9.3)

---

*We refer to the reasoning that led to equation (9.5). Conceptually, totally uncorrelated consumptions between two winters can be thought of as the consumptions of random pairs of houses: house number 17 in the first winter and house number 28 in the second, etc. We symbolize this by the "randomly paired" relative consumption RC_{ij}, where i, j label random pairs of houses. Though in this analysis we use random pairs of movers, we have found that random pairs of stayers have an almost identical distribution of relative consumption.

Stayers: $$RC_{ii}^{S} = \frac{C_i(t_3)}{C_i(t_1)}$$ (9.7a)

Movers: $$RC_{ii}^{M} = \frac{C_i^{new}(t_3)}{C_i^{old}(t_1)} \cdot \frac{L_i^{new}(t_3)}{L_i^{old}(t_1)}$$ (9.7b)

Random Pairs of Movers: $$RC_{ij}^{RM} = \frac{C_j^{new}(t_3)}{C_i^{old}(t_1)} \cdot \frac{L_j^{new}(t_1)}{L_i^{old}(t_1)} \cdot \frac{Q_j(t_3)}{Q_i(t_1)}$$ (9.7c)

The superscript "new" refers to the new owners in the second winter; the subscript j refers to the jth house in the second winter, randomly paired with the ith house in the first winter.

From the data we know the variances of the logarithms of the left-hand sides of the three equations (9.7a), (9.7b), and (9.7c); we can derive the variances of each of the three factors on the right-hand side if the following three assumptions hold: (1) the three factors, C, L, Q, are uncorrelated with each other; (2) the variance of each factor does not change between the two winters; (3) the variables representing the new owners, $C^{new}(t_3)$ and $L^{new}(t_3)$, and the variables representing the old owners, $C^{old}(t_1)$ and $L^{old}(t_1)$, are uncorrelated and of identical variances. While the lack of correlation between old and new owners in assumption (3) seems reasonable, the variation between individual lifestyles of the new occupants may need some time to "settle" to that of the old occupants. In fact, Table 9-2 shows that the movers' normalized gas consumption in the second winter has a slightly wider distribution than that of the stayers and that of the movers in the first winter, but an F test on the variances is not significant at the 5 percent confidence level. Assumption (2) is made plausible by the constancy of the standard deviation of the stayers' normalized gas consumption across three winters: 14.1, 14.4 and 15.0 in 1971–1972, 1972–1973, and 1973–1974, respectively. The slight increase over three years cannot be regarded as significant. Assumption (1) is the hardest to confirm: it implies, for instance, that there is no interaction between occupants and their houses (e.g., a "tight" house encouraging some occupants to save energy or, conversely, decreasing their alertness to energy conservation), a claim questioned by many social scientists. Though no evidence could be found supporting or refuting this assumption and no direct test could be devised, this author is confident that interactions between the three factors, if they exist, would not be so large as to seriously alter the quantitative results derived below.

With these assumptions, the propagation of variance can be written as

Stayers: $\qquad \sigma^2 [LRC^S] = .01148 \pm .00004$

$$= 2\sigma^2 [LC] \cdot (1 - \rho [LC(t_1), LC(t_3)]) \qquad (9.8a)$$

Movers: $\qquad \sigma^2 [LRC^M] = .03576 \pm .00034$

$$= 2\sigma^2 [LC] + 2\sigma^2 [LL] \qquad (9.8b)$$

Random Pairs
of Movers: $\quad \sigma^2 [LRC^{RM}] = .05011 \pm .00048$

$$= 2\sigma^2 [LC] + 2\sigma^2 [LL] + 2\sigma^2 [LQ] \qquad (9.8c)$$

where $LRC^S = ln\ (RC^S)$, and so forth.

$\rho [LC(t_1), LC(t_3)]$ is the correlation coefficient between these variables in the two winters (see below).

Working with the logarithms of the variables was necessary in order to stay within the conventional linear framework of the analysis of variance (ANOVA). The following results involve the movers only (equations [9.8b] and [9.8c]):

"quality": $\qquad\qquad\qquad \sigma^2 [LQ] \ = .00718 \pm .00029 \quad (9.9a)$

"change" and
"lifestyle": $\quad \sigma^2 [LC] \ + \ \sigma^2 [LL] \ = .01788 \pm .00017 \quad (9.9b)$

How can we separate the individual contributions of LC and LL to the total variance in equation (9.9b)? The stayers (equation [9.8a]) do not yield enough information to distill "change," C, from "lifestyle," L; The correlation coefficient $\rho [LC(t_1), LC(t_3)] = \rho_{LC2}$ expresses the degree to which the stayers reproduce their consumption level over two years. Since $\rho_{LC2} \geq 0$, we can state merely that $\sigma^2 [LC] \geq .00574$. The limited amount of data (too few houses, too few winters) does not warrant an exact evaluation of ρ_{LC2}, although more information is available and will be discussed in the next section. Thus, the certain quantitative results so far are expressed by equations (9.9a) and (9.9b).

Summing up what we have learned until now, we can state that the observed variation in gas consumption among identical houses ($\sigma^2 [LGN]$ = $(.158)^2$ = $.02505 \pm .00024$) is caused 71.4 percent by different occupant-related consumption patterns ($\sigma^2 [LC]$ + $\sigma^2 [LL]$ = $(.134)^2$ = $.01788 \pm .00017$) and 28.6 percent by different house-related characteristics ($\sigma^2 [LQ]$ = $(.085)^2$ = $.00718 \pm .00029$). Translated into physical units, the average observed standard deviation among identical houses is 3.71 MWh per six-month winter, compared to an average consumption of 23.46 MWh per six-month winter. Occupant-related consumption patterns alone would cause a standard deviation of 3.14 MWh per six-month winter, while persistent quality differences between houses alone would cause a standard deviation of 1.99 MWh per six-month winter.

TIME DEPENDENT CHANGES IN CONSUMPTION PATTERNS

Concerning the variation in consumption among our nominally identical houses in one particular heating season, we are done: the occupants are responsible for 71 percent of the observed variation, the houses for 29 percent. However, the stayers sample provides more information related to the partition between persistent and nonpersistent consumption patterns.

"Change," the nonpersistent factor, can be thought of as the result of a continuous series of random decisions by the occupants affecting energy consumption. The factor "change" is represented by the variable $C(t)$. The "decision status" of the ith family at time t determines its value, $C_i(t)$, of the variable $C(t)$. A histogram of the values $C_i(t)$ of all families (or houses) at a given time, t, yields the distribution of the variable $C(t)$ for that time.* The limited number of possible decisions, the workings of peer pressure, and other "stabilizing influences" prevent the distribution of consumption over many houses from broadening indefinitely: no statistically significant broadening in gas consumption distribution has been observed in Twin Rivers over the years. Thus we can visualize the nonpersistent consumption pattern of an individual family as a "random walk" within a finite range $\pm\sigma [LC]$; the "speed" at which an individual family randomly "walks" can be observed in the widening of the stayers' relative consumption distributions over one, two, or more years up to a maximum of $\pm\sqrt{2}\,\sigma [LC]$. The relative consumption of the movers, in turn, shows no widening. Since the move totally

---

*One can show that the resulting mean and the standard deviation are practically the same for movers and stayers.

separates the identities of the families before and after the move (separating $C_i^{old}(t_1)$ from $C_i^{new}(t_3)$), the relative consumption already has the full width $\pm\sqrt{2}\,\sigma[LC]$.

Figure 9-4 shows the logarithmic variances of the relative consumption of the stayers among the three winters 1971–1972, 1972–1973, and 1973–1974. The variances are 0.0077, 0.0071, and 0.0115, respectively. The relative consumption distribution over two years is clearly wider than the two relative consumption distributions over one year. For short periods of time or for a very large maximum range of the "random walk," one can apply the law of diffusion, whereby the variance is proportional to elapsed time:

$$\sigma^2[LC(t') - LC(t)] = 2\sigma^2[LC] \cdot (1 - \rho[LC(t), LC(t')]) \propto (t' - t) \quad (9.10)$$

$$t' - t \geq 0 \quad .$$

For large periods of time or for a small maximum range, one would expect the dependence on elapsed time to level off, since the variance of the random walk (l.h.s. of equation [9.10]) cannot exceed $2\sigma^2[LC]$. In a rather speculative manner, one could postulate the correlation coefficient in equation (9.10) to "decay" exponentially, with increasing elapsed time:

$$\rho[LC(t), LC(t')] = \exp(-(t' - t))/T \quad (9.11)$$

$$t' - t \geq 0$$

where T is a time constant associated with changes in consumption patterns of the occupants.

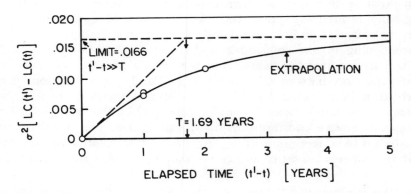

Figure 9-4. Variance of Stayers' Relative Consumption as a Function of Time

From the data in Figure 9—4, averaging the two relative consumptions for $t' - t = 1$ year, we obtain $T = 1.69$ years and $\sigma^2[LC] = 0.00830 = (0.091)^2$. In other words, the variation in normalized gas consumption over the years, of the same family in the same house, is likely to stay within ± 9.1 percent of their average consumption. Though the set of decisions affecting this variation in gas consumption is assumed to be continuously under review, it is not likely to change drastically in less than a year or so. Over two or more years, however, the family progressively resembles itself no more or less than any other family, concerning energy behavior that is susceptible to change.

These results fit well into the previous analyses. Now one could state that: the observed variation in gas consumptions among identical houses is caused 33 percent by nonpersistent changes in consumption patterns, 38 percent by persistent occupant-related patterns, and 29 percent by persistent house-related quality differences. However, given the scant number of winters for which consumption data are available at present, such a conclusion is speculative and awaits confirmation by further research.

CONCLUSION

The variation in a six-month winter's gas consumption among a sample of 205 townhouses has been explained to about 54 percent by "obvious" physical features, like the number of bedrooms; the area of insulated glass, if any; and whether the house is an end unit. The main thrust of this chapter has been to determine the factors responsible for the remaining 46 percent variation that cannot be explained by conventional factors.

The strategy was to observe the changes in consumption levels of the houses in three different samples: (1) "stayers," where houses and occupants remain the same in every winter; (2) "movers," where the houses remain the same, but the occupants change; and (3) "random pairs," where both houses and occupants change. The measure for the change in consumption over time is defined as "relative consumption" between two winters—the ratio of the consumption in the second winter divided by the consumption in the first. The data allow three different factors to be discerned: (1) nonpersistent consumption patterns of occupants and/or house, "change"; (2) persistent behavior patterns of the occupants, "lifestyle"; and (3) persistent consumption patterns of the house, "quality." Assuming that these factors are uncorrelated and that their variances remain constant for different winters and for different sets of occupants (concerning "movers"), we can state that 71 percent of the variation unexplained by conventional factors is caused by occupant-related consumption patterns, a combination of the first two factors above, and 29 percent by persistent house-related quality differences. Close scrutiny of the stayers' consumption across one and two years suggests, somewhat speculatively, that the 71 percent is the sum of 33 percent nonpersistent patterns ("change") and 38 percent persistent, occupant-related patterns ("lifestyle").

We have proved experimentally that (so far) unpredictable behavior patterns of the occupants introduce a large source of uncertainty into the computation of residential space heating energy requirements. The lesson to be learned is twofold: first, there is little practical usefulness in pushing too far the detail of any deterministic model for the prediction of heating load requirements. Second, the effect of retrofits, weather, or other factors physically influencing the heat load of a house should be tested on many houses occupied by real people. These conclusions may be the strongest a posteriori justification for the approach of the Twin Rivers project. That approach placed special emphasis on the monitoring of a large number of populated houses, to be modeled in relatively simple fashion, instead of testing a sophisticated model under laboratory conditions.

Chapter 10 describes how questionnaires have identified the importance of considerations of health and comfort in determining level of summer use of air conditioning. Another way in which our group addressed variability was through on-site inspection of identical houses. This work uncovered numerous structural problems that merited attention, but it disclosed only a few structural problems across houses that correlated with level of energy use.* Yet another study involved direct monitoring of interior temperatures across houses. This revealed a rough correlation of higher interior temperatures with higher consumption of natural gas. Thus, our various attempts to clarify the variability in energy consumption across houses are broadly consistent, all pointing to the significant role of the resident. It follows, we believe, that constructs of the problem of achieving energy conservation in housing that exclude the resident are seriously incomplete.

---

*For example, Schrader [3] finds a weak correlation ($r^2 = 0.33$) between the dimensions of the gaps at the firewall (see Figure 1-8) and the slope parameter (see Chapter 9). The correlation may be interpreted as a 6 percent increase in furnace gas consumption for each additional inch (2.5 cm) of crack width at any of the firewall gaps.

APPENDIX: DATA ACQUISITION

The data presented in this chapter were gathered from the monthly readings of the Public Service Electric and Gas Company, Twin Rivers' natural gas supplier. The utility records list four digit readings (in units of 100 cubic feet, corresponding to 0.0300 MWh) and special flags for missing or estimated readings. All meters in our sample are read near the end of the month, normally on the same day.

There are 248 townhouses in Quad II, upon which we concentrated our efforts. In a first elimination process, all houses with missing or estimated readings that influence the computation of the six-months (November–April) consumption were eliminated. The monthly electric consumption records of the Jersey Central Power and Light utility for the same houses were consulted to establish when and where a change in ownership occurred: when the billing address of a customer changes, a special code number is increased by one. All houses for which a move occurred during any of the eight winter months (October–May) in either 1971–1972 or 1973–1974 were also eliminated. Subletting a house to another family was considered a "de facto" move. Such occurrences could be detected from the change in the resident's name in the utility records, although the billing address remained unchanged. The electric utility records proved very useful in detecting a prolonged absence by the owners: under such circumstances the electric consumption, a good measure for the "activity" inside the house, would drop to very low levels, while a sizeable gas consumption would remain even if the thermostat were set back to $12°C$ ($55°F$), the minimum possible setting on the thermostats employed in these houses. Such absences over several months were also excluded.

As a result of these successive eliminations, the original 248 townhouse sample was reduced to a "clean" sample of 205 townhouses. This sample, in turn, was split into "movers" and "stayers," according to whether a change in ownership occurred between the heating seasons under consideration.

REFERENCES

1. Mayer, L.S., and Robinson, J.A. 1975. A statistical analysis of the monthly consumption of gas and electricity in the home. CES Report No. 18. Princeton, N.J.: Princeton University, March.
2. Fox, J.M. 1973. Energy conservation for residential space heating—a case study. Master's thesis, AMS Department, Princeton University (also issued as CES Report No. 4.
3. Schrader, T.F. 1978. A two-parameter model for assessing the determinants of residential space heating. MSE thesis, Department of Aerospace and Mechanical Sciences, Princeton University.

Chapter 10

Behavioral Approaches to Residential Energy Conservation*

Clive Seligman
John M. Darley
Lawrence J. Becker

Center for Environmental Studies
Princeton University

Abstract

This chapter outlines some of the research conducted by social psychologists to reduce residential energy consumption. The results of two attitudinal surveys demonstrated that homeowners' summer electricity consumption could be predicted from their energy-related attitudes. Personal comfort and health concerns were the best predictors of consumption. Psychologically derived techniques to reduce summer electricity consumption were experimentally examined in three separate studies. In study 1, almost daily consumption feedback was found to reduce electricity usage 10.5 percent. In study 2, subjects receiving frequent feedback, who were also asked to adopt a difficult conservation goal, reduced their electricity consumption 13.0 percent. In study 3, a device that signaled homeowners when they could cool their houses without air conditioning by opening their windows led to a reduction in consumption of 15.7 percent. It was concluded that the resident can play an important role in energy conservation that complements engineering solutions.

INTRODUCTION

The social sciences, including psychology, have been far less involved than the physical and engineering sciences in efforts to conserve en-

*The authors would like to thank the following individuals for their advice, help, and support during the conduct of this research: Jan Beyea, Ellen Fagenson, Russ Fazio, David Harrje, Mitchell Kriss, Larry Mayer, John Pryor, Vita Rabinowitz, Frank Sinden, Robert Socolow, and Tom Woteki.

ergy. As a consequence, much less is known about the human (as opposed to the technological) side of the energy crisis, even though it is people who make the decisions to use the machines that consume energy. Only recently have we begun to learn about how people perceive and respond to their "energy environment" and how their attitudes and motivations affect their energy consumption behavior. Nonetheless enough has been learned to indicate that people have an important role to play in any comprehensive energy conservation plan.

Three pieces of evidence collected by the Twin Rivers project (see Chapter 1) clearly show the importance of the human role in residential consumption. First, in a sample of twenty-eight identical townhouses, variation in energy consumption was found to be as great as two to one (see Figure 1–13). Since these houses are identical in floor plan, position in the interior of a townhouse row, builder, construction materials, and climate, it is likely that most of the consumption variance is due to the different behavior of the people in the houses. Second, in houses where there has been a change in residents, it has been found that the energy consumption of the house with the new residents cannot be predicted from the energy consumption of the same house with the previous residents (see Chapter 9). Third, even after houses had been successfully retrofitted (with 20–25 percent savings), the variance in energy consumption among the houses remained almost the same as it was before the retrofits took place, and the rank order hardly changed [1].

These results demonstrate quite convincingly that the energy consumption of a house cannot be completely understood without reference to the people in the house. In the remainder of this article, we will review the research that our group has conducted in applying psychological theory and procedures to the problems of encouraging residential energy conservation. First, we will discuss research aimed at finding the attitudinal determinants of residential energy consumption. Second, we will present several psychologically derived strategies to induce people to reduce their energy consumption and discuss the evidence we have collected bearing on the success of these strategies.

ATTITUDES AND ENERGY CONSUMPTION

Does it matter what people think of the energy crisis? Obviously many people think that it does. The consumers of polls of attitudes toward energy issues include politicians, government bureaucrats, journalists, and businessmen. The politician may be in search of votes, the newspaperman of a good story, the oil company executive of guidance with advertising campaigns; nevertheless, all share the critical assumption that what people think about energy directly affects how much energy they consume.

Is this assumption reasonable? For example, do people who think the energy crisis is a hoax consume more energy than people who think it is genuine? In spite of the large number of energy attitude surveys that have been conducted [2], there is surprisingly little evidence that relates homeowners' attitudes to their actual energy consumption. First, because it is hard to obtain, many surveys have not collected actual energy usage data, assuming instead that homeowners' self-reports of past, present, and future consumption accurately reflected real energy consumption patterns. But we regard this as an unwarranted assumption. For instance, just after a national fuel shortage, people are likely to say that their most recent fuel bills show savings, because they feel that the interviewer would regard any other answers as unpatriotic. But whether they actually did save is a separate matter. Second, partially because of complex and difficult-to-decipher bills, and partially because until recently energy has been sufficiently cheap so as not to have been worth monitoring, people are often quite unaware of the rates at which they consume energy. For these reasons, until someone documents that there is a strong relationship between actual and self-reported energy consumption patterns, we are skeptical of this assumption.

It is perhaps for the reason that previous surveys have not looked at actual energy consumption that attempts to predict conservation behavior have failed. Murray et al. [3] were not able to find any statistically significant relationships between reported temperature reduction or use of major appliances and any nondemographic variables. Curtin [4] tried without success to predict reported past conservation behavior and expected difficulty of future conservation from fourteen demographic and attitudinal variables. Newman and Day [5] did collect actual energy consumption data but, because they were primarily interested in describing how consumers use energy, they did not attempt to relate consumption to attitudinal dimensions.

TWIN RIVERS SURVEYS

In the summer of 1976, we conducted two energy attitude surveys [6]. Our purposes were twofold: First, we wanted to see whether we could distill from the many varied attitudes that people have about energy a few basic attitudinal dimensions that reflect people's conceptualizations of energy consumption. Second, we wanted to know whether these attitudinal dimensions relate to actual energy consumption.

The respondents of our first summer questionnaire were fifty-six couples living in Twin Rivers, New Jersey. The respondents are relatively homogeneous: the average husband is in his midthirties, his wife in her early thirties. The majority of couples have one or two children. Forty-two of the couples in the survey sample live in three bedroom townhouses, and fourteen live in two bedroom townhouses. Within each bedroom size, the townhouses are identical in floor plan and have identical central air conditioning systems. In the summer, electricity use for the air conditioner accounts for 70 percent of all electricity usage in these houses.

Notice that by concentrating the survey in Twin Rivers something was lost and something was gained. Because of the relative homogeneity of the residents, it is not possible to be sure that the attitudinal patterns that emerge from an analysis of their data are representative of the national pattern. However, because of the physical homogeneity of the houses, the variance in energy consumption is greatly reduced. Therefore, differences in energy consumption due to attitudinal patterns can be detected more easily.

What attitudes and patterns of thought determine an individual's energy consumption decisions? On initial analysis, it seemed likely that the answer to this question depended on the kind of energy consumption under consideration. Gasoline consumption, for instance, would be likely to relate to a person's perceptions of the convenience of public transportation alternatives, while attitudes determining air conditioning consumption would be more likely to involve dimensions such as the comfort consequences of hotter inside temperatures.

To get an initial fix on attitudes relevant to air conditioning usage, we generated twenty-eight attitudinal questions (see Table 10−1) that represented seven attitudinal categories. The categories were: (1) perceived bother of conserving energy (e.g., "It is just not worth the trouble to turn off the air conditioner and open the windows every time it gets a little cooler outside"); (2) discomfort in conserving energy (e.g., "While others might tolerate turning off the air conditioner in the summer, my own need for being cool is high"); (3) health questions (e.g., "It's essential to my health and well-being for the house to be air conditioned in the summer"); (4) the legitimacy of the energy crisis (e.g., "The energy crisis is a hoax"); (5) belief in science (e.g., "Science will soon provide society with a long lasting source of energy"); (6) morality (e.g., "It is immoral for America to

Table 10-1. Rotated Factor Loadings. *(Study 1)*

Variable	Factor 1	Factor 2	Factor 3	Factor 4
1. Consumers have the right to use as much energy as they want and can pay for.	0.19	(0.53)*	0.29	0.04
2. I find it very difficult to fall asleep without an air conditioner on at night.	(0.61)	0.28	0.38	-0.03
3. Nuclear power will eventually provide us with most of our energy needs.	0.06	-0.11	0.02	0.01
4. Science will soon provide society with a long lasting source of energy.	0.26	0.10	-0.06	0.22
5. It's essential to *my* health and well-being for the house to be air conditioned in the summer.	(0.76)	0.28	0.16	-0.06
6. It is just not worth the trouble to turn off the air conditioner and open the windows every time it gets a little cooler outside.	0.27	(0.62)	0.19	0.00
7. How uncomfortable would you be if you turned your thermostat setting up 3 degrees from its usual setting?	(0.55)	0.00	0.11	-0.01
8. How much of a savings per month on your summer electricity bill *would it take to induce you* to turn your thermostat setting up 3 degrees from its usual setting?	0.25	0.23	0.05	-0.16
9. I never feel guilty about having my air conditioner on.	0.30	0.17	0.25	0.11
10. It is immoral for America to consume 40 percent of the world's energy resources.	-0.02	-0.25	-0.28	0.03

(Table 10-1. continued overleaf)

Table 10–1. continued

Variable	Factor 1	Factor 2	Factor 3	Factor 4
11. If everyone in the country tried to conserve energy at home, there would probably be *little or no real impact* upon the nation's overall energy consumption.	0.22	0.03	0.33	0.07
12. To what degree has overconsumption by individuals contributed to this country's energy problem?	-0.23	-0.22	(-0.65)	0.16
13. The energy crisis is largely due to real worldwide shortages of fuels needed to produce energy.	-0.02	-0.02	-0.09	(0.69)
14. I almost never think about the energy needs of Americans 100 years from now.	0.07	0.18	-0.06	-0.16
15. It is immoral to consume any more energy than I absolutely need.	-0.02	-0.39	-0.03	(0.51)
16. American technology in the past has come to grips with all major crises and it will no doubt soon discover a solution to the energy problem.	0.19	-0.09	-0.07	0.22
17. While others might tolerate turning off the air conditioner in the summer, my own need for being cool is high.	(0.74)	0.30	0.00	-0.08
18. How difficult would it be for you to adjust to an indoor temperature of not less than 75° F in the summer months?	0.40	(0.49)	0.13	0.00
19. To what degree would more conservation of energy on the part of individuals alleviate the energy problem?	-0.04	-0.21	(-0.79)	0.13

20. It's not worth it at all to sweat a little in the summer to try to save a little energy.	0.21	(0.58)	0.11	-0.05
21. The energy crisis is largely due to the federal government's lack of an adequate energy policy.	-0.13	0.16	0.08	0.12
22. The energy crisis is largely due to supply and price manipulations by the major oil companies.	0.17	0.01	0.00	-0.16
23. Trying to save pennies a day conserving energy is just not worth it.	0.41	(0.48)	0.33	-0.17
24. It's essential to my family's health and well-being for the house to be air conditioned in the summer.	(0.74)	0.19	0.13	0.02
25. It's just *not* worth the trouble to turn the thermostat up every time it gets a little cooler outside.	0.08	(0.59)	0.22	-0.15
26. I would only conserve energy if I could not afford to pay for it.	0.25	(0.76)	0.00	-0.12
27. The energy crisis is a hoax.	0.23	0.21	0.13	-0.44
28. If we were able to put a man on the moon within ten years, we could certainly solve the energy crisis within a short time period.	0.16	0.14	0.13	-0.29

* ( ) indicates loading > .45.

consume 40 percent of the world's energy resources"); (7) the role of the individual (e.g., "To what degree has overconsumption by individuals contributed to this country's energy problem?"). Responses to the questions were made on seven point scales. Except for some background questions, which were asked first, the questions were randomly ordered on the questionnaire.

During the first week of July, potential respondents were telephoned and asked if they would be willing to answer an attitudes-toward-energy questionnaire that had been developed by a group of university researchers. People who agreed were told to expect two questionnaires to be dropped off at their home on a certain day. Wives and husbands were to fill out their questionnaires independently. All of the questionnaires were distributed and picked up from the residents' homes within a two week period. The respondents were also asked to give us their permission to obtain a record of their electricity consumption from the local utility company's files. All residents agreed. Actual electric consumption (kilowatt hours) for June, July, and August was determined for each couple in the sample.

A statistical technique called factor analysis [7] was used to reduce the respondents' attitude scores to a relatively few attitudinal factors. Four factors emerged,* and Table 10−1 shows the factor loadings (i.e., the correlations between particular attitude variables and factors). The conventional way of interpreting the meaning of a factor is to examine the content of those attitudinal variables that load highly on a factor. An examination of those variables that have loadings of 0.45 or greater on a rotated factor suggests the interpretation of factors shown in Table 10−1:

Factor 1. The five variables (2, 5, 7, 17, and 24) having loadings greater than 0.45 are clearly concerned with personal comfort and health. This indicates the importance of personal comfort and health in decisions to regulate the use of the air conditioner. People who score high on this factor are not necessarily more concerned with their health and comfort than other people, but they do perceive a close connection between those variables and air conditioning usage. For them, to be cool is to be healthy and comfortable.

---

*The twenty-eight questions were subjected to a principal factor analysis, with squared multiple correlations used as communality estimates. Eight factors were extracted with eigenvalues greater than 1, and the factors were varimax rotated. As the first four factors accounted for 48 percent of the total variance of the attitudinal variables and 80 percent of the total eight factor variance, only these four were interpreted.

Factor 2. This factor seems to reflect two related concepts. Variables 6, 18, 20, and 25 indicate a concern for the effort or bother involved in conserving energy. Variables 1, 23, and 26 are concerned with the individual's ability to pay for his energy needs. These two concepts are related in that we can characterize this factor with the statement: "Conserving energy in the home requires a great deal of effort for too little dollar savings." We might name this the high effort, low payoff factor.

Factor 3. The two variables (12 and 19) loading highest on this factor point to the role of the individual in contributing to and alleviating the energy crisis. Individuals who score high on this factor regard the ordinary homeowner as having little or no role in the national energy consumption crisis. Feeling this, a person who scored high on this factor could be quite convinced of the reality of the national energy crisis and still not take steps to conserve, because he would consider his energy savings irrelevant to the aggregate consumption pattern.

Factor 4. The two variables (13 and 15) loading greater than 0.45 reflect the extent of individuals' beliefs about whether there are real shortages of fuels and whether it is immoral to consume too much energy. We can tentatively label this factor as a concern with the legitimacy of the energy crisis—that is, those who believe there is a real shortage of fuels believe it is immoral to overconsume. Variable 27, "the energy crisis is a hoax," loads third highest on this factor, -0.44, consistent with our tentative interpretation of the factor.

On the basis of the factor analysis, a picture begins to emerge of how homeowners perceive their energy consumption. The basic considerations seem to involve judgments about effects of conservation on health and comfort, monetary return for one's conservation efforts, the impact of the individual consumer on conservation, and the legitimacy of the energy crisis. Since men and women might be educated differently about energy, and since this might be reflected in their having differential attitudinal structures about the abstract topic of energy, separate factor analyses on males and females were conducted. Happily for the simplicity of our data analysis, the same four factors as reported above were apparent for both males and females.

For any individual in the sample, then, a score on each of these four factors can be calculated. To predict a particular house's consumption, one would want to know the factor scores of both husband and wife. Thus eight factor scores (four from the husband and four from the wife) were employed as predictors of each household's summer electric consumption. An overall multiple regression analysis revealed that a total of 55 percent of the variance in consumption was accounted for by the predictors, $R^2 = 0.553$, $F (8, 47) = 7.26$, $p < 0.001$. In psychological research, this is a strikingly high attitude-behavior correlation. Thus, our attitudinal variables were very successful in predicting energy use.

The relationship between each factor and energy use was examined by correlating the two spouses' scores on a given factor with consumption. Table 10–2 presents males' and females' correlation for each factor. The combined effect of the male and female scores on the comfort and health factor was highly significant, accounting for 30 percent of the variance in actual electric consumption, $R^2 = 0.301$, $F (2, 53) = 11.41$, $p < 0.001$. The more a household perceived conservation as leading to discomfort and ill-health, the more energy the household consumed. Moreover, the health and comfort attitude of the female was more strongly linked to air conditioner usage than was that of the male. This makes sense. Other information we have indicates that the wife is more likely than the husband to be home during the day and to control the energy use during that time.

Scores of the high effort, low payoff factor also significantly predicted consumption, $R^2 = 0.245$, $F (2, 53) = 8.61$, $p < 0.001$, as did the households' scores on the role of the individual factor, $R^2 = 0.115$, $F (2, 53) = 3.43$, $p < 0.05$. The more energy conservation was perceived as requiring great effort for little monetary return and the

Table 10–2. Predicting Actual Summer Electric Consumption from Attitudinal Factors: Correlations Between Attitudinal Factors and Electricity Consumption. *(Survey 1)*

	Simple Correlations		
Factor	*Male Factor Score*	*Female Factor Score*	*Multiple Correlation*
Comfort and health	0.40**	0.53***	0.55***
High effort, low payoff	0.41**	0.42**	0.50***
Role of the individual	0.33*	0.03	0.34*
Legitimacy of energy crisis	−0.08	0.19	0.26

   * $p < 0.05$
  ** $p < 0.01$
*** $p < 0.001$

less importance attached to the role of the individual in contributing to and alleviating the energy crisis, the more energy was consumed. Scores on the factor involving the legitimacy of the energy crisis accounted for only a trivial proportion of variance, $R^2 = 0.066$, $F(2, 53) = 1.88$, $p > 0.10$.

The results have shown (1) that homeowners' attitudes toward energy can be conceptualized into a few basic factors, and (2) that these attitudinal factors can predict actual energy consumption. Homeowners perceived their use of energy according to their judgement of the effect of energy conservation on personal comfort and health, the effort required to conserve and the monetary payoff for doing so, the ability of the individual to have an impact on the energy problem, and their belief that the crisis is legitimate. Together, these factors were capable of explaining a total of 55 percent of the variance in actual electric consumption. Examined singly, the comfort and health factor, the high effort, low payoff factor, and the role of the individual factor were significant predictors of energy use. The comfort and health factor emerged as the best single predictor of consumption, accounting for a greater percentage of consumption variance than any other factor.

A second survey of sixty-nine couples was conducted in September 1976 in the same community to attempt to confirm the general results of the first survey [6]. The results of the second survey showed that the same factors reemerged and that together they again accounted for a significant portion of the variance. However, in the second survey the comfort and health factors were the only statistically significant predictors of actual energy consumption.

A major result of these analyses is the importance of the resident's attitudes toward his or her own comfort and health as a determinant of actual energy consumption. While individuals do indeed perceive the energy crisis in terms other than simply comfort and health, only comfort and health concerns were consistently predictive of actual energy consumption in both surveys. It is necessary to remain cautious about the importance of the high effort, low payoff factor and the role of the individual factor, since they were not statistically significant predictors in the second survey. Finally, we also need more information about the connection between people's perceptions of the reality of the energy crisis and their energy consumption patterns. Is there really as little relationship as our results seem to suggest?

If larger scale surveys confirm the present results, the design of national energy conservation campaigns can be more sensibly addressed than one suspects it has been. What does medical research show about the links between health and air conditioning usage? If, contrary to what many people now assume, there is no positive relationship between air conditioning and health, then air conditioning usage might be reduced. For people who regard air conditioning as essential to their comfort, the high effort, low payoff factor ought to be addressed. They ought to be informed that there are highly cost-effective low effort ways of cooling without air conditioning, for example, by installing window and attic fans, by regulating the use of window shades and drapes, and by opening windows in the evening when outside temperature falls below inside temperature. National energy saving appeals have their best chance of being successful if they are fitted to the actual patterns of existing attitudes of energy consumers.

MOTIVATING THE RESIDENT TO CONSERVE: FEEDBACK RESEARCH

Survey research represents one approach that psychologists have taken to study the relationship between people and their energy consumption. As we have seen, surveys can tell us a great deal about the characteristics or attitudes of people that are important for energy consumption. Another approach to the problem is to be less concerned with individual differences in attitudes and habits and to be more concerned with the immediate environments in which people live that make them more or less conscious of their energy behavior and that facilitate or hinder energy conservation.

Since we are concerned with residential energy use, let us consider the house as an "energy environment." Appliances are run, the air conditioning cycles, hot water is used, lights are turned on and off, and the homeowner has no way of determining what amounts of energy are used by these devices. The utility bill that the homeowner gets does not break down energy usage into these components. Nor does the bill appear at or near the time of the energy usage; it arrives on a monthly basis at best. Frequently, the bill is an estimate. Clearly, the homeowner lives in an information-deficient energy environment. But what would happen if we gave the homeowner more information about his energy consuming behavior—if we closed the "feedback loop" between the homeowner and his or her house? The resident has a number of controlling actions available, the most important of which is thermostat control. In general, feedback research has shown that performance feedback, displayed to the human operator, is critical in producing effective performance [8]. During the individual's learning of the control tasks, informational feedback has been repeatedly shown to improve the rate and level of learning [9, 10]. It can also improve motivation to perform the task [11], and in general, the more immediately the feedback follows the control action, the more optimal the performance [9].

We have now conducted several summer feedback experiments in Twin Rivers aimed at reducing electricity consumption.

Study 1

The purpose of the first feedback study [12] was to determine the effects of an immediate consumption feedback procedure on the reduction of electricity consumption. Electricity consumption was examined because the study was conducted during the summer when, in the studied houses, 70 percent of the electricity used is for central air conditioning. Moreover, air conditioning use can be modified to a large degree by the homeowner. In this particular case, a 1°F increase in thermostat setting would result in an approximately 12 percent savings in air conditioning consumption [13].

The subjects of this study were twenty-nine homeowners who lived in identical three bedroom townhouses. The homeowners were randomly assigned either to a feedback group or to a control group. Beginning in July 1975, the electric meters at each home in both groups were read by a research assistant each weekday afternoon for a month. A daily average temperature was computed from the hourly readings for each day (the twenty-four hour day began at 5:00 P.M. to coincide with the meter readings). For each house, a regression line was plotted to predict daily electric consumption from the daily average temperature. The squared multiple correlations of these regression lines ranged from 0.57 to 0.98. By inference, the electric meter reading was proportional to a reading that would have been taken from a meter on the air conditioning system plus a constant. For each house, then, it was possible to predict its future rate of energy usage based on outdoor temperature.

Beginning in August, the research assistant not only read the electric meters each weekday but also, from Tuesday through Friday for the houses in the feedback group, calculated the ratio of actual over predicted consumption. (Predicted consumption was based on inserting the temperature readings for the twenty-four hours immediately preceding into the regression equation for each house.) This ratio was displayed in a lucite device that was attached to the outside of the kitchen window in each home. The display was approximately twelve by eight centimeters (five inches by three inches), consisting of a holder and small plastic numbers that could be inserted to show the percentage consumption reading. If the homeowner's predicted performance was that he would use ten units of energy and he actually used eight units, then his display for that day would read "80 percent." Note that this means that an individual who received feedback attempted to improve his electricity consumption relative to a standard derived from his past consumption rather than a theoretical standard or one derived from other units.

The feedback ran for three weeks. The same day the feedback began, each household in the feedback group received a letter explaining the feedback procedure—that is, how predictions of their electricity consumption were made and what the numbers in the lucite device meant. The letter also focused the homeowners' attention on air conditioning; they were told that in the summer, the largest use of electricity was due to air conditioning. The control group was sent the same letter, except for the part dealing with the feedback procedure. Therefore, summarizing the similarities between conditions, all households, regardless of condition, had their electric meters read five days a week and were told that they were in an energy study, that air conditioning was the largest use of electricity, and that we hoped they would reduce their air conditioning usage. Thus, both demand characteristics to reduce electricity consumption and information received about how to do it were the same for both groups. The feedback group differed from the control group in that it received the daily information about its consumption and an explanation of how that information was presented.

The results are shown in Table 10−3. Before looking at the effects of the experimental treatment, it is necessary to test whether the groups differed prior to the treatment. The average daily consumption in the pretreatment period was computed. The feedback and control groups did not differ, $F(1, 27) = 0.04$. The mean daily consumption of the feedback group during the feedback period was 10.5 percent less than the control during the same period. This dif-

Table 10−3. **Mean Daily Electric Consumption (kWh): Study 1—Feedback**

	Condition	
	Feedback	*Control*
Sample size	15	14
Pretreatment	68.33	69.14
	(10.45)	(11.04)
During treatment	48.56	54.25
	(7.94)	(5.12)

Note: Standard deviations are given in parentheses.

ference between the feedback and control groups was statistically significant, $F(1, 21) = 4.81, p < 0.04$, in an analysis of variance that included the feedback factor, as well as subjects' pretest scores as a blocking factor.

The results have shown that providing homeowners with feedback information about their rate of energy consumption can be an effective strategy for conserving energy. Feedback is thought to be effective for two reasons. First, feedback cues individuals to the procedures that are most successful in achieving the task. Feedback given frequently to homeowners can show them which of their attempts to reduce energy was effective. Of course, in the present study homeowners were cued right from the beginning to focus on their air conditioning use. However, by attending to the feedback, homeowners may have found other ways to cool their homes, for example, by opening and closing drapes. Second, feedback serves to motivate a person to try harder or to persist longer at a task to reach a goal. If a person has a particular conservation goal and the feedback informs him that his performance falls short of that goal, there would typically be an attempt made to improve subsequent performance. If a person meets his conservation goal, only the amount of effort needed to maintain that level of achievement may be expended. The implication is that a difficult conservation goal should lead to greater effort being expended than an easy goal, with the possibility that more energy conservation would follow from increased effort.

Study 2

Our second feedback study [14] was conducted to test the hypothesis that feedback would lead to more energy conservation if individuals were asked to adopt a difficult conservation goal rather than an easy one. One hundred Twin Rivers families who lived in identical three bedroom townhouses were recruited to participate in the study. The households were randomly assigned to five groups. The households in two of the groups were asked to set an easy conservation goal and those in two other groups were asked to set a difficult conservation goal. Within each of these levels of goal difficulty, the households in one group were given feedback concerning their conservation performance, while those in the other group were not given feedback. The households in one group were asked simply to continue using electricity as they normally would; they constituted a control group.

The easy conservation goal was to reduce electric consumption 2 percent for the treatment period, and the difficult goal was to reduce it 20 percent. These figures were chosen on the basis of an examination of the conservation achieved by the subjects in the previous study. Reduction in consumption was measured against the predicted consumption for each household on the basis of its consumption during the first half of the summer. Predicted consumption contained an adjustment for weather differences between the earlier period and the treatment period. The adjustment was accomplished in the following way: The median difference in average daily consumption between the earlier period and the treatment period to date was computed for the control group and was then subtracted from the average daily consumption during treatment for each subject in the feedback groups before feedback was computed. Feedback was given in terms of the percent of electricity conserved or wasted by a household from the beginning of the treatment period to the day the feedback was given. It was computed by subtracting actual from predicted consumption and dividing the difference by predicted consumption.

Every Monday, Wednesday, and Friday morning during August 1976, all households had their electric meters read. Each time after all meters were read, feedback was calculated and plotted on a fifteen by twenty-three centimeters (six inches by nine inches) graph attached to the kitchen windows of the homes in the two feedback groups. To control for the effects of the experimenters' attention, the homes in the other three groups also had charts attached to their kitchen windows that were marked each meter-reading day. These charts were the same size as the graphs on the feedback homes, but simply allowed for a mark to be made that indicated that the meter had been read on that day.

The results are given in Table 10-4. There are no significant difference among the groups in mean daily consumption during the pretreatment period, $F(4, 95) < 1$. During the treatment period, the only experimental group with significantly lower electric consumption than the control group was the difficult goal with feedback group, $F(1, 94) = 9.22, p < 0.005$. This group used 13.0 percent less electricity than the control group. In addition, the two groups that received feedback saved significantly more energy than the two (noncontrol) no feedback groups, $F(1, 94) = 8.35, p < 0.005$.

These results show that feedback is especially effective if the homeowners are motivated to save a considerable amount of energy. Homeowners who received feedback but who were only trying to save a little energy did not conserve more than a control group that was not given feedback nor asked to save energy.

The results also showed that three of the experimental groups did not conserve significantly more energy than the control, despite the

Table 10–4. Mean Daily Electric Consumption (kWh): Study 2 – Feedback and Goal Setting

		Condition			
	Difficult Goal Feedback	Easy Goal Feedback	Difficult Goal No Feedback	Easy Goal No Feedback	Control
Sample size	20	20	20	20	20
Pretreatment	38.68 (14.21)	36.82 (8.03)	39.02 (10.86)	39.37 (11.19)	36.85 (14.23)
During treatment*	34.70 (8.31)	38.03 (3.62)	39.35 (4.05)	40.34 (5.14)	39.87 (4.33)

Note: Standard deviations are given in parentheses.
*Adjusted for pretreatment differences by analysis of covariance.

considerably greater amount of attention paid to them—they were asked to adopt a conservation goal, in one group feedback was also given, all had charts on the patio window that were marked several times a week, and all knew they were in an energy conservation study and that their energy usage was being monitored. Therefore, it is not likely that the energy conservation effect of feedback plus goal setting can be explained away by the Hawthorne effect, which argues that performance improvements can sometimes be the result simply of increased attention paid to subjects.

The magnitudes of the percent reductions in average daily consumption between each of the two feedback groups and the control group can be compared to the percent reduction achieved in the feedback group in the previous study. The latter figure, 10.5 percent, falls between the percent reduction for the easy goal with feedback group (4.6 percent) and the percent reduction for the difficult goal with feedback group (13.0 percent). Although there were differences between the two experiments in how feedback was computed and reported to the subjects, the percent reduction figures can be taken as a rough indication that, on the average, the subjects in the first feedback study (who were asked simply to do the best they could with respect to reducing their consumption) adopted (either consciously or unconsciously) a consumption reduction goal that was somewhere between 2 and 20 percent.

Study 3

Feedback is a way of providing information to homeowners that informs them whether they are consuming too much energy. Presumably, homeowners whose feedback indicates wasteful consumption take corrective actions to reduce their energy usage. Feedback is thus a signal that some energy control action is required. For our feedback studies, we have explicitly told our subjects that their best energy-saving action is thermostat control. Thus waste-indicating feedback means, to our homeowners, that they should modify the thermostat setting to reduce consumption. But there are also other ways to highlight the importance of thermostat control and to indicate when it should be exercised.

In the third study [15], we wanted to look at the effects of a device that signaled homeowners when the outside temperature was below 68°F and their air conditioner was still running. Homeowners were informed that when the outside temperature was below 68°F, air conditioning was no longer necessary, and the house could be cooled effectively just with the windows open.

The device used a blue light that was displayed in the homeowner's kitchen. The blue light was connected both to the air conditioner and to a thermostat situated on the outside wall of the house. The blue light would blink repeatedly when the air conditioner was on and when the outside temperature was below 68°F. The only way the homeowner could stop the blue light from blinking was to shut off the air conditioner. When the outside temperature was 68°F or higher, the blue light was off regardless of whether the air conditioner was on or off.

Forty residents were randomly assigned to one of four conditions: blue light plus feedback, feedback only, blue light only, and a control (no feedback and no blue light). The feedback was given three times a week in a manner similar, except for the computation of feedback, to that described in the previous study. In the present study, consumption per degree hour was computed for each house before the study began, and predicted consumption was based only on the consumption per degree hour index. In addition, feedback was given only for the period between the last feedback point and the current one. It was not based on all the days since the study began, as was the case in the preceding experiment. The experiment lasted from mid-August to mid-September.

There were no significant differences among the groups before the treatments began, $F(3, 36) < 1$. During the treatment period, only those days in which the outside temperature dropped below 68°F were included in the analysis, since the blue light was operative only then. The results are shown in Table 10-5. Homeowners who had the blue light device used 15.7 percent less electricity than the homeowners who did not, $F(1, 35) = 4.64, p < 0.04$. Thus, the blue light device proved effective in alerting the homeowners to a savings opportunity, and they took it.

In view of the previous studies in which consumption feedback had an effect, the failure of the feedback manipulation in the present study requires explanation. From interviews with the subjects after the experiment was over, it was revealed that most residents did not believe the feedback. The credibility of the feedback was not an issue in the previous two successful feedback studies. Apparently, in this study, the feedback scores jumped around too much to be believeable. Residents repeatedly saw no relationship between their conservation actions and the feedback scores. As a result, the feedback was ignored. The main differences between the feedback given in the different experiments were in the methods of computation and display. In the two previous experiments, feedback was based on either a regression model or a control group correction. In this study, consumption per degree hour was the basis. In the first study, feedback

Table 10–5. Mean Daily Electric Consumption (kWh) Study 3—Feedback and Blue Light Signaling Device

	Blue Light Feedback	Feedback Alone	Blue Light Alone	Control
Sample size	10	10	10	10
During treatment*	18.30 (2.96)	20.61 (5.69)	18.24 (4.50)	22.76 (6.02)

Note: Standard deviations are given in parentheses.
*Adjusted for pretreatment differences by analysis of covariance.

was not displayed over time, only for each feedback period. Thus, swings in feedback over time were less salient. In the second experiment, feedback was displayed over time on a chart, but each feedback score was based on the whole period since the experiment began. The feedback, being averaged over longer times, was actually smoother than it would have been if individual feedback periods were used. Thus it appears that in the third experiment, both the method of computation and the way it was displayed served to exaggerate the swings in the feedback, making it less credible. This result, of course, underscores the importance of providing feedback that is credible.

CONCLUDING COMMENTS

As the last study reminds us, our research on consumption feedback is hardly finished. But we are encouraged to continue. It appears that frequent, credible energy consumption feedback coupled with encouragement to adopt a reasonable but difficult energy conservation goal can be an effective conservation strategy for homeowners. One of the most urgent questions that arises concerning consumption feedback is its effectiveness over time. For practical application of the feedback technique, its efficacy over long periods of time would need to be demonstrated. Our studies looked only at periods of about one month. Practical consideration would also require that the development, building, and installation of feedback devices be cost-effective. Finally, future research should address the issue of the best kind of feedback to display to the homeowner. In our studies, we have concentrated on feedback that compared an individual's rate of energy use to his rate at an earlier time. Would feedback that promoted comparisons with other people be more effective?

State-sensing information systems, such as the blue light signaling device that we designed, also seem promising sources of energy consumption savings. More than general consumption feedback, these systems focus people's attention on specific conservation actions and do so exactly when these actions are appropriate. Indeed, it is not hard to envision an energy control panel, perhaps situated somewhere in the kitchen, that provides homeowners with detailed information about the house's energy performance and also indicates which energy-conserving actions are appropriate to take at different times.

Sinden (see Chapter 2) has suggested a variety of techniques and devices for promoting energy conservation in the home. Some of these retrofits, once done, are continually effective, for example, attic insulation. Here the psychological analysis is directed at convincing people to make the one time decision to initiate the retrofit. Others, for example, close-fitted window shades to be drawn at night, require the individual to act habitually on a frequent basis to achieve the conservation benefits. Here a different sort of psychological thinking is required. First, are there groups of individuals who are likely to be able to develop the habitual action patterns necessary for these innovations? Second, are there psychological elements that can be included in the design of these "action-requiring" conservation innovations that induce all people to use them successfully? Here, too, feedback has a role to play; it can demonstrate to the homeowner that his actions to reduce energy consumption do in fact succeed. Again, one needs to recall that it is enormously difficult for the homeowner to recover this information from his utility bills. For instance, if the effectiveness of a thermal conservation device is under test, then some sort of temperature-corrected feedback is absolutely essential. Therefore, one use of energy consumption feedback is a temporary one demonstrating to the innovator that the energy-conserving innovation is successful. This demonstration, occurring at the beginning of the innovation period, would be important in motivating the innovator to develop the set of habits necessary to use the innovation.

One final point. When social scientists, engineers, and physical scientists discuss energy conservation, the discussion all too frequently turns to the potential energy savings that each discipline can "produce." It seems to us that this is an unprofitable form in which to cast what could otherwise be an important discussion. Research leads us to suspect that over 50 percent of the energy used in residential space thermal regulation could be saved by a variety of retrofits [16] (see also Chapter 2). Exactly which retrofits make sense for any particular structure must be determined by physical scientists and engineers. Economists can define economic incentive structures so that these modifications are economically feasible for the homeowner. Above and beyond general questions of economic feasibility, homeowners will need to be convinced that they will be able to get a trustworthy, reliable, and effective installation of an energy-conserving innovation, a task for the psychological researcher. And the innovations will need to be designed to enable the homeowner to use them effectively, a task for the human factors specialist. As a matter of public policy, legislation may be passed mandating the construction of new energy-efficient residential units; political scientists and others will need to work with physical scientists and engineers on the specification of such standards. Accomplishing these goals with any degree of success requires the efforts of all of these disciplines and requires these efforts to go forward in interdependent and closely coordinated fashion. The research reported in this article and other articles in this issue has indicated the importance that must be attached to the homeowner in conservation efforts.

REFERENCES

1. Woteki, T. 1977. The Princeton omnibus experiment; some effects of retrofits on space heating requirements. CES Report No. 43. Princeton, N.J.: Princeton University.

2. Lopreato, S.C., and Meriwether, M.W. 1976. Annotated bibliography of energy attitude surveys. Center for Energy Studies, University of Texas at Austin.

3. Murray, J.R.; Minor, M.J.; Bradburn, N.M.; Cotterman, R.F.; Frankel, M.; and Pisarski, A.E. 1974. Evolution of public response to the energy crisis. *Science* 184: 257–63.

4. Curtin, R. 1976. Consumer adaptation to energy shortages. *Journal of Energy and Development* 1.

5. Newman, D.K., and Day, D. 1975. *The American Energy Consumer.* Cambridge, Mass.: Ballinger.

6. Seligman, C.; Kriss, M.; Darley, J.M.; Fazio, R.H.; Becker, L.J.; and Pryor, J.B. Predicting residential energy consumption from homeowners' attitudes. *Journal of Applied Social Psychology* (in press).

7. Harman, H. 1967. *Modern factor analysis.* 2nd ed. Chicago: University of Chicago Press.

8. McCormick, E.J. 1976. *Human Engineering* 2nd ed. New York: McGraw-Hill.

9. Ammons, R.B. 1956. Effects of knowledge of performance: a study and tentative theoretical formulation. *Journal of General Psychology* 54: 279–99.

10. Bilodeau, E.A., and Bilodeau, I. McD. 1961. Motor-skills learning. *Annual Review of Psychology* 12: 243–80.

11. Locke, E.A.; Cartlege, N.; and Koeppel, J. 1968. Motivational effects of knowledge of results: a goal-setting phenomenon? *Psychological Bulletin* 70: 464–85.

12. Seligman, C., and Darley, J.M. 1977. Feedback as a means of decreasing residential energy consumption. *Journal of Applied Psychology* 67: 363–68.

13. Socolow, R., and Sonderegger, R. 1976. The Twin Rivers program on energy conservation in housing: four year summary report. CES Report No. 32. Princeton N.J.: Princeton University.

14. Becker, L.J. 1977. The joint effect of feedback and goal setting on performance: a field study of residential energy conservation. *Journal of Applied Psychology* (in press).

15. Becker, L.J., and Seligman, C. 1977. Reducing air conditioning waste by signaling it is cool outside. *Personality and Social Psychology Bulletin* (in press).
16. Ross, M.H., and Williams, R.H. 1976. Energy efficiency: our most under-rated energy resource. *The Bulletin of the Atomic Scientists*, November, pp. 30–38.

Chapter 11

Energy Conservation Techniques as Innovations and Their Diffusion*

John M. Darley
*Center for Environmental Studies
and Department of Psychology
Princeton University*

Abstract

Many effective products, procedures, and techniques for achieving energy conservation have been discovered by researchers. This chapter focuses on the conditions under which these procedures and techniques will be adopted voluntarily. It is suggested, first, that an economic incentive for the utilization of those energy-conserving techniques is not a sufficient condition for their adoption, and second, that a psychologically based theory of the diffusion of innovation will identify the critical variables for promoting the adoption of energy-conserving products and techniques. Based on preliminary, small-scale observations of homeowners' reactions to a complex, time-controlled thermostat, the initial parameters of a diffusion theory for energy innovation are suggested.

BACKGROUND

The federal government's approach to the problem of energy resources can be characterized at the moment as heavily physical sciences oriented. Relatively little interest, place, or priority has been

*This chapter is based on an informal paper given at a symposium entitled Psychological Perspectives on Encouraging Energy Conservation, organized by Clive Seligman and presented at the American Psychological Meetings held in San Francisco, August 26–30, 1977. The author gratefully acknowledges the advice and assistance of Larry Becker, Clive Seligman, and Toby Kriss. This research was made possible by the resources of the Center for Environmental Studies of Princeton University.

accorded to social science approaches, a point about which many social scientists have complained—and rightly, for we have a great deal to say.

Some of what social scientists have to say has a negative import. From what we know about attitude change, we can estimate to what extent campaigns indiscriminately addressed to changing the energy usage attitudes of Americans are likely to be effective. The answer is likely to be, "not very." These campaigns, for example, are not likely to be more effective than other "persuasive" campaigns organized for public health reasons, such as antismoking campaigns. In other directions we can be more positive. For instance, in our own research, we have shown the utility of providing individuals with meaningful feedback on their energy conservation attempts. We are learning to design devices that give homeowners useful feedback about their energy consumption that enables them to reduce it [1]. Also, as McClelland and Cook have pointed out, we know techniques for aggregating individuals into groups in ways that may cause individuals to reduce their energy consumption even when their consumption is not individually monitored [2].

There is another critical point of application of psychological theory to energy conservation. Suppose that tomorrow engineers were to produce a reliably functioning "energy reducer." Would this theoretically wonderful device get into the hands of a significant percentage of homeowners? Only after the application of a considerable amount of psychological expertise.

The fact that a device, a procedure, or a technique is demonstrably effective in ideal settings does not guarantee its adoption by real people in the real world. We know this is true in general. Contemplate the toothbrush, a device of known efficacy in reducing dental cavities. Good studies concerning the actual patterns of its use among various populations reveal that it has by no means gained universal acceptance. Indeed, its utilization is startlingly infrequent. We know that this is also true in the field of energy conservation devices. For some years now, a device has been commercially available that would provide a night setback on the thermostat, thus reducing the amount of energy used to heat the house. It is possible to estimate rather precisely how quickly this sort of device will pay for itself, and it will pay for itself quite quickly. However, companies manufacturing these thermostats are rather depressed about their market prospects. Their market penetration, compared to theoretical estimates of their potential market, is very small.

The problem here is one of the diffusion of innovation. The excellence of an innovation or its cost-effectiveness in an ideal setting does not guarantee its successful diffusion. This is not always appreciated in national policies directed to the dissemination of energy conservation methods. Innovations are developed, then economic incentives are manipulated to bring about the adoption of these innovations. As is apparent from the night setback thermostat example, the actual diffusion of innovation process requires more complex theoretical analysis than this.

In our research in Twin Rivers, we have had considerable contact with real homeowners attempting to decide how they might conserve energy in their own homes. Further, theoretical perspectives from various fields of psychology are available that provide elements for a theory of the diffusion of energy innovation. Drawing very impressionistically on both those sources, we can add a few notes toward what will eventually become a more general theory.

The origins of the theory of the diffusion of innovation are found in rural sociology, represented, for example, by the work of Torsten Hägerstrand [3]. The innovations in question included contour plowing and new strains of wheat. In this context, remarkably few variables were needed to account for diffusion patterns. Basically, the critical determinant of the adoption of an innovation was information about it, and this information was observed to diffuse in a spatial pattern, spreading from farm to neighboring farm. Under the leadership, especially, of Everett M. Rogers [4], other innovations were considered, and the theory became both more complex and more psychological. Studies continue [5].

AN EXPERIENCE IN THE FIELD

Let us consider an innovation such as adding an insulation package to an attic, wrapping insulation around a water heater, or purchasing and installing a clock-controlled night setback thermostat. What is likely to bring this about? In order that we consider this in a specific context, consider an innovation we rather absentmindedly constructed, and some very preliminary evidence that we have about its diffusion.

The innovation in question is a three stage thermostat [6]. The "psychostat" is a clock-driven thermostat for the home that has three key characteristics.

1. It is clock driven and selects its various temperature settings automatically, after they have been programmed in by the homeowner.
2. It has the capability for a night setback and also for a day setback. This latter setback capitalizes on the fact that a good many

homes are empty for significant periods of the day (e.g., homes of single persons, dual career couples without children, and dual career couples with children at school). This day setback roughly doubles the savings achievable by a night shutdown thermostat. Imagine, for example, a winter day. The homeowner might set the thermostat to a normal comfortable temperature from 7:00 to 9:00 in the morning, perhaps 68°F. At 9:00, when the home is empty, the temperature setting is 55°F and remains there until the children return home at 3:00 P.M. At that time, it reverts to the comfortable normal temperature of 68°F until a 10:00 P.M. bedtime, when it sets to 62°F.

3. The third feature, and one that is critical to its acceptance (and one that stems from psychological wisdom) is the override feature. The homeowner can at any time override the time-selected setting and cause the thermostat to deliver the normal comfortable setting. If, for instance, a child is home sick during the day, the child need not be in a 55°F house. However, the override feature is itself time controlled, and the psychostat returns to its normal cycle after a number of hours. And when it operates in its normal mode, it is maximally energy conserving. An effort is required of the homeowner to deviate from this conserving mode, and the deviation will be only a temporary one. Nonetheless, the homeowner perceives he has control of the device.

For the diffusion research, we targeted a subarea of three blocks at Twin Rivers, New Jersey. We mailed homeowners a letter announcing that we had some possible energy-saving innovations to try and asked them to contact us if they were interested in participating in the research. Those who contacted us were sent, in the traditional ungrateful fashion of researchers, a questionnaire. From those questionnaires we identified a few households in which to try this particular innovation. During the winter of 1976–1977, we installed psychostats in their houses; measured the savings and, more importantly, the homeowners' reactions; and collected some preliminary information on the diffusion of this innovation.

In energy conservation terms, the innovation was wildly successful. We had expected that it would save the users about 10 percent of their heating energy use; instead it saved between 18 and 47 percent. This figure we found sufficiently unbelievable so that we calculated it several ways and checked and rechecked it. It is accurate. Our field notes indicate that the saving has two sources: first, and obviously, the setbacks themselves; and second, a feature we had included in our agenda for discussion with the homeowners. As will be remembered, people are being asked to maintain their houses at reduced temperature settings. Building on this, we simply "negotiated" with people lower values for the normal setting of the thermostat at the time we installed it in their homes. If the setting proved too cold, they could then adjust it. Perhaps because they perceived that they had this control, most of the homeowners tolerated the lower settings, which contributed considerably to the higher than expected savings achieved.

THE BEGINNINGS OF AN ENERGY DIFFUSION THEORY

With the impressions formed from this experience, plus other project experiences, plus general psychological knowledge, we can begin to indicate the elements of a theory of the diffusion of energy conservation innovations in residential settings.

Principle One: Only a subset of the target population initially will feel the need for any particular innovation.

Many people in Twin Rivers reported a feeling that energy bills were too high and that this was the cause for the desire to innovate. But many other people, who are making approximately the same income, do not feel "pinched" by their fuel bills. We conclude that "energy costs" are a psychological rather than an economic press. In our test community, some people have no idea of the size of their fuel bills, others know them and find them acceptable, and the people who are interested in innovation are aware of them and find them too high. None of this shows any particular correlations with income.

Rather surprisingly, two innovations that are similar in their conservation effects cause different subsets of the population to be interested in them. Some people perceive a close correlation between ambient temperature levels and comfort and health, so, for instance, to be "warm" is to be comfortable, while to be "cold" is to be risking "a cold." These people tend not to be interested in the clock-driven thermostat because it lowers house temperatures. But they are very interested in increasing the effective insulation in their house, because this will eventually save money without requiring them to lower temperatures. The people willing to contemplate the thermostat, however, were willing to tolerate lower temperatures.

Principle Two: Not only is it necessary to feel a negative state, it is necessary to feel that, in general, it is possible to change the negative state.

This principle arises both from our previous attitudinal research [7] (see also Chapter 10) and from general psychological theory. One factor that emerged from our analysis was a "high effort, low payoff" factor. People high on this factor seemed to believe that there was little they could do to achieve significant energy savings in the home. (Here, rather than in other directions seems a useful focus for a national attitudinal campaign.) This factor, specifically discovered in the energy area, is likely to be the projection of a very general psychological construct that has been focused in many other areas of human action and that can be generally characterized as feeling a lack of internal control over events and outcomes.

Principle Three: To "complete the circuit," a person must believe that a specific, durable, usable innovation is available that will actually make a significant dent in his problem.

Here psychologists know a great deal, although what we know we haven't always categorized as "diffusion of innovation." Instead we call it "attitude change" or the "acceptance of persuasive communications." From this large body of research we take two conclusions: first, that we are more persuaded by an individual who does not stand to gain if he persuades us; and second, that persuasion seems to be most effective when it is between individuals rather than when it is between an individual and an audience.

What this means is that we are most convinced of the efficacy of an energy conservation innovation when we see an acquaintance making the innovation and having it work for him. Our thermostat study confirms this. Each innovator has identified at least five other homeowners who are interested in being involved in future research. (Obviously, here we need to face a limitation of the research. Initially we were "giving it away for free," as it were; our thermostats didn't cost anything, because we wanted to take them back. By a series of not entirely satisfactory questions, we attempted to probe the willingness of these second stage targets to pay for the innovation and found that their interest remained high. More needs to be done here, however.)

Classic theory, as we have said, looked for the diffusion of innovation to occur spatially. Greatly influenced by this, we looked forward to presenting a map of our three block target area, showing the diffusion of the psychostat through the neighborhood. Unfortunately, the map would be blank. None of the second stage targets came from the neighborhood. However, there is a conclusion to be extracted from our disappointment: diffusion proceeds along sociometric rather than spatial networks. The second stage innovators were friends, colleagues, or office coworkers of the initial innovators, not neighbors. Again, this is in agreement with later theories of innovation diffusion. The innovation diffused sociometrically from the initial innovation, not spatially, and diffused only to that subset of the innovator's acquaintances who felt a need that was satisfied by the innovation.

Principle Four: If an individual adopts an innovation, certain conditions are necessary for him to regard it as successful.

First, the individual must believe that the innovation worked effectively for him and did not cause him unanticipated problems. That an innovation works is not always immediately obvious. Our thermostats may have worked, but if we installed them in a cold December following a warm November, the fuel bills wouldn't confirm this. We took complex readings to be able to calculate fuel savings on a degree day basis. This proved extremely important in convincing people of the innovation's effectiveness. In general, it is worth considering carefully how innovations might be made to show their effectiveness.

One of our families simply had a bad time with the thermostat. It didn't seem accurate to them (it was, we checked it). It annoyed them, although they gave it a fair chance. It saved them over 20 percent of their fuel bill, but this didn't overcome the unanticipated difficulties. They were not a source of second stage innovators. It is worth considering whether they might not be a source of "second stage resistance." In general, innovation theory suggests that a person who feels that an innovation that he made was unsuccessful will be a significant deterrent to other people's adopting the innovation.

More positively, a successful innovation will create increased willingness on the part of the innovator to consider other innovations to which he was initially resistant. Success in innovation increases one's feelings of control. And, in addition, in ways that need to be conceptualized carefully, success of one innovation leads to heightened trust in the source of that innovation. Our homeowners who tried the thermostat now do some "do it yourself" insulating, with our guidance. They are eager to buy the thermostat if it becomes commercially available.

We are joining the optimists in this business, who postulate that without a great deal of increased discomfort or cost to the owner, it is technically possible to reduce the heating energy consumption of an average house at least 50 percent (see Chapter 2). Can this be done on a national basis, effectively, without compulsion, and without creating massive exploitation and disillusionment of the homeowner? Social and physical scientists can design techniques so that it can. Whether they will be called on to do so remains to be seen.

REFERENCES

1. Seligman, C., and Darley, J.M. 1977. Feedback as a means of decreasing residential energy consumption. *Journal of Applied Psychology* 62: 363–68.
2. McClelland, L. 1977. Encouraging energy conservation as a social psychological problem. Institute of Behavioral Science, University of Colorado. Talk presented at the symposium, "Psychological Perspectives on Encouraging Energy Conservation," American Psychological Association, August.
3. Hägerstrand, T. 1967. *Innovation Diffusion as a Spatial Process*, Allan Prad, trans. Chicago: University of Chicago Press.
4. Rogers, E.M. 1962. *Diffusion of Innovations.* New York: Free Press.
5. Saint, W.S., and Coward, E.W. 1977. Agriculture and behavioral science: Emerging orientations. *Science* 187: 733–37.
6. Mertz, H. and Darley, J.M. 1976. Versatile thermostat for the Twin Rivers project to encourage energy conservation. Princeton University, Center for Environmental Studies, Working Paper No. 29.
7. Seligman, C.; Kriss, M.; Darley, J.M.; Fazio, R.H.; Becker, L.J.; and Pryor, J.B. Predicting residential energy consumption from homeowners' attitudes. *Journal of Applied Social Psychology* (in press).

Appendixes

Appendix A

Facts About Twin Rivers

THE PRICE OF ENERGY

Energy at Twin Rivers is supplied in two forms: natural gas and electricity. In the townhouses analyzed in most of this book (the Quad II townhouses), gas is used exclusively for space heating (and, rarely, for an outdoor barbecue), while electricity powers all appliances and the air conditioner. The structure of the price of both fuels, as seen by the resident, is essentially the same: The bill is calculated monthly, and the price of a unit of energy decreases in steps (or "blocks") as the quantity consumed increases.

The price schedules for natural gas and electricity that governed the billing in December 1975 are shown in Figures A-1 and A-2. The shaded areas at the bottom of Figures A-1 and A-2 represent the energy adjustment charge, and the unshaded areas above reflect the rate schedule negotiated between the gas or electric utility and New Jersey's Public Utility Commission. The energy adjustment varies each month, which allows the utility to pass on changes in the price it pays for fuel. The rate structure, recently, has been renegotiated more than once a year.

Also shown in Figures A-1 and A-2 is the mean and standard deviation of the level of consumption of gas and electricity in the townhouses in December.[1] Virtually the entire townhouse sample is seen to confront the same marginal price in winter, the price of the

1. Actually, December 1973 is used rather than December 1975, for which data are unavailable. A small conservation effect for gas is therefore absent. The data shown agree with those in Figure I-20.

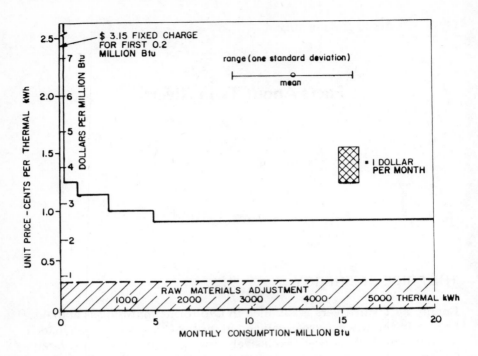

Figure A-1.   Gas Rate Schedule for Quad II Townhouses, December 1975.

outermost block. This is not the case for gas in summer, when consumption by the furnace pilot light (about 7 therms[2] or 0.7 million Btu per month, or 300 Watts) dominates the summer bills in Quad II, which lands one on the innermost step.

The history of the rate structure and fuel adjustment allowance, as seen by the Quad II resident from 1970 to 1976, is found in Tables A-1 and A-2. The rate structure for electricity has two complexities, not seen in the rate structure for natural gas, that deserve further discussion—a discount for the electric water heater and a penalty for the use of large amounts of electricity in the summer months (June through October).

The discount for the electric water heater in December 1975 took the following form: the price per kilowatt hour for monthly consumption of the 301st through the 800th kilowatt hour was discounted 1.11 cents, a total monthly discount of $5.55, or $66.60

2. One therm = 10^5 Btu is the unit in which the gas rate structure is expressed.

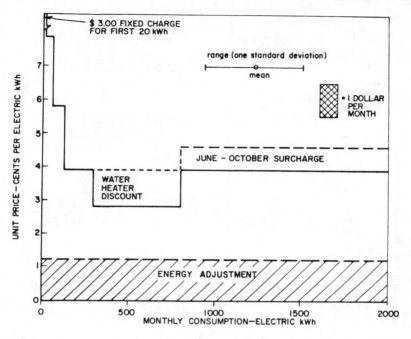

Figure A–2.   Electric Rate Schedule for Quad II Townhouses, December 1975.

each year. This discount, seen as a notch in Figure A–2, should be compared to the cost of 8,000 kilowatt hours of electricity, our estimate of the average annual consumption of electricity by the Quad II water heater. Roughly, this comes to $320 without the discount and $250 with the discount, so the discount amounts to about 20 percent. (One can calculate the cost of operating the water heater in various ways. The estimate of $320 per year is the product of 8,000 kWh per year and 4.0 cents per kWh, the latter factor being the sum of an energy adjustment charge that averaged 1.26 cents per kWh during the period from July 1, 1975, through June 30, 1976, and a base charge of 2.71 cents per kilowatt hour for monthly consumption above 130 kilowatt hours that applied throughout that period, except for the summer.)

The builder of Twin Rivers chose electric water heaters for Quads I and II but gas water heaters for Quads III and IV, the Quads being built about a year apart. The switch to gas in 1972 was motivated in part by changes in the rules of the Public Utility Commission governing the relationship between the electric utility and the builder. The switch to gas water heaters (discussed further later in this Appendix), under the prices paid in recent years for gas and electricity at Twin

Table A-1.   Rate Schedule for Gas 1970-1976. Public Service Electric and Gas, Residential Service.

	Date Effective								
	1/3/66	12/3/70	3/23/72	6/1/73	1/7/74	9/23/74	6/15/75	11/7/75	10/21/76
Fixed fee (first 2 therms)	$1.05	$1.08	$1.08	$1.14	$1.24	$1.30	$2.28	$3.15	$4.50
Unit price (¢/therm)									
Next 7 therm	21.40	21.90	22.50	23.72	25.83	27.00	25.89	27.83	27.23
Next 17 therm	18.50	18.90	19.50	20.53	22.38	23.38	22.45	24.19	27.23
Next 24 therm	14.50	14.80	15.50	16.34	17.78	18.57	17.78	19.52	27.23
Over 50 therm	11.40	11.66	12.80	13.50	14.69	15.35	14.69	16.43	27.23

Raw Materials Adjustment (¢/therm)

	1970	1971	1972	1973	1974	1975	1976
January	1.0200	1.4414	1.8190	1.9448	2.7608	4.9535	10.0785
February	1.0200	1.4414	1.3728	1.5787	1.8162	4.9535	10.0785
March	1.0200	1.4414	1.8190	1.9448	2.7685	4.9535	10.0785
April	1.0800	1.6817	1.7503	2.0020	3.4892	8.6578	6.6626
May	0.3000	1.6817	1.7503	2.0020	3.4892	8.6578	10.0785
June	1.0800	1.6817	1.7503	2.0020	3.4892	8.6578	10.0785
July	1.0800	1.3270	1.6474	2.0020	2.8714	7.5618	10.0785
August	1.0800	1.3270	1.6474	2.1850	2.8714	7.5618	10.0785
September	1.0800	1.3270	1.6474	2.1850	2.8714	7.5618	10.0785
October	1.0800	1.3270	3.3290	4.0498	6.1890	8.3039	9.4750
November	1.0800	1.3270	3.0202	4.0498	5.6170	8.3039	5.8540
December	2.2079	3.4206	3.3290	4.0498	6.1890	8.3039	5.8540

NB: 1 therm = 10^5 Btu = 29.3 thermal kWh = 105.5 MJ

Table A–2.   Rate Schedule for Electricity 1970–1976. Jersey Central Power and Light, Residential Service

	Date Effective										
	10/1/66	7/13/70	11/6/70	6/5/72	10/1/73	6/1/74		6/17/75		7/19/76	
Fixed fee (first 14 kWh)	$1.00	$1.06	$1.09	$1.15	$1.20	(first 20 kWh) $2.00		(first 20 kWh) $3.00		(no kWh) $5.38	
Unit price (¢/kWh)											
Next 46 kWh	5.60	5.98	6.13	6.50	6.70	Next 40	6.50	Next 40	6.70	First 300	3.30[b]
Next 70 kWh	3.50	3.72	3.83	4.06	4.18	Next 70	4.40	Next 70	4.60	First 300	4.00[c]
Next 20 kWh	2.00	2.13	2.19	2.32	2.40	Next 20	2.48	Next 170	2.71		
Next 500 kWh[a]	1.30	1.38	1.42	1.50	1.55	Next 500[a]	1.59	Next 500[a]	1.60	Next 500[a]	2.00
Next 650 kWh	2.00	2.13	2.19	2.32	2.40	Over 650	2.48	Over 800	2.71[b]	Over 800	3.30[b]
									3.41[c]		4.00[c]

Energy Adjustment (¢/kWh)

	1971	1972	1973	1974	1975	1976
January	0.0000	0.1189	0.1841	0.4486	0.8169	1.1649
February	0.0000	0.1254	0.1941	0.3873	0.8365	1.3000
March	0.0000	0.1299	0.1972	0.5055	0.7376	1.4258
April	0.0000	0.1314	0.1926	0.5443	0.6783	1.3987
May	0.0000	0.1417	0.2038	0.8257	0.7053	1.5421
June	0.0000	0.1351	0.2112	1.0217	0.9403	1.3051
July	0.0589	0.1789	0.2296	1.4926	1.2751	1.2393
August	0.0589	0.2026	0.2478	1.6002	1.3891	0.9095
September	0.0589	0.2314	0.2608	1.6591	1.2098	0.8311
October	0.0589	0.2232	0.3518	1.6242	0.9927	1.0489
November	0.0752	0.1913	0.3368	1.4742	0.9320	0.8192
December	0.0927	0.1933	0.4387	1.0261	1.2071	0.6465

[a] Special rate for customers with electric heaters.
[b] November–May.
[c] June–October.

Rivers, carried with it a substantial dollar savings for the resident. During the same twelve month interval, estimating the gas water heater consumption to be 36,000 cubic feet (1000 m^3) per year and the average price of gas at the last block in the rate structure (including energy adjustment) to be $2.46 per million Btu ($2.52 per thousand cubic feet or 8.9 cents per cubic meter or 0.84 cents per thermal kilowatt hour), the gas for the Quad II water heater would have cost $90.

Thus there was a difference of $160 dollars per year, in the 1975–1976 year, in the annual energy charges for the gas water heater ($90) versus the electric water heater ($250). This extra cost of annual operation is several times the dollar value per house of the arrangement between builder and electric utility that was discontinued in 1973.

In June of 1975, New Jersey's Public Utility Commission instituted a surcharge for use of energy during the summer (the months of June through October), which took the form of a 0.7 cent per kilowatt hour increase in the cost of all but the first 800 kWh of electricity consumed monthly in these five months. Estimating the air conditioner to use 2,500 kWh per year, and assigning all of these kilowatt hours to the outermost block in the summer rate structure, this represents a $17.50 per year surcharge on residential air conditioning.

THE LOCAL WEATHER [3]

Twin Rivers is located in central New Jersey at 40.3° north latitude and 74.5° east longitude. Although only twenty-six miles (forty-two kilometers) from the Atlantic Ocean, its climate is largely continental, mainly as a result of winds from the interior of North America. The temperature extremes lie at about 0°F (−18°C) (recorded about one winter in eight) and 100°F (38°C) (recorded about one summer in five). Summer relative humidity can be as high as 90 percent for a stretch of a few days, alternating with more comfortable periods.

Weather data have been gathered both from our own weather station on top of a bank at Twin Rivers and from the U.S. weather station located in downtown Trenton, N.J., fourteen miles west of Twin Rivers. Simultaneous observations from the two locations differ by an average of 1°F (0.6°C) in temperatures and by about one mile per hour (two kilometers per hour) in wind velocity. Figures A−3, A−4, A−5, and A−6 show Trenton data.

Figure A−3 displays the annual average temperature for the past forty years. The worldwide temperature peak during World War II is clearly visible. The heating trend since 1960 may be a consequence of Trenton gradually becoming a local heat island as urban energy use increases.

The monthly average temperatures and the monthly means of daily highs and lows, shown in Figure A−4, reflect data going back to 1893. Notice how the daily temperature excursions are larger in summer than in winter.

The heating degree days and cooling degree days in each calendar month are shown in Figure A−5, based on averages over twenty-one years and six years, respectively. A reference temperature of 65°F (18.3°C) is used for all calculations.[4]

Figure A−6 shows the variation over the year in the thirty year average of monthly average wind velocity, monthly sunniness, and monthly rainfall. The monthly average wind velocity goes through a smooth yearly cycle, peaking in March at 10.7 miles per hour (17.2 kilometers per hour) and receding to a minimum of 7.6 miles per

---

3. Adapted from data compiled by Robert Sonderegger.

4. The concept of heating degree days is discussed in detail in Chapters 2 and 8. Cooling degree days are accumulated in an analogous fashion; if the average of the daily high and the daily low exceeds 65° F by N° F, a day is said to have had N Fahrenheit cooling degree days. If N is negative, no cooling degree days are accumulated, but N heating degree days are accumulated. Thus, although no single day can have both heating and cooling degree days, a stretch of mild days can have some days with one and some days with the other—and thus a nonzero sum for both.

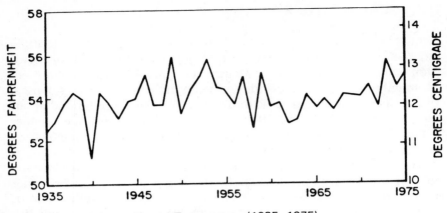

Figure A—3. Average Annual Temperature (1935—1975).

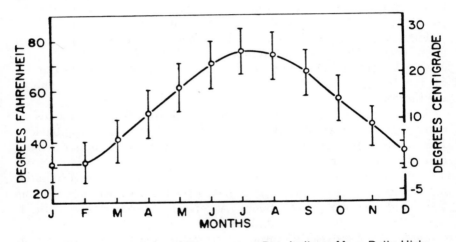

Figure A—4. Monthly Average Temperature. Bars Indicate Mean Daily Highs and Lows.

hour (12.2 kilometers per hour) in August. The fraction of the maximum possible sunshine peaks in July at 65 percent and drops to 48 percent in December, with a yearly average of 59 percent. The average rainfall is relatively constant at about 3.4 inches (90 millimeters) per month except for July and August, when it increases to 4.6 and 5.0 inches (120 and 130 millimeters) respectively.

Table A—3 permits the estimation of the total monthly solar flux on the surfaces of interest for Quad II townhouses at Twin Rivers. The estimate is obtained by first multiplying the direct radiation on the surface by the sunniness factor, and then adding either the full

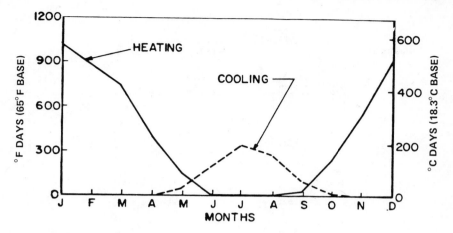

Figure A–5. Monthly Average Heating and Cooling Degree Days.

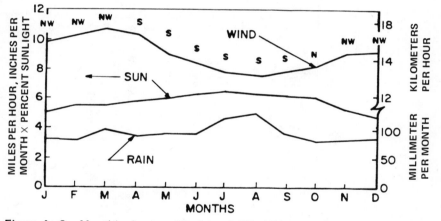

Figure A–6. Monthly Average Windspeed, Wind Direction, Sunlight (Percent of Possible), Precipitation.

diffuse radiation (for horizontal and roof surfaces) or half the diffuse radiation (for wall surfaces). Table A–3 considers nine cases: a horizontal surface; vertical walls oriented 10° east of north, 10° south of east, 10° west of south, and 10° north of west; and roofs with a slope of 5/12 (elevation of 22.6°), oriented in the horizontal plane exactly as the walls. Except for one block of Quad II townhouses (rotated 45° from the others), these nine cases cover all of the orientations relevant to the estimation of incident solar flux.

Table A–3. Solar Flux [Btu/day–ft^2] in Twin Rivers.

	Diffuse[a]	Direct[b]									Sunniness[c]
		Horizontal	"E"[b]	"S"	"W"	"N"	"RE"	"RS"	"RW"	"RN"	
January	120	776	599	1607	316	0	841	1334	642	133	.51
February	148	1133	766	1644	477	0	1181	1678	975	425	.55
March	200	1553	905	1417	657	4	1560	1977	1377	891	.55
April	282	1919	963	988	797	48	1867	2133	1740	1410	.58
May	367	2135	954	626	868	141	2033	2160	1962	1784	.60
June	424	2214	930	453	889	215	2088	2139	2047	1952	.63
July	423	2141	916	507	858	178	2026	2107	1975	1850	.65
August	363	1925	904	783	779	75	1852	2050	1753	1504	.63
September	272	1602	866	1185	658	11	1585	1930	1431	1028	.62
October	191	1224	772	1514	507	0	1256	1708	1064	558	.61
November	138	864	632	1589	352	0	923	1408	767	209	.53
December	117	680	544	1547	271	0	746	1222	555	76	.48
Average	254	1514	813	1155	619	56	1497	1821	1357	985	.59

[a]Diffuse radiation on a horizontal surface, about twice what strikes a vertical surface.

[b]"E": Solar flux striking a vertical wall oriented 10° south of east; "S": Solar flux striking a vertical wall oriented 10° west of south; etc. "RE": Solar flux impinging on a roof surface (inclined by 22.6°) facing 10° south of east.

[c]Monthly average fraction of the maximum possible sunshine for Central New Jersey (also plotted as Sun in Figure A-6).

NB: 1 Btu/day–ft^2 = 0.131 W/m^2.

CHRONOLOGY OF CONSTRUCTION
AND PATTERNS OF LAND USE

One of the initial tasks in our research program was to document the process that led to the building of Twin Rivers. Interviews were held with local officials, inspectors, installers of heating equipment, representatives of utilities, the developer's architects and staff, and some residents.[5] The chronology below was assembled from these interviews. Tables A−4 and A−5 present the pattern of land use and the housing density that emerged.

Chronology[6]

	1963	Gerald Finn, a local developer, engages the architectural firm of Whittlesey and Conklin to design a planned unit development (PUD) for East Windsor Township, New Jersey. The target is 3,000 residential units. The model is Reston, Virginia.
	1964	Whittlesey and Conklin submit a regional analysis and proposed land use sketches.
	1965−1968	Finn meets with town officials throughout this period to convince them of the desirability of a PUD. They visit Reston and attend discussions of PUDs by professionals. A model of Twin Rivers is displayed.
	1967	Finn acquires an additional 200 acres (81 hectares) in response to pressures from town for additional industrial acreage.
May	1967	Planned Unit Development Enabling Act passed by the state of New Jersey.
October	1967	Zoning Ordinance Amendment, Planned Unit Development, passed by East Windsor Township.
	1967	Herbert Kendall, of Kendall Development Corporation, Princeton, becomes a co-venturer. He assumes the mortgage on the land.
December	1967	Twin Rivers Holding Corporation established, with Kendall as president.

5. The subjects of these interviews are listed in Appendix C.

6. Adapted from Appendix II of H. Fraker, Jr., and E. Schorske, *Energy Husbandry in Housing: an Analysis of the Development Process in a Residential Community* (Princeton, N.J.: Princeton University, Center for Environmental Studies Report No. 5, 1973).

December (*continued*)	1967	Finn and Kendall negotiate financing with American Standard.
March	1968	Application made by Twin Rivers Holding Corporation for tentative approval by Township Planning Board, which holds the public hearings prescribed by the PUD ordinance.
May	1968	East Windsor Planning Board gives tentative approval to Quad I.
	1968	Sewer and water contract negotiated by developer with East Windsor Municipal Authority.
	1968	Whittlesey, Conklin and Rossant, architects (New York City), replaced by Robert J. Hillier, architect (Princeton, N.J.).
February	1969	American Standard acquires Windsor Properties (Finn's corporation, which had a 25 percent share in the development) and becomes financial backer and co-partner with Kendall Development Corporation.
March	1969	East Windsor Township issues construction permit for Quad I following local planning board approval.
April	1969	First model houses built.
October	1969	Veterans Administration approval of Quad I.
November	1969	Community Trust agreement signed with First Charter National Bank to manage resident payments for community services.
April	1970	State Department of Community Affairs approval of Quad I.
April	1970	First families move in.
June	1970	East Windsor Township issues construction permit for Quad II following partial approval by local planning board. Final approval delayed until commercial center and industrial buildings are more fully developed.
July	1970	Twin Rivers Holding Corporation becomes a wholly owned subsidiary of American Standard.
July	1970	Veterans Administration approval of Quad II.
December	1970	East Windsor Planning Board issues final approval of Quad II.
	1971	Developer exercises options to purchase forty-eight acres (nineteen hectares) for a town park and eighty acres (thirty-two hectares) for industry.
March	1971	State Department of Community Affairs approval of Quad II.

August	1971	East Windsor Planning Board approval of Quad III.
November	1971	Veterans Administration approval of Quad III.
March	1972	State Department of Community Affairs approval of Quad III.
September	1972	Community Trust acceptance of Quads I and II delayed until performance bond of $300,000 is posted by developer.
December	1972	Community Trust acceptance of Quad III.
March	1973	East Windsor Planning Board partial approval of Quad IV, permits issued for one-half of construction only.
March	1973	State Department of Community Affairs approval of Quad IV.
	1975	Completion of Quad IV.

Table A-4. Land Use at Twin Rivers (acres[a]).

	Quads					Total
	I	II	III	IV		
Residential	44.7	77.0	63.0	67.1		251.8
Commercial	26.6	5.4	11.8	1.3		45.1
Open Space	32.9	35.8			100[c]	168.7
Dedicated Right of Way	8.2	4.5			12[c]	24.7
Private Institutional					1[c]	2
Industrial	1[b]					208
	208[b]					
Total	444.1[b]			207.9[c]		700.3

[a]NB: 1 hectare = 2.47 acres.
[b]Quads I and II combined.
[c]Quads III and IV combined.

Table A—5.   Distribution of Housing.

	Quad				Total Dwelling Units	Average Dwellings per Acre (per hectare)
	I	II	III	IV		
Low density						
Single family houses	—	83	30	26	139	
Dwellings per acre (per hectare)	—	4.1 (10.1)	4.1 (10.1)	4.1 (10.1)		4.1 (10.1)
Medium density						
Townhouses	264	401[a]	450	511	1,626	
Garden apartments	323	144	240	192	899	
Total	587	545	690	703	2,525	
Dwellings per acre (per hectare)	13.2 (32.6)	12.4 (30.6)	12.4 (30.6)	11.5 (28.4)		12.4 (30.6)
Town Center Apartments	—	43	—	—	43	
Total residential units	587	671[b]	720	729	2,707[b]	

[a] 248 two floor and 153 split level townhouses.

[b] There are thirteen additional acres (5.1 hectares) in Quad II that were originally zoned for 234 dwelling units in two high rise apartment buildings. The acres were rezoned for 82 townhouses in 1977, but no construction has begun as of January 1978.

THERMAL CHARACTERISTICS OF BUILDING MATERIALS, COMPOSITE WALL SECTIONS, AND THE OVERALL TOWNHOUSE[7]

Thermal Characteristics of the Buildings Materials

Table A—6 shows some physical properties of the building materials used in the construction of the Twin Rivers townhouses. Listed are the density, ρ [kg/m^3], the heat capacity per unit mass, c [Wh/ (kg°C)], the conductivity k [W/(m°C)], the material thickness, d, in the direction of heat transfer [m], the resulting conductance U = k/d [W/(°Cm^2)], and capacitance (capacity per unit surface) C_s = ρcd [Wh/(°Cm^2)].

Thermal Characteristics of Composite Wall Sections

Using the conductance, U, and the capacitance, C_s, of each layer listed in Table A—6, the U-value and the overall capacitance of all composite wall sections are calculated in Table A—7. The R-values shown in Table A—7 are the reciprocals of the U-values shown in Table A—6. Because the components of a composite wall section are thermal resistances in series, the R-value of the composite is the sum of the R-values of the components.

The heat conductance through studs and trusses is added to the conductance of the medium surrounding them (air spaces, insulation batts, etc.) after weighting by the respective areas. Where studs and trusses protrude significantly into open spaces (attic, basement), acting like fins, their conductance [W/(°Cm^2)] perpendicular to the wall surface is doubled, to account for the conductive heat losses through the sides of the trusses.

If a wall extends below grade, as the basement walls do, its U-value will decrease with depth below grade. An approximation[8] to the dependence of U-value on depth follows from solving the two dimensional heat conduction equation (appropriate for an infinitely long wall):

$$U(y) = (R_w + \frac{\pi}{2} \cdot r_E \cdot y)^{-1} \tag{A.1}$$

7. Drawn from Appendix v. of Robert C. Sonderegger, "Dynamic Models of House Heating Based on Equivalent Thermal Parameters" (Ph.D. thesis, Department of Aerospace and Mechanical Sciences, Princeton University, 1977).

8. See F. Sinden, *Conductive losses from basements* (Princeton, N.J.: Princeton University, Center for Environmental Studies, Twin Rivers Note No. 4, 1976).

where U is the equivalent U-value between basement air and outdoor air $[W/(°Cm^2)]$;

R_w is the composite resistance of the below grade basement wall or floor, excluding the surrounding earth $[°Cm^2/W]$;

r_E is the resistivity of the earth $[°Cm/W]$;

y   is the depth below grade $[m]$.

The resistivity of earth varies between $r_E = 1.16 \text{ m}°C/W$ (dry soil with stones) and $r_E = 1.91 \text{ m}°C/W$ (wet earth). An average resistivity of $\bar{r}_E = 1.53 \text{ m}°C/W$ was used with an average depth, $\bar{y}$, in the computation of the equivalent below grade U-values in Table A−7.

Table A–6. Physical Properties of Building Materials.

Item	ρ [kg/m³]	c [Wh/(kg °C)]	k [W/(°Cm)]	d [m]	U [W/°Cm²]	C_s [Wh/(°Cm²)]
Plywood	550	0.337	0.115	0.013	9.08	2.3
Wood Siding, lapped	510	0.361	0.088	0.013	6.98	2.3
Studs and Joists[a]	510	0.384	0.118	0.092	1.28	18.1
" "	510	0.384	0.118	0.143	0.823	28.1
" "	510	0.384	0.118	0.194	0.608	38.1
Gypsum Board	801	0.302	0.162	0.013	12.8	3.1
Building Paper	—	—	—	—	94.8	—
Asphalt Shingles	1,120	0.260[b]	0.160[c]	0.013[c]	12.9	3.6[c]
Cinder Blocks	890	0.186	0.670	0.203	3.30	33.7
Brick	1,900	0.230	0.722	0.203	3.58	90.9
Concrete	2,300	0.186	0.935	0.102	9.20	43.6
Stone Fill	1,520	0.230	1.800	0.102	17.7	35.9
Linoleum Tile	800[c]	0.350	1.440[c]	0.013[c]	114.0	3.6[c]
Rug (with fibrous pad)	800	0.558	0.035	0.013	2.73	5.7[c]
Window Glass	—	—	1.021	0.003	321.0	—
Insulation, Batt R–7	14	0.210	0.047	0.057	0.812	0.2
" " R–11	14	0.210	0.047	0.089	0.517	0.3
" " R–19	14	0.210	0.047	0.156	0.301	0.5
Earth (dry, stony)	1,920	0.230	0.870	—	—	—
Earth (wet)	1,920	0.230	0.520	—	—	—
Film coefficients						
indoor, vertical	—	—	—	—	8.29	—
outdoor, horizontal	—	—	—	—	9.26	—
attic	—	—	—	—	12.5	—
outdoor (5 m/s wind)	—	—	—	—	28.0[d]	—
Airspace						
vertical	1.20	0.280	—	0.025–0.100	6.36	—
horizontal (2.5 cm)	1.20	0.280	—	0.025	6.19	—
horizontal (10 cm)	1.20	0.280	—	0.100	5.17	—
horizontal (20 cm)	1.20	0.280	—	0.200	5.11	—

Table A–6. continued (Notes)

[a] One dimensional heat transfer only

[b] Asphalt, pure

[c] Estimates

[d] Approximate dependence on wind: $U[W/(°Cm^2)] = 10.2 + 3.56 \cdot v\,[m/s]$

Conductance $U = \dfrac{k}{d}$. Capacitance (Capacity per unit area) $C_s = \rho \cdot c \cdot d$

ρ = Density

c = Specific Heat

k = Conductivity

d = Thickness

Table A–7.   Description, Overall U-Value, and Overall Thermal Mass of all Wall Sections of the Townhouse.

Outside Walls

	$R\,[°Cm^2/W]$	$C_s\,[Wh/(°Cm^2)]$
Indoor Film Coefficient	0.121	—
Gypsum Board	0.078	3.1
R–7 Insulation/9.2 cm Studs[a]	1.355	2.0
Plywood Sheathing	0.110	2.3
Building Paper	0.011	—
Wood Siding (lapped)	0.143	2.3
Outdoor Film Coefficient (5 m/s wind speed)	0.036	—
	1.853	9.7

Overall U-Value $U = 0.540\ W/(°Cm^2)$

Front Door

Overall U-Value $U = 3.07\ W/(°Cm^2)$

Windows (Double and Single Pane)[b]

	Wind:	5 m/s	2 m/s
Overall U-Value [W/(°Cm²)]	Double Pane	4.29	3.98
	Single Pane	6.14	5.45

Ceiling

	$R\,[°Cm^2/W]$	$C_s\,[Wh/(°Cm^2)]$
Indoor Film Coefficient	0.108	—
Gypsum Board	0.078	3.1
R–11 Insulation/14.3 cm Joists[a]	1.761	2.2
Attic Film Coefficient	0.080	—
	2.037	5.2

Overall U-Value $U = 0.493\ W/(°Cm^2)$

Roof

	R [$°Cm^2/W$]	C_s [Wh/($°Cm^2$)]
Attic Film Coefficient	0.080	—
Plywood/14.3 cm Joists[a]	0.117	4.3
Building Paper	0.011	—
Asphalt Shingles	0.078	3.6
Outdoor Film Coefficient	0.036	—
	0.322	7.9

Overall U-Value   3.11 W/($°Cm^2$)
Attic Ventilation[c]   0.84
Roof Equivalent U-Value   U = 3.95 W/($°Cm^2$)

Above Grade Basement Walls

	R [$°Cm^2/W$]	C_s [Wh/($°Cm^2$)]
Indoor Film Coefficient	0.121	—
Cinder Blocks	0.304	33.7
Outdoor Film Coefficient (5 m/s wind speed)	0.036	—
	0.460	33.7

Overall U-Value   U = 2.17 W/($°Cm^2$)

Below Grade Basement Walls

Indoor Film Coefficient	0.121	—
Cinder Blocks	0.304	33.7
	R_W = 0.425	33.7

Equivalent U-Value[d]   U = 0.566 W/($°Cm^2$)

Basement Floor

Indoor Film Coefficient	0.108	—
Concrete Floor	0.109	43.6
Stone Fill	0.056	35.9
	R_W = 0.273	79.6

Equivalent U-Value[d]   U = 0.095 W/($°Cm^2$)

Table A–7. continued

Basement Ceiling (carpeted)

	C_s [Wh/(°Cm^2)]	R [°Cm^2]
Indoor Film Coefficient	—	0.108
Plywood/19.4 cm Joists[a]	6.3	0.121
Carpet (fibrous pad)	5.7	0.367
Indoor Film Coefficient	—	0.108
	12.0	0.704

Overall U-Value $U = 1.42$ W/(°Cm^2)

Basement Ceiling (tiled)

	C_s [Wh/(°Cm^2)]	R [°Cm^2]
Indoor Film Coefficient	—	0.108
Plywood/19.4 cm Joists[a]	6.3	0.121
Linoleum Floor Tiles	3.6	0.009
Indoor Film Coefficient	—	0.108
	9.9	0.346

Overall U-Value $U = 2.89$ W/(°Cm^2)

Basement and Attic Firewalls:

	C_s [Wh/(°Cm^2)]	R [°Cm^2]
Indoor Film Coefficient	—	0.121
Cinder Block	—	0.304
Indoor Film Coefficient	—	0.121
	33.7	0.545

Overall U-Value $U = 1.84$ W/(°Cm^2)

Living Space Firewalls:

	C_s [Wh/(°Cm^2)]	R [°Cm^2]
Same as Basement and Attic Firewalls	33.7	0.545
Gypsum Board (twice)[e]	6.1	0.155
10 cm Air space/9.2 cm studs[a] (twice)[e]	3.7	0.342
	43.6	1.284

Overall U-Value $U = 0.965$ W/(°Cm^2)

Upstairs Floor (carpeted)

Indoor Film Coefficient	0.108	—
Gypsum Board	0.078	3.1
20 cm Air space/19.4 cm trusses[a]	0.215	3.9
Plywood	0.110	2.3
Carpet (fibrous pad)	0.367	5.7
Indoor Film Coefficient	0.108	—
	0.986	15.0

Overall U-Value $U = 1.01$ W/(°Cm²)

Upstairs Floor (tiled)

Indoor Film Coefficient	0.108	—
Gypsum Board	0.078	3.1
20 cm Air space/19.4 cm trusses[a]	0.215	3.9
Plywood	0.110	2.3
Linoleum Floor Tiles	0.009	3.6
Indoor Film Coefficient	0.108	—
	0.628	12.9

Overall U-Value $U = 1.59$ W/(°Cm²)

Partition Walls

Indoor Film Coefficient	0.121	—
Gypsum Board	0.078	3.1
10 cm Air space/9.2 cm studs[a]	0.171	1.9
Gypsum Board	0.078	3.1
Indoor Film Coefficient	0.121	—
	0.569	8.0

Overall U-Value $U = 1.76$ W/(°Cm²)

[a] Aggregated as described in text.

[b] Including correction for 80 percent glass area and metal sash.

[c] Calculated as: Air Infil. (Attic) × c(Air) × Volume (Attic)/Surface (Roof).
The result is: 3 exch./hr. × 0.336 Wh/(°Cm³) × 70.7 m³ /84.2 m² = 0.84 [W/(°Cm²)].

[d] U-Value combines wall and earth, as described in text.

[e] Resistance and capacitance are double the value listed in Table A-6 because there is one layer on both "our" side and the neighbor's side.

Thermal Characteristics
of the Overall Townhouse

The overall heat conductances H [W/°C] of each wall section are given in Table A−8. They are obtained by multiplying the area of the wall section by the appropriate U-value from Table A−7. The thermal masses, C [kWh/°C], are obtained in the same fashion. The mass-transport-induced heat loss due to air infiltration is presented in Table A−8 as an overall heat conductance, based on 0.75 exchanges per hour of the volume of air between upstairs ceiling and ground level; this is the nominal exchange rate and air volume recommended by ASHRAE for heat loss calculations for townhouses.

Table A−8 is calculated for the particular townhouses rented by our group. It had double pane windows but a single pane patio door; it also had some carpet and some linoleum tile on each floor. The townhouse is described as built, before the shell is modified by any retrofits.

A plausible value for the effective conductance (lossiness) of the whole townhouse is obtained by summing the conductances (AU) presented above the dashed line in Table A−8. The result is 289 W/°C, a sum of three approximately equal terms—air infiltration (96 W/°C), heat flow through glass (84 W/°C), and heat flow through opaque surfaces (109 W/°C). However, this is likely to be an underestimate, because the attic bypasses discussed in Chapter 3 are not included. Any temperature drop across a side wall, for example, would lead to further heat flow.

The last six lines of Table A−8 are included to elucidate the effective heat capacity of the townhouse. The combined heat capacity of 17.6 kWh/°C for all the elements included in Table A−8 is seen to include 6.9 kWh/°C from firewalls, 5.4 kWh/°C from the basement cement floor, 0.8 kWh/°C from the basement front and back masonry walls below grade, 0.7 kWh/°C from the asphalt roof, and 3.9 kWh/°C from the structure of interior and exterior walls, ceilings, and floors. By comparison, the heat capacity of the roughly 500 cubic meters of air contained between basement floor and upstairs ceiling is 0.2 kWh/°C. Time-dependent effects in the townhouse will reflect the interaction of these heat capacities with a variety of thermal resistances, including the effective thermal resistance between the interior air and the interior skin of the structure.

Table A–8. Overall Conductances and Thermal Masses for Three Bedroom Wood Frame Townhouse.

Wall Sections	A [m²]	U[W/(°Cm²)]	AU[W/°C]	C_s[Wh/(°Cm²)]	C[kWh/°C]
Outside Walls	63.3	0.540	34.2	9.7	0.61
Front Door	1.9	3.07	5.7	—	—
Double Pane Windows	11.7	4.29[a]	50.1	—	—
Single Pane Patio Doors	5.6	6.14[a]	34.3	—	—
Ceiling	70.9	0.493	35.0	5.2	0.37
Roof	84.2	3.95	332.6	7.9	0.67
Attic[b]	—	—	31.6	—	—
Air Infiltration	382[c]	0.75 exc./hr	96.4	—	—
Basement:					
Above Grade Walls	6.0	2.17	13.0	35.4	0.20
Windows	0.77	5.45	4.2	—	—
Below Grade Walls	22.9	0.566	13.0	33.7	0.77
Floor	67.4	0.095	6.4	79.6	5.37
			Lossiness 288.9		
Ceiling	67.4	1.98[d]	133.4	11.1	0.75
Firewalls	49.1	1.84	90.3	33.7	1.66
Living Space Firewalls	104.2	0.965	100.6	43.6	4.54
Attic Firewalls	21.1	1.84	38.8	33.7	0.71
Upstairs Floor	67.4	1.12[e]	75.5	14.5	0.98
Partition Walls	119.4	1.76	210.1	8.0	0.96
				Capacity	17.59

[a] Wind at 5 m/s.
[b] Ceiling and roof added as series resistances: 1/AU (Attic) = 1/AU (Ceiling) +1/AU (Roof).
[c] Indoor *volume* above grade [m³] listed under areas "A."
[d] 62% carpet, 38% tile.
[e] 81% carpet, 19% tile.

APPLIANCES

Average Levels of Use

The builder of the Quad II townhouses at Twin Rivers purchased nearly all the major energy-using appliances and installed them prior to occupancy. In the case of the range and the refrigerator, the resident could select among a small number of options. Table A–9 displays the rated power of these appliances and our estimates of the annual energy use attributable to most of them. The quotient of the two entries in each row gives our estimate of the number of hours of use each year at rated power, which, for an appliance that operates only at full power (like the water heater, but unlike the range), is the same as the number of hours of operation each year.

Our estimates of hours of operation each year of the furnace and air conditioner are 900 hours and 700 hours respectively. Our estimates of the energy consumption of the fan that powers the forced air distribution system (a total of 600 kWh per year, roughly half in the heating mode and half in the cooling mode) follow from these estimates of hours of use. The water heater, which accounts for roughly half of the electricity use in the house, operates one or the other of its two 4.5 kW heating elements 1,800 hours each year, or 5 hours each day. More detailed data analysis (see below) indicates that the refrigerators operate roughly half of the time—in fact, roughly half of each hour of the year.

The air conditioner is a two ton unit; that is, it is expected to remove heat from the interior at a rate of 24,000 Btu per hour (7.0 kW) when it is operating. Its coefficient of performance (COP) is obtained by dividing this heat removal rate by the power demand, which is either 3.2 kW or 3.7 kW, resulting in an estimated COP of either 2.2 or 1.9, depending on whether one excludes or includes the energy to drive the fan that circulates the cold air.[9] Our models of the summer energy balance in Twin Rivers townhouses are still preliminary, but they appear to confirm that the air conditioner actually operates with a COP of about 2.0.

Extensive data on appliances in Twin Rivers have been acquired in parallel research by the National Bureau of Standards. It is likely that some of the estimates in Table A–9 will have to be revised as results emerge from their data analysis. However, our most provocative result, the 8,000 kWh per year consumption at the electric water heater, is based on a larger sample of houses than our estimates of refrigerator, range, and dryer, and is not likely to change.

9. The corresponding energy efficiency rating (EER), which is 3.414 times the COP, is therefore either 7.5 or 6.5.

Table A—9. Rated Power and Estimated Annual Use of Gas Furnace and Major Electric Applicances in a Quad II Townhouse at Twin Rivers.

	Rated Power (kW)	*Estimated Annual Use (kWh)*
Provided By Builder		
Gas		
Furnace		
Running (80,000 Btu/hr "input")	23.4	20,800 (as gas)
Off, but pilot on (1000 Btu/hr)	0.3	2,600 (as gas)
Electric		
Air conditioner compressor	3.2	2,200
Blower fan (heating mode)	0.34a	300
(cooling or manual mode)	0.47a	300
Water heater (each of two elements)	4.5	8,000
Refrigerator (12 cu.ft., 0.34m³)	0.14a	
(15 cu.ft., 0.42m³)	0.35a	2,000
(18 cu.ft., 0.51m³)	0.54a	
Dishwasher	1.0a, b	d
Range (regular)	10.3	
(self-cleaning)	12.0	700
Clothes washer	0.3a, c	
Clothes dryer (cold)	0.2a	
(warm)	2.9	500
(hot)	5.6	
Three bathroom fans	0.3	d
Acquired By Typical Resident		
Lighting (30 light bulbs)	2.25	d
Two TV sets	0.5	d
Humidifier	0.12	d
Stereo	0.2	d
Freezer	0.3	d
Total electric consumption		16,200

a Including a power factor that takes into account the phase shifting characteristics of the component electrical motors.

b 0.5 kWh per load.

c 0.2 kWh per load.

d Breakdown not available, but estimate of subtotal is 2200 kWh, dominated by lighting and TV.

Load Profiles Over the Day

During which hours of the day do appliances draw electric current, and how much? Among those interested in the answers to this question are virtually all those concerned with meeting or diverting peak demand. These include the professionals in the utility industries, first of all, but also the designers of solar energy and fuel cell systems for the home and, rather soon, the residents who will confront peak power pricing and will want to try to do something in response.

Our group's approach has been to generate average load profiles from a stretch of data obtained at twenty minute intervals over several days, by averaging over days for each twenty minute segment of the day. For each data channel and each house, a seventy-two-point sample results that represents an average day's profile. Figure 1–21 displayed such a load profile for three water heaters in winter. Figures A–7 through A–10 present such profiles in summer, drawn from the same three townhouses.[10] These summer load profiles were derived from twenty-two days of data, running (with a gap) from Saturday, August 24, through Thursday, September 19, 1974.

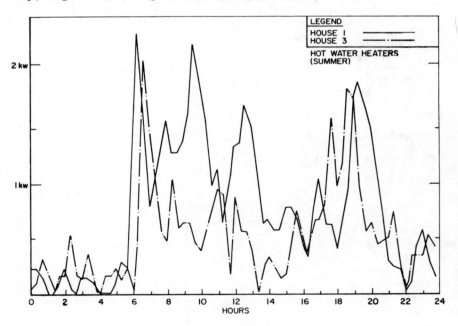

Figure A–7. Load Profile—Water Heater (Summer)

10. Data reduction was carried out by Jeffrey Robinson, Johnny Yeung, and Linda Shookster, under the direction of Lawrence Mayer.

The pattern of the water heater over the day in summer, seen in Figure A–7, is remarkably consistent with the pattern over the day in winter, seen in Figure 1–21. Both patterns show a double peak in the morning in House 1, each peak at an average rate of two kilowatts, one at 6 A.M. and one at 9 A.M. House 3 shows its own double-peaked structure, a morning peak just after the one in House 1 (the alarm must go off about twenty minutes later) and an evening peak at 6 P.M. Unfortunately, there were no summer data from the water heater in House 2; at least in winter, it uses much less energy than the other two, averaging 690 Watts, versus 870 Watts and 900 Watts for the water heaters of House 1 and House 3, respectively. As

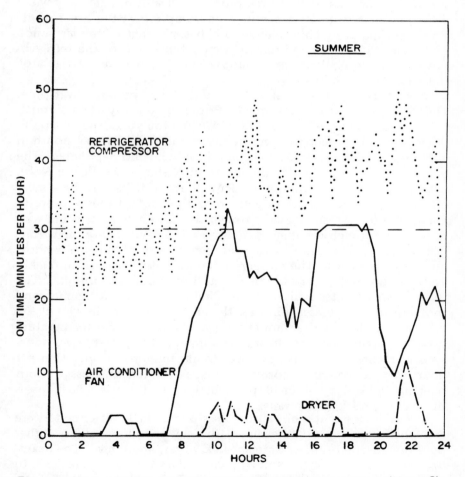

Figure A–8. Load Profile—Air Conditioner Fan, Refrigerator, Dryer (House 2)

discussed in some detail in conjunction with Figure 1–21, the consumption during the night, when power is cheapest to generate, is virtually nil. Yet these water heaters store an entire day's hot water in their eighty gallon (0.30 m^3) tanks, so that the decoupling of time of water heating from time of hot water use ought to be a realizable objective.

Figure A–8 gives profiles over the day in House 2 for the air conditioner fan, the refrigerator compressor, and the dryer, in minutes of operation per hour. As each of these always operates at full power, these profiles of appliance use are indirect measurements of the profiles of energy consumption of the same appliances. However, the relative heights of the three profiles will shift dramatically when drawn in energy units: the power consumption of the dryer on its "hot" setting is roughly one and a half times that of the air conditioner (including fan) and ten to twenty times that of the refrigerator. (See Table A–9: House 2 has a 15 cu.ft. = 0.42 m^3 refrigerator that draws about 350 Watts.)

These three appliances show totally different patterns over time. The dryer is used for about one-half hour, once a day, right through the year, and consumes about 500 kWh for the year. The air conditioner uses all its electricity in summer, about 800 kWh per month in July and August, 400 kWh per month in June and September. The pattern of use over the day manifests an M shape (see Figure A–8), with a dip between noon and 3 P.M. that we believe to be a solar effect: As the sun passes directly over the roof of these houses at about 1 P.M., the solar load through the east- and west-facing windows goes through a minimum. (Houses 1, 2, and 3 have their front doors facing 10° south of east, and they have roughly equal window area front and back.) The refrigerator consumption pattern is roughly constant not only over months but also over hours of the day. The refrigerator operates a bit more than half of the time in summer, and (not shown) it operates a bit less than half of the time in winter, the difference reflecting the warmer kitchen and the warmer temperature outdoors beside the kitchen wall in summer. The pattern over hours seen in Figure A–8 remains above twenty minutes of operation per hour even in the early morning hours, indicating that usage (door opening) adds only a small perturbation on the basic heat losses through the refrigerator walls.

In our instrumentation, all the uses of the 110 volt circuits were combined in a single data channel (thereby combining all uses other than the air conditioner, water heater, dryer, and range). The resulting load, labeled "Lights and Appliances," is seen in Figure A–9. In all three townhouses the profile is quite flat, both over the day and over the year, in large part because the refrigerator is included and

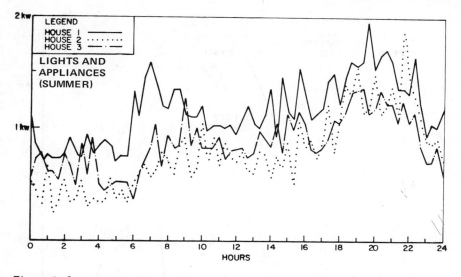

Figure A–9. Load Profile—Lights and Appliances *(total except water heater, air conditioner, dryer, range)*

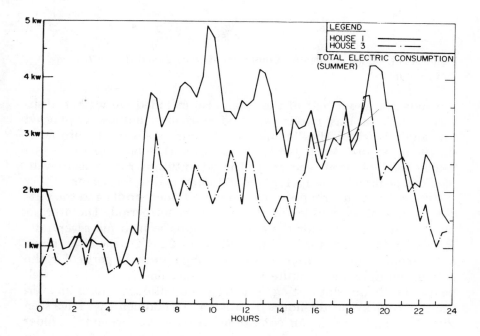

Figure A–10. Load Profile—All Uses of Electricity

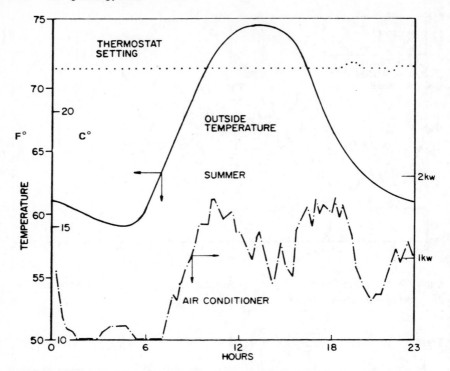

Figure A–11. Load Profile—Air Conditioner (House 2) and Hourly Average Temperature

accounts for about half of the total; also included are washer, dishwasher, TVs (at least two in each house), freezer (not always plugged in), and all lights. The "grand total" summer electricity profile is shown in Figure A–10 (with House 2 omitted because the water heater had not been recorded). The adventurous reader can try to pick out peaks due to dryer, air conditioner, and water heater.

Figure A–11 superimposes the air conditioner profile and the outdoor temperature profile for the same summer period. The average outdoor temperature for the entire period is seen to fall several degrees below the thermostat setting ($72°$F, or $22.2°$C), the latter being a reasonable index of desired interior temperature. In particular, the average outdoor temperature in the late evening is seen to lie well below the thermostat setting. Yet the air conditioner runs at an average rate of 1 kW in the hours from 9 P.M. to midnight. We have seen this pattern, where the air conditioner is used even when it is colder outside than in, in data from many Twin Rivers townhouses. An alternative energy-conserving strategy is available to the Twin Rivers resident in this situation—opening the windows![11] The "blue light" experiment, described in Chapter 10, in which a light blinked in the kitchen whenever the air conditioner was running and the outside temperature was below 68°F (20° C), was our psychologists' attempt to confirm that such energy-conserving strategies would be implemented if the residents had the energy-wasteful mode of their house called to their attention. The experiment appears to have been successful.

A Comparison of Gas and Electric Appliances

In Quad III at Twin Rivers, townhouses identical to those in Quad II were built, but gas replaced electricity as the energy source for the water heater, range and dryer. Figure A–12 shows the consumption of gas and electricity in three-bedroom townhouses, averaged over 138 Quad II or 146 Quad III townhouses. Close study of the monthly differences reveals the following:

1. During the eight nonsummer months of October through May, the difference in average rate of consumption of electricity was nearly constant, averaging 710 kWh per month, or 1,000 Watts. In Table A–9, we estimated the combined electricity consumption of the Quad II water heater, range, and dryer to be 9,200 kWh per year, or 770 kWh per month, which agrees with this independent estimate to within 10 percent.
2. During the same eight month period, the difference in the average rate of gas consumption averaged[12] 4,500 cubic feet per month (or 4.9 GJ per month, or 1,900 Watts). This estimate of the combined rate of consumption of gas by the water heater, range, and dryer in Quad III is seen to be roughly double our estimate of the rate of consumption of electricity by the same three appliances in Quad II (1,900 W versus 1,000 W)—when energy consumption at

11. The Twin Rivers air conditioner is not designed to admit and circulate outside air, a feature known as an "economizer." Such a feature is energy-conserving, assuming the fan is approximately as large as at Twin Rivers, where the fan draws one-eighth the power drawn by the fan plus compressor together. From a comparison of Figures A–8 and A–11, we see that the fan is apparently never used alone, for the two load profiles nearly coincide. We also see that during the hours from 9 P.M. to midnight, the air conditioner runs about one-third of the time. Therefore, even if in the alternative mode the fan would run continuously with the air conditioner off, this mode would consume only about three-eighths as much power.

12. There is a small phase difference between the two winter peaks that results from meters being read six days apart, though on the same day for all townhouses in a Quad. This explains the artifact that differences vary sharply over months around the winter peak.

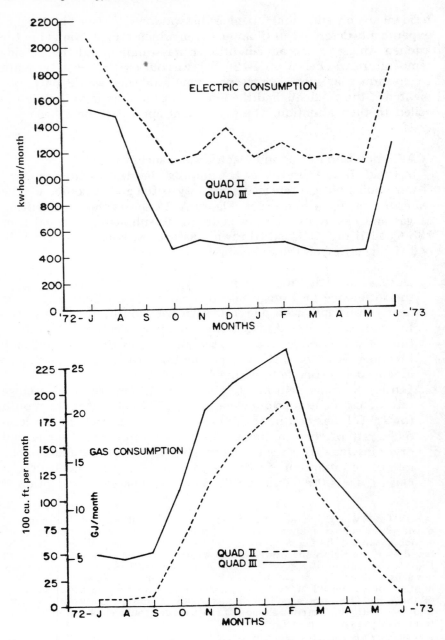

Figure A–12. Average Energy Consumption in Identical Townhouses: Quad II (Electric Appliances) and Quad III (Gas Appliances).

the house is considered.[13] Comparing energy use by the economy as a whole (by multiplying the electricity consumption by three), we attribute energy use at a rate of 3,000 W to the three electric appliances and energy use at a rate of 1,900 W to the three gas appliances, a ratio of 1.6 to 1.

3. The difference in monthly gas consumption in the summer has the same average value as in the winter, but this is not true of electricity. The excess electricity consumption in Quad II is substantially diminished in summer, and the excess is diminished more in July and August than in June and September. This strongly suggests that the Quad III electric air conditioner consumes more energy than the Quad II electric air conditioner for the same outside weather. Assuming that the rate of use of electricity in the eight nonsummer months is the same as the rate of use of electricity in the four summer months for all uses other than air conditioning, we find from Figure A—12 that the Quad II air conditioner used 2,300 kWh and the Quad III air conditioner used 3,200 kWh over the summer.

4. The excess air conditioning in Quad III, 900 kWh per summer, can be compared to the excess heat generated in the Quad III townhouses, arising from the use of gas instead of electric appliances (900 Watts for four months, or 2,600 kWh). At a COP of 2.0, the 900 kWh of excess air conditioning would remove 1,800 kWh of heat from the house, which is most but not all of the 2,600 kWh excess heat produced at the house by gas appliances. We should not have expected all of the excess heat from gas appliances to require removal by the air conditioner, since (a) some of the excess heat will be generated in mild weather when the air conditioner is not used, and (b) some of the excess heat from gas appliances is vented directly to the outside.

5. The differential use of air conditioning in Quad III relative to Quad II, 900 kWh per summer, translates to 2,700 kWh of extra energy use at the power plant and cancels roughly 30 percent of the energy advantage of gas appliances, previously calculated to be 1,100 Watts for a year, or 9,600 kWh. The annual savings for the economy in using gas appliances, therefore, becomes 6,900 kWh per townhouse. Of course, the energy form used to accomplish this energy saving, natural gas, would be judged by many to be a resource whose value relative to the nuclear power, coal, and

13. A large part of the excess energy consumption at the house by the gas appliances can be associated with five pilot lights, three at the range, and one each at the water heater and dryer.

residual fuel oil used at the power plant is not fully captured by measurements in energy units.

Among the conservation opportunities suggested by this brief discussion are, surely, the elimination of pilot lights, the venting of appliances differently in summer and winter, and the abandonment of electric resistive water heating. The list becomes longer as soon as one considers individual appliances in detail, as we are now doing in collaboration with the National Bureau of Standards.

Appendix B

Selected Reports and Publications

NOTE: Unpublished works were produced for Princeton University. They have been disseminated from the Center for Environmental Studies (CES), Princeton University, Princeton, New Jersey.

PROGRAM REVIEW

Grot, R., and Socolow, R.H. 1974. Energy utilization in a residential community. In *Energy: Demand, Conservation, and Institutional Problems*, ed. M.S. Mackrakis, pp. 483–98. Cambridge, Mass: MIT Press.

Socolow, R.H. 1976. Energy utilization in a planned community in the United States. In *Energy Conservation in the Built Environment*, ed. R.G. Courtney, pp. 447–57. Proceedings of the CIB Symposium held at The Building Research Establishment, Garston, Watford, April 1976. Hornby, Lancaster, England: The Construction Press.

Socolow, R.H., and Sonderegger, R.C. 1976. The Twin Rivers program on energy conservation in housing: four-year summary report. CES Report No. 32.

Harrje, D.T.; Socolow, R.H.; and Sonderegger, R.C. 1977. Residential energy conservation—the Twin Rivers project. *ASHRAE Transactions* 83, pt. 1.

CONSTRUCTION OF TWIN RIVERS

Fraker, H., Jr., and Schorske, E. 1973. Energy husbandry in housing: an analysis of the development process in a residential community, Twin Rivers, N.J. CES Report No. 5.

Hackney, L.D. 1975. A political analysis of the development process in East Windsor Township. Senior thesis, Department of Politics, Princeton University.

PSYCHOLOGY AND THE RESIDENT

Seligman, C., and Darley, J. 1977. Feedback as a means of decreasing residential energy consumption. *Journal of Applied Psychology* 67: 363–68.

Seligman, C.; Darley, J.; and Becker, L.J. 1976. Psychological strategies to reduce energy consumption. CES Report No. 41.

Becker, L.J. 1978. The joint effect of feedback and goal setting on performance: a field study of residential energy conservation. *Journal of Applied Psychology* (in press).

Seligman, C.; Kriss, M.; Darley, J.M.; Fazio, R.H.; Becker, L.J.; and Pryor, J.B. 1978. Predicting residential energy consumption from homeowners' attitudes. *Journal of Applied Social Psychology* (in press).

Becker, L.J., and Seligman, C. 1978. Reducing air conditioning waste by signaling it is cool outside. *Personality and Social Psychology Bulletin* (in press).

AGGREGATE ENERGY CONSUMPTION

Fox, J. 1973. Energy consumption for residential space heating—a case study. MSE thesis, Department of Aerospace and Mechanical Sciences (also issued as CES Report No. 4).

Cheung, M. 1974. The effect of the energy crisis on the winter gas consumption of quad II split-level townhouses at Twin Rivers, New Jersey. Junior independent work, Department of Statistics, Princeton University.

Mayer, L., and Robinson, J. 1975. A statistical analysis of the monthly consumption of gas and electricity in the home. CES Report No. 18.

Schrader, T.F. 1978. A two-parameter model for assessing the determinants of residential space heating. MSE thesis, Department of Aerospace and Mechanical Sciences, Princeton University.

Alpert, R.A. 1976. Electricity: residential consumption and conservation. Senior thesis, Department of Statistics, Princeton University.

Horowitz, C.E., and Mayer, L.S. 1977. The relationship between the price and demand for natural gas. *Energy Research* 1: 193–222.

Mayer, L.S. 1976. Estimating the effects of the onset of the energy crisis on residential energy demand. *Energy and Resources* (in press).

EQUIVALENT THERMAL PARAMETERS
TO CHARACTERIZE A HOUSE

Socolow, R.H. 1975. Time-series models for the energy balance in a house. CES Working Paper No. 19.

Socolow, R.H. 1975. A model of heat flow in an attic. CES Working Paper No. 20.

Sinden, F. 1976. Conductive losses from basements. Twin Rivers Note No. 4.

Pollack, A. 1976. Modeling attic temperature in three highly instrumented townhouses in Twin Rivers, New Jersey. Junior independent work, Department of Statistics (also issued as CES Report No. 28).

Dutt, G.S., and Harrje, D.T. 1977. Influence of attics on residential energy conservation. CES Working Paper No. 33.

Woteki, T., and Dutt, G. 1977. The two-resistance model for attic heat flow: Theory and results from a retrofit experiment. CES Report No. 52.

Dutt, G., and Beyea, J. 1977. Attic thermal performance: a study of town-houses at Twin Rivers. CES Report No. 53.

Sonderegger, R.C. 1977. Modeling residential heat load from experimental data: the equivalent thermal parameters of a house. *Proceedings of the International Conference on Energy Use Management* (Tucson, Arizona; October 1977), eds. R.A. Fazzolare, and C.B. Smith, II, 183−94. New York: Pergamon.

Sonderegger, R.C. 1977. Diagnostic tests determining the thermal response of a house. Paper presented at the ASHRAE meeting, Atlanta, Georgia, February 1978.

Sonderegger, R.C. 1977. Dynamic models of house heating based on equivalent thermal parameters. Ph.D. thesis, Department of Aerospace and Mechanical Sciences (also issued as CES Report No. 57).

AIR INFILTRATION

Harrje, D.; Hunt, C.; Treado, S.; and Malik, N. 1975. Automated instrumentation for building air infiltration measurements. CES Report No. 13.

Mattingly, G., and Peters, E. 1977. Wind and trees—air infiltration effects on energy in housing. *Journal of Industrial Aerodynamics* 2: 1−19.

Sinden, F. 1978. Theoretical basis for tracer gas measurements of air infiltration. *Building and Environment* 13:21−28.

Sinden, F. 1977. Passive device for controlling ventilation. Patent disclosure dated January 31, 1977 (CES).

Sinden, F. 1977. Decentralized heat recovery devices. Patent disclosure dated March 8, 1977 (CES).

Harrje, D., and Grot, R. 1977. Automated air infiltration measurements and implications for energy conservation. In *Proceedings of the International Conference on Energy Use Management* (Tucson, Arizona; October 1977), eds. R.A. Fazzolare, and C.B. Smith, I, 457−64. New York: Pergamon.

Malik, N. 1977. Air infiltration in homes. MSE thesis, Department of Aerospace and Mechanical Sciences, Princeton University.

ELECTRICAL APPLIANCES

Meyer, J.; Niemiec, D.; and Harrje, D. 1974. Energy efficient design of household appliances. CES Report No. 11.

Robinson, J., and Yeung, J. 1975. Summer air conditioning and appliance use patterns: a graphical analysis. CES Report No. 22.

ANALYSIS OF RETROFITS

Harrje, D.T. 1976. Retrofitting: plan, action, and early results using the townhouses at Twin Rivers. CES Report No. 29.

Woteki, T. 1976. The Princeton Omnibus experiment: some effects of retrofits on space heating requirements. CES Report No. 43.

Woteki, T. 1977. Some effects of retrofits on interior temperatures in a sample of houses. CES Working Paper No. 31.

Pollack, A. 1977. Residential energy conservation: the effects of retrofits on summer electricity demand. Senior thesis, Department of Statistics, Princeton University.

INSTRUMENTATION

Fox, J.; Fraker, H., Jr.; Grot, R.; Harrje, D.; Schorske, E.; and Socolow, R.H. 1973. Energy conservation in housing: first annual progress report (1973). CES Report No. 6.

Hall, S., and Harrje, D. 1975. Instrumentation for the Omnibus experiment. CES Report No. 21.

Grot, R.; Harrje, D.; and Johnston, L. 1976. Application of thermography for evaluating effectiveness of retrofit measures. In *Third Biennial Infrared Information Exchange*. St. Louis, Mo.: AGA Corporation.

RELATED PUBLICATIONS

Socolow, R.H. 1973. New tasks for the energy industries. *Public Utilities Fortnightly* 91 (12): 40–43.

Socolow, R.H. 1975. Energy conservation in housing: concepts and options. In *Future Land Use: Energy, Environmental and Legal Constraints*, eds. R.W. Burchell, and D. Listokin, pp. 311–23. New Brunswick, N.J.: Rutgers University Press.

Ford, K.W.; Rochlin, G.J.; Ross, M.; and Socolow, R.H. eds. 1975. *Efficient Use of Energy: A Physics Perspective*. AIP Conference Proceedings No. 25. New York: American Institute of Physics.

The Study Group on Technical Aspects of Efficient Use of Energy, 1975. Efficient use of energy. *Physics Today* 28 (8): 23–33.

Socolow, R.H. 1976. Energy conservation in existing residences: Your home deserves a house call. Presented at the conference *Energy Efficiency as a National Priority*. Washington, D.C., May 20, 1976.

Socolow, R.H. 1977. The coming age of conservation. *Ann. Rev. Energy* 2: 239–89.

Socolow, R.H. 1978. Four anxieties about a vigorous energy conservation program in the United States. *Annals of the New York Academy of Sciences* (in press).

Appendix C

Dramatis Personae

PRINCETON UNIVERSITY

Senior Researchers

Lawrence Becker
Jan Beyea
John Darley
Gautam Dutt
Harrison Fraker, Jr.
Richard Grot
David Harrje

George Mattingly
Lawrence Mayer
Clive Seligman
Frank Sinden
Robert Socolow
Thomas Woteki

Graduate Students

Yoav Benjamini
Ellen Fagenson
Russ Fazio
John Fox
Miriam Goldberg
Jeff Jacobs
Mitchell Kriss
Nicholas Malik

Andrew Persily
John Pryor
Vita Rabinowitz
(Northwestern University)
Thomas Schrader
Robert Sonderegger
Robert Stine

Undergraduate Students

Rosalind Alpert
Bradley Bellows
Heidi Bode
Martin Booker
Charles Buckley
Anthony Caine, Jr.
John Cella

Malcolm Cheung
Karl Danz
José Davila
David Donoho
Bruce Duncan
Jonathan Eckstein
Jon Elliott

Undergraduate Students *(continued)*

Rick Ferris
Steven Fisher
Miles Gessow
Michael Guerin
Lucy Hackney
Shawn Hall
Walter Hallagan
William Holstein
Cindy Horowitz
John Kadyszewski
Jeff Kang
  (Harvard University)
Raymond Kang
  (Cornell University)
Larry Krakauer
Sylvia Kuzmak
David La Plante
Adrienne Lavine
  (Brown University)
Andrew Lazarus
Robert Levin
Peter Maruhnic

David Matchar
Herbert Mertz
Thomas Mills
Walter Moberg
Donald Niemiec
Mark Nowotarski
Gene Peters
Alison Pollack
Mark Ramsey
Robert Rowse
  (Hampshire College)
Lauren Sarno
Stewart Sender
Molly Sherrick
Linda Shookster
Steve Silverman
John Spriegel
Francis Sweeney
Johnny Yeung
Douglas Zaeh
David Zuckerman

Faculty Advisors

Irvin Glassman, director, Center for Environmental Studies, 1973–
George Reynolds, director, Center for Environmental Studies, 1971–1973

Peter Bloomfield
Robert Geddes
Robert Gutman

Suzanne Keller
Norman Kurtz

Technical Staff

Jack Cooper
Roy Crosby
Kenneth Gadsby

Victor Warshaw
Richard Whitley
Tom Williams

Research Associates

Corinne Black
Cal Feinberg
Joan Hall
Judith Hunt
Toby Kriss

James Meyer
Pam Pinkham
Jeffrey Robinson
Elizabeth Schorske

Administrative Staff

Terry Brown
Deborah Doolittle

Selma Lapedes
Jean Wiggs

ADVISORY COMMITTEE

James B. Comly, General Electric Corporate Research and Development, Schenectady, New York

Maurice Gamze, consulting engineer, Gamze, Korobkin, and Caloger, Chicago, Illinois

John Meyers, Oak Ridge National Laboratory

William Schluter, former senator, state of New Jersey

John Senders, Department of Industrial Engineering, University of Toronto, Ontario, Canada

Charles F. Sepsi, professor, Department of Mechanical Engineering, Ohio State University

Bernard Spring, dean, School of Architecture, City College of New York

N. Richard Werthamer, director, New York State Energy Research and Development Administration

John Tukey, professor, Department of Statistics, Princeton University

PROGRAM SUPERVISION

National Science Foundation—RANN

Paul Craig	Thomas Sparrow
Harold Horowitz	Charles Thiel
Roland Radloff	Seth Tuttle
Alex Schwarzkopf	William Wetmore
David Seidman	

Department of Energy—Conservation

John Cable	David Pellish
Lynn Collins	Howard Ross
Bruce Hutton	Maxine Savitz
Gerald Leighton	

COLLABORATORS

Nation Bureau of Standards

Jacquie Elder	Dan Quigley
Lawrence Galowin	Lynn Schuman
Richard Grot	Chock Siu
Max Hunt	Jack Snell
Tamani Kusuda	Heinz Trechsel
Frank Powell	

Public Service Electric and Gas

Walter Browning	Edward Nelson
John Casazza	J. Papsycki
Gene Fornarotto	Paul Platt
Arthur Fowler	Robert Reinauer
James Griffith	Louis Rizzi
Edward Monteverdi	Richard Skank

Jersey Central Power and Light

Shephard Bartnoff   Charles Gurner

Richard Green

SUBJECTS OF INTERVIEWS (1972–1974)*

Original Developer

Gerald Finn, president, The Nilsen Group, New Hope, Penn. 1964–1968

The Developer's Staff: Twin Rivers Holding Corporation**

Aaron Kenton, vice president

Arthur Rothschild, vice president, finance

William Lynch, vice president, sales and marketing

Architects

Robert Hillier, assisted by Edward Wilson, Princeton, N.J.

William Conklin, Conklin and Rossant, NYC, original architect

   1964–1968 (Whittlesey and Conklin 1964–1966)

Town Officials of East Windsor

Dana Miller, town manager   1970–1972

Richard Lee, selectman   1964–1969

Planning Board, East Windsor

John Orr, member, 1968; chairman 1969–1971, 1972–

Douglas Miller 1971–1972

William B. Harvey, secretary, 1963–1971, and town engineer to 1971

William E. Harvey, chairman 1968–1969

Eugene O'Connor, vice chairman 1968–1969

Inspectors

George Hill, chief building inspector, East Windsor Township

Robert Aasen, building inspector, East Windsor Township

Thomas Tang, Inspection Division, State Department of Community Affairs

Abe Marland, site inspector, Veterans Administration

Utilities

Ted Bowman, sales representative, Public Service Electric and Gas Co.,

   Princeton, N.J.

Donald Philipps, industrial-commercial representative, Public Service Electric

   and Gas Co., Princeton, N.J.

Thomas Brennan, sales manager, Public Service Electric and Gas Co.,

   Trenton, N.J. (formerly Princeton office)

   *Interviews were conducted by Harrison Fraker, assistant professor of architecture; and Elizabeth Schorske, research associate of the Center for Environmental Studies.

   **Developer: Herbert Kendall, president.

Norman Foy, sales manager, Jersey Central Power and Light,
Morristown, N.J.
Arthur Chasey, builder representative, Jersey Central Power and Light,
Lakewood, N.J.
William Farrer-Baynes, director, Technical Division, Oil Heat Council
of New Jersey, Springfield, N.J.
Fred Bauer, superintendent, East Windsor Municipal Authority (sewer and
water), East Windsor, N.J.

Board of Public Utilities Commissioners, Newark
Charles Sheppa, principal engineer, Engineering Division
Michael Mehr, hearing examiner

Installers (HVAC systems)
Sterling Apgar, Apgar Heating and Cooling, Quad I
I. Harris, Harris Heating, Quad II and III

Construction Supervisor
Barry Fiske, Kendall Development Corporation

Civil Engineers
James Kovacs, Kovacs, Inc., Civil Engineers for Twin Rivers, 1971—
Peter Tobia, engineer, Twin Rivers Holding Corporation

Veterans Administration
Thomas McCarthy, chief, Construction and Valuation Section

Residents
Charles Matteson, president, Home Owners Association   1971–1972
Myra Epstein, Twin Rivers Ecology Committee   1971–1972

Appendix D

Relations Among
Physical Units

Conversion factors are generally given to four significant figures, except when calorific values of fuels are concerned. To convert from an SI unit to a non-SI unit, multiply by the factor given in the equation. To convert from a non-SI unit to an SI unit, multiply by the reciprocal factor given in parentheses at the right.

Length (meter)

1 m	=	3.281 ft	(0.3048)
1 km	=	0.6214 mile	(1.609)
1 cm	=	2.540 inch	(0.3937)

Area (square meter)

1 m^2	=	10.76 ft^2	(0.09290)
1 hectare	=	10^4 m^2	(10^{-4})
	=	2.471 acres[a]	(0.4047)

[a]640 acres = 1 square mile

Volume (cubic meter)

1 m^3	=	6.102 × 10^4 cu. in.	(1.639 × 10^{-5})
	=	10^3 liter	(10^{-3})
	=	264.2 U.S. gallon	(3.785 × 10^{-3})
	=	220.0 British Imperial gallon	(4.546 × 10^{-3})
	=	35.31 cu. ft.	(0.02832)
	=	6.290 U.S. barrel[b]	(0.1590)
	=	0.2759 cord[c]	(3.625)

[b]1 U.S. barrel (oil) = 42 U.S. gallon
[c]1 cord (wood) = 128 ft^3

Velocity (meter per second)

$$
\begin{aligned}
1 \text{ m/s} &= 3.600 \text{ km/h} && (0.2778) \\
&= 3.281 \text{ ft/s} && (0.3048) \\
&= 2.237 \text{ mph (miles per hour)} && (0.4470)
\end{aligned}
$$

Flow Rate (cubic meter per second)

$$
\begin{aligned}
1 \text{ m}^3/\text{s} &= 2119 \text{ cfm (cubic foot per minute)} && (4.719 \times 10^{-4}) \\
&= 22.82 \text{ Mgd (million U.S. gallon per day)} && (0.04381)
\end{aligned}
$$

Mass (kilogram)

$$
\begin{aligned}
1 \text{ kg} &= 10^{-3} \text{ t (metric tonne)} && (10^3) \\
&= 2.205 \text{ lbm (pound mass)} && (0.4536) \\
&= 1.102 \times 10^{-3} \text{ U.S. ton} && (907.2)
\end{aligned}
$$

Density (kilogram per cubic meter)

$$
1 \text{ kg/m}^3 = 0.06243 \text{ lbm/ft}^3 \qquad\qquad (16.02)
$$

Pressure (Pascal)

$$
\begin{aligned}
1 \text{ Pa} &= 1 \text{ N/m}^2 \text{ (newton/m}^2) \\
&= 1 \text{ J/m}^3 \text{ (joule/m}^3) \\
&= 1 \text{ kg/m sec}^2 \\
&= 10 \text{ dyne/cm}^2 && (0.1) \\
&= 2.089 \times 10^{-2} \text{ lbf/ft}^2 \text{ (pound force/ft}^2) && (47.88) \\
&= 1.547 \times 10^{-2} \times \text{wind at 10 m/s (22.4 mph)}^{\text{d}} && (64.65) \\
&= 7.502 \times 10^{-3} \text{ mm Hg} && (133.3) \\
&= 4.015 \times 10^{-3} \text{ inch H}_2\text{O (at } 39°\text{F)} && (249.1) \\
&= 2.953 \times 10^{-4} \text{ inch Hg} && (3386) \\
&= 1.450 \times 10^{-4} \text{ psi (pound force/inch}^2) && (6895) \\
&= 10^{-5} \text{ bar} && (10^5) \\
&= 9.87 \times 10^{-6} \text{ standard atmosphere} && (1.013 \times 10^5)
\end{aligned}
$$

[d]Stagnation pressure ($\frac{1}{2}\rho v^2$) for standard air (dry, $0°$C, sea level: $\rho = 1.293$ kg/m^3)

Temperature (Kelvin)

$$
\begin{aligned}
1 \text{ K} &= 1°\text{C} && (1) \\
&= 1.8°\text{F} && (5/9)
\end{aligned}
$$

$$
T(°\text{K}) = T(°\text{C}) + 273
$$

$$
T(°\text{C}) = \frac{5}{9}[T(°\text{F}) - 32]
$$

Energy (Joule)

1 J	=	10^{-3} kJ (kilojoule)	(10^3)
	=	10^{-6} MJ (megajoule)	(10^6)
	=	10^{-9} GJ (gigajoule)	(10^9)

1 J	=	0.7377 ft − lbf	(1.356)
	=	0.2390 cal	(4.184)
	=	9.485×10^{-4} Btu	(1054)

1 GJ	=	277.8 kWh (kilowatt hour)	(0.003600)
	=	26.2 m^3 natural gas[e]	(0.0382)
	=	9.488 therm[f]	(0.1054)
	=	7.7 U.S. gallon gasoline[g]	(0.130)
	=	0.164 barrel crude oil[g]	(6.1)
	=	0.036 t coal[g]	(28)
	=	0.023 t crude oil[g]	(44)

[e]Natural gas at Twin Rivers: 1025 Btu/cu. ft.
[f]1 therm = 10^5 Btu
[g]approximate value

Power (Watt)

1 W	=	1 J/s (joule/second)	(1)
	=	3.414 Btu/h	(0.2929)
	=	0.03156 GJ/year	(31.69)
	=	1.340×10^{-3} hp (horsepower)	(746)
	=	2.845×10^{-4} "ton" of cooling[h]	(3514)

[h]1 "ton" of cooling = 12,000 Btu heat removed per hour.

Energy Composites (heat storage)

Specific energy:	1 kJ/kg	= 0.4302 Btu/lbm	(2.324)
Thermal mass:	1 kJ/°C	= 0.5269 Btu/°F	(1.898)
Integrated flux:	1 kJ/m^2	= 0.08811 Btu/ft^2	(11.35)
		= 0.02390 langley[j]	(41.84)
Specific heat:	1 kJ/kg°C	= 0.2390 Btu/lbm°F	(4.184)
Thermal capacitance:	1 kJ/m^2°C	= 0.04895 Btu/ft^2 °F	(20.43)

[j]1 langley = 1 calorie/cm^2 .

Power Composites (heat flow)

Specific power:	1 W/kg	= 1.549 Btu/h-lbm	(0.6457)
		= 6.082×10^{-4} horse-power/lbm	(1644)
Conductance ("lossiness")	1 W/$^\circ$C	= 1.896 Btu/h$^\circ$F	(0.5272)
Flux	1 W/m^2	= 0.3172 Btu/h ft^2	(3.152)
Heat transfer coefficient (U-value)	1 W/m^2 $^\circ$C =	0.1762 Btu/h ft^2 $^\circ$F	(5.674)
Conductivity	1 W/m$^\circ$C	= 0.5782 Btu/h ft $^\circ$F	(1.730)
		= 6.938 Btu/h ft^2 $^\circ$F/inch	(0.1441)

Other Composites

Fuel economy:[k]	1 MJ/km	= 1526 Btu/mile
		= 2.9 liter of gasoline/100 km
		= (81 miles/U.S. gallon of gasoline)$^{-1}$
		= (34 km/liter of gasoline)$^{-1}$
Cost of energy:[k]	1 ¢/kWh (thermal)	= 10.6 ¢/m^3 natural gas
		= 36¢/U.S. gallon of gasoline
		= $2.93/million Btu
		= $16.94/U.S. barrel crude oil
		= $71/U.S. ton coal
		= $78/metric tonne coal

[k]At calorific values listed under "Energy" above.

Index

Aggregate demand for natural gas, 190–94

Air conditioners
and average level of use, 290–91
vs. cost of energy, 239–40
effect on health, 234–40
and electricity consumption, 1, 13–14, 21, 47, 57, 207, 231, 234–42, 248, 266, 270, 299
and energy consumption, 1, 13–14, 21, 207, 248, 299
vs. energy crisis, 47
fan load profile, 294
vs. feedback, 243–51
measurement of "on time," 175, 177
vs. outdoor temperature, 296–97
and price, 265, 270
and rate structures, 266, 270
and retrofit, 96, 98

Air flow. *See also* Air infiltration rate
and attic insulation, 104, 107–10
mathematical expression of, 139–42
through a crack, 133–34
and wind-temperature relationship, 132–33, 134–38

Air infiltration rates, xxi, 8, 33–35, 49, 144–46
and basement retrofit, 86–87
and conductance, 288–89
and convection, 131, 133
effects of weather on, 88–89, 131–33, 140–43, 146–49, 165
and furnace firing time, 143, 146–49, 152, 161, 165
and gas consumption, 143–46, 152
and lossiness, 75, 88–89, 91

measurement of, 167–68, 177–79
and open door time, 143, 146–49
vs. outdoor-indoor temperature difference, 131–34, 134–38, 138–42, 143–46, 148, 161
in retrofit program, 4–5, 55, 63, 88–90, 123–28
and thermal performance, 4
vs. wind direction, 35, 143, 155–65
vs. wind-temperature interaction, 131–33, 134–38, 143, 161–64
vs. wind velocity, 33, 132, 136–37, 143, 146, 149–55, 155–65

Air layers, 76

Air leaks, 67, 75, 87–89, 91. *See also* Cracks; Lossiness

American units, xxiii
conversion tables for, 311–14

Anticipator, 53

Appliances
average levels of use, 290–91
and conservation, 13, 57, 300
effect on space heating, 7, 13, 49, 57, 208
and energy consumption, 1, 13–14, 21, 49, 51, 294, 297–99
and energy use, 3, 13, 51, 57
as free heat, 67, 99
and gas consumption, 51, 297–99
gas vs. electric, 297–99
-generated heat, 49, 51, 57, 144
load profiles over day, 292–97
measurement of energy consumption by, 170–72, 177
in retrofit program, 4, 63
and thermal performance, 4

315

About the Contributors

Lawrence J. Becker is Research Associate at the Center for Environmental Studies and Lecturer in Psychology at Princeton University. Since receiving his Ph.D. from the University of California at Davis, he has conducted research concerning psychological strategies to reduce residential energy consumption. His current focus is on the use of feedback as a technique to encourage residential energy conservation.

Yoav Benjamini is a candidate for the Ph.D. degree in the Department of Statistics at Princeton University. He was born in Petah-Tikva, Israel, in 1949. He received the B.Sc. (1973) and M.Sc. (1976) degrees in Mathematics from Hebrew University, Jerusalem. He was a Research Assistant in the Department of Atmospheric Sciences at Hebrew University, 1975–76.

Jan Beyea, a physicist, received his Ph.D. from Columbia University. He pursued post-doctoral studies at Columbia, taught at Holy Cross College, and is now a member of the Research Staff at Princeton University's Center for Environmental Studies. His research activities include residential energy conservation (especially thermal modeling) and risk analysis of nuclear reactors. Dr. Beyea has been particularly concerned about the policy implications of technical studies and testifies frequently before governmental bodies. He has carried out risk studies for the State of California and the Swedish Energy Commission. He currently serves as a consultant to the State of New Jersey's Department of Environmental Protection.

John M. Darley is Professor of Psychology at Princeton University. He received his Ph.D. in Social Relations at Harvard University in 1965. He was an Assistant Professor of Psychology at New York University, 1964—68, before joining the faculty at Princeton. Aside from environmental psychology, his research interests include people's behavior in emergencies and principles of moral judgment. His book, coauthored with Bibb Latane, *The Unresponsive Bystander*, won the AAAS Sociopsychological Prize in 1968.

Gautam S. Dutt is a member of the Research Staff of the Center for Environmental Studies at Princeton University. He was born in Calcutta, India, in 1949. From 1966 to 1971 he was an engineering trainee with Rolls Royce Ltd. in Derby, U.K. and a student at the University of London from which he received a B.Sc. (Engineering) in 1970. He received a Ph.D. in electric propulsion from the Department of Aerospace and Mechanical Sciences of Princeton University in 1976. His interests include energy policy for the less developed countries.

Richard A. Grot is Mechanical Engineer in the Service Systems Program of the Center for Building Technology at the National Bureau of Standards, Washington. After receiving his Ph.D. from Purdue University in Aeronautics and Astronautics and Engineering Science in 1966, he was a post-doctoral research associate in the Department of Civil Engineering at Northwestern University and Visiting Professor at the Universidad Nacional de Trujillo, Peru, with the U.S. Peace Corps. From 1969—1974 he worked at Princeton University as an Assistant Professor of Aerospace and Mechanical Sciences and a member of the Research Staff of the Center for Environmental Studies.

David T. Harrje is Senior Research Engineer and Lecturer in the Department of Aerospace and Mechanical Sciences at Princeton University. He received a B.S. in Engineering Physics from New York University and an M.S. in Engineering from Princeton. He has spent four years at Rocketdyne and at the Jet Propulsion Laboratory of California Institute of Technology. His research interests over the past twenty years range from energy conservation in housing to combustion instabilities associated with liquid-propellant rocket systems. He is currently a member of the Standards Committee for Ventilation of the American Society of Heating Refrigerating and Air Conditioning Engineers (ASHRAE), the Committee on Air Infiltration Measurements of the American Society for Testing and Materials (ASTM), and the Subcommittee on Air Infiltration Research and Development of the International Energy Agency (IEA).

Nicholas J. Malik received his B.E. with distinction from the American University of Beirut, Lebanon. Subsequently, he earned his M.A. and M.S.E. in Engineering from Princeton University. At present he is Energy Systems Analyst with Gamze-Korobkin-Caloger, Inc., Chicago. Mr. Malik specializes in the analysis and conceptual design of solar and community systems.

Lawrence S. Mayer is Research Statistician and Lecturer with rank of Associate Professor in the Department of Statistics at Princeton University. After receiving his Ph.D. in Mathematics and Statistics from Ohio State University in 1971, he was an Assistant Professor of Statistics at Virginia Polytechnic Institute, 1971–74. At Princeton University he is an Associate Master of Princeton Inn College.

Clive Seligman is currently Assistant Professor of Psychology at the University of Western Ontario in London, Canada. Previously, he was a Lecturer in Psychology and a Member of the Research Staff of the Center for Environmental Studies at Princeton University. Seligman received his Ph.D. in social psychology from Northwestern University in 1974. In addition to his research interests in studying peoples' attitudes toward energy and in developing strategies to encourage residential energy conservation, he is also interested in evaluating the effectiveness of energy conservation programs and in studying the conditions under which energy conservation programs can be initiated as experiments.

Frank W. Sinden divides his time between Princeton's Center for Environmental Studies and the Mathematics Research Center of Bell Laboratories at Murray Hill, N.J. He holds a doctorate in Applied Mathematics from the Swiss Federal Institute of Technology. Over his twenty year career he has contributed to a variety of fields including topology, convex programming, satellite communication, computer-animated films, mathematics education, energy and environment.

Robert H. Socolow is Acting Director of the Center for Environmental Studies and Professor of Mechanical and Aerospace Engineering at Princeton University. He received his Ph.D. in theoretical physics from Harvard University in 1964 and taught physics at Yale University from 1966 to 1971. Socolow is the co-editor of *Patient Earth* (Holt Rinehart, 1971), *Efficient Use of Energy* (American Institute of Physics, 1975), and *Boundaries of Analysis: An Inquiry into the Tocks Island Dam Controversy* (Ballinger, 1976). In 1976–77, he studied international aspects of energy policy at the Cavandish Laboratory, Cambridge, England, while holding fellowships from the German Marshall Fund and the Guggenheim Foundation.

Robert C. Sonderegger is a researcher in residential energy conservation at the Energy and Environment Division of Lawrence Berkeley Laboratory, and a visiting lecturer at the Mechanical Engineering Department of the University of California at Berkeley, California. He is currently working on dynamic thermal performance of building envelopes and on building energy performance parameters. He received a Ph.D. in Engineering in 1977 at the Center for Environmental Studies of Princeton University, Princeton, New Jersey, and a Master's Degree in Physics in 1973, at the Federal Institute of Technology, Zurich, Switzerland.

Thomas H. Woteki was a senior investigator in the Twin Rivers research program from 1975 to 1978. During that time he was also an Assistant Professor in the Department of Statistics and a member of the Center for Environmental Studies, Princeton University. Currently he is associated with the Energy Information Administration of the U.S. Department of Energy. His interests include energy data methodology, with particular emphasis on the data needs of local decision-makers.